WILL POWER!

WILL POWER!

USING SHAKESPEARE'S INSIGHTS

TO TRANSFORM YOUR LIFE

GEORGE WEINBERG AND DIANNE ROWE

ST. MARTIN'S PRESS ⚘ NEW YORK

Book design by Gretchen Achilles

Library of Congress Cataloging-in-Publication Data

Weinberg, George H.
        Will power! : using Shakespeare's insights to transform your life /
        by George Weinberg and Dianne Rowe.—1st ed.
                p.   cm.
        Includes index.
        ISBN 0-312-14764-3 (hardcover)
        1. Self-actualization (psychology)   2. Shakespeare, William,
1564–1616 Psychology.   3. Psychology and literature.   I. Rowe,
Dianne.   II. Title.
        BF637.S4W44   1996
        158'.1—dc20   96–8517
                                                                                        CIP

First Edition: September 1996

10   9   8   7   6   5   4   3   2   1

CONTENTS

STAGE FOUR: PRESERVING YOUR "SELF" IN RELATIONSHIPS

BE ACTIVE, NOT REACTIVE 121

STAGE FIVE: KEEPING THE DEMONS OUT OF YOUR LIFE

AVOIDING OBSESSIONS AND COMPULSIONS 159

STAGE SIX: NURTURING YOUR SOUL

SPIRITUALITY AS THE ULTIMATE SENSE OF BEING 193

ACKNOWLEDGMENTS

The authors are thankful to many people for their help with this book. Especially to Robert Weil, our editor at St. Martin's Press, who did everything from conceiving the form of the book to improving it in many small details. Also, we'd like to thank Andrew Graybill at St. Martin's for his editorial help.

Our agent, Russell Galen, himself a Shakespeare student, gave us the benefit of his sensitivity and fine literary judgment.

We would also thank our friend Jan Miller, whose vibrancy and all-embracing worldview, as well her keen insights, are invaluable.

Also, we thank our dear friend Dr. Louis Ormont, a playwright and renowned group analyst, for his many helpful suggestions and his abiding friendship.

Introduction
UNDERSTANDING THE SIX
STAGES OF WILL POWER!

Shakespeare is under attack today. There are many who say that he is no longer useful to us or even important, and that he need not be taught in high school or college. He has been removed from the curriculum of required reading in many places. As a result, many children will learn nothing about such plays as *Julius Caesar, Hamlet,* and *Macbeth*. These children will spend their lives imagining that the Bard speaks only old-fashioned language, irrelevant to their lives.

This is a tragedy because no one tell us more about ourselves and other people than Shakespeare.

We have written this book expressly to show that the Bard can still be vitally helpful to us in family life, in work-related problems—in understanding ourselves and other people. Shakespeare's greatness is undiminished, and if we do not allow ourselves to see it, we are the losers.

Will Power! is not an academic book. We are celebrating the joy and the usefulness of what Shakespeare has given us for the taking. There is no need to understand every word he says, but so many of his sentences can mean so much and can be so helpful at every stage of our lives that it would be a great loss not to learn from him.

We hope that this book will bring many useful truths to you through Shakespeare.

In the complex world of the 1990s, happiness and success in relationships and jobs require more than hard work, a good appearance, or even good luck. While these help at the start, what counts most is how developed you are as a person. Do you come across to people as whole and steady? Or as fragmented, unformed, and therefore undependable?

In every person's psychological life, there are stages of evolution. Your success in life will depend on how far up the ladder of psychological evolution you climb.

This book, which uses William Shakespeare as a therapist and guide, will teach you to understand yourself and other people better. It will show you how to move up the ladder of psychological evolution, and as you do, to move ahead in life and in your relationships. You will discover a whole lifestyle, which we call "Will Power!"

The "I" in this book refers to Dr. George Weinberg, a psychotherapist in practice for over thirty years. In that time, he has done therapy with a wide range of people. Many came during a crisis or after realizing that their pattern of living had not been successful. His task has been to help them understand themselves in order to change—or merely in order to persevere until their situation changed. He has sought to help them improve themselves where possible, but above all to develop self-love, peace of mind, and harmony with the world.

It was in the course of his practice that he developed the system of Will Power! It came out of a need that he saw in many people which the writings of Shakespeare would satisfy. His system has succeeded time and time again, and we believe that if you follow it, it will work for you.

William Shakespeare wasthe greatest of all psychologists. He was the foremost genius at knowing what people will do in virtually all situations. Shakespeare understood why people act as they do, what they fear, and what they want. Shakespeare grasped the magnificence and complexity of even the smallest moments in life.

The greatness of Shakespeare's psychology is that in examining the motives and purposes of his characters, he arrived at brilliant insights useful in the lives of all of us. These insights can help us in our most critical and intimate moments.

Of course, Shakespeare used no psychological terms in his work. He was writing essentially to entertain people. We, who have the leisure to study him and the tools of modern psychology at our disposal, can finally understand the psychological techniques that he left for us.

Shakespeare constantly considered his characters as being on higher or lower rungs of personal evolution. He saw his great heroes as formed people, typically with a tragic flaw that prevented them from reaching the highest rung. He wanted his audiences to perceive some of his characters as dislikable, people he conveyed, in effect, as unformed or unfinished.

In the great diversity of his characters, we see people at different levels of psychological evolution, much the way people are in reality. Shakespeare's characters succeed or fail by how they cope with a series of challenges in their own lives.

You face challenges that are in essence quite similar. They are part of human nature and development.

Will Power! isolates many of these challenges and studies them. We will take you through each challenge, and as you surmount them you will travel through Six Stages of Psychological Evolution. They are six stages of wholeness achieved through the wisdom of Will Power! If Shakespeare were writing a textbook today, we believe, he would give us these six stages.

Shakespeare often spoke of life as a journey, by which he clearly meant a psychological journey. The happiest and most successful people are those who enjoy the journey and who pursue it all their lives.

The richest life is the one that is most evolved emotionally. It does not fixate on single emotions, as on hatred or even on love. It does not give itself over to repetition, but it sweeps onward. It enjoys inner freedom but also devotion to values, to something higher than itself—to faith, to hope. Many people continue to strive all their lives for such richness.

Unfortunately, however, many people stop their psychological journey very early in life. Like children who haven't been socialized, they go on seeing themselves as in a struggle to survive against all others. They create barriers and walls that prevent them from learning about Will Power! Their lack of evolution results in a wide range of symptoms.

You can often recognize these unevolved people by your desire to avoid them or, if you know them well, by an impulse to fix them. They may have trouble listening to you; they may say hurtful things without meaning to. They often seem to miss the essence of what's going on, and you may wonder if they know what they themselves are feeling.

Some of these people can be physically attractive and have attended to themselves superficially. You might even be unlucky enough to fall in love with one. They get by in certain businesses, so you might have one as a boss or a client. But no matter how passable they may seem on the outside, there remains a core of isolation about them.

Often you can spot them by their money desperation, no matter how much they have. Their real problem, though is not money at all. It is their continual sense that they are poor, which in fact they actually are. They are low on the scale of psychological evolution.

It's important to be able to spot these people.

And it's vital not to be one yourself.

Times and customs have of course changed in many ways since Shakespeare's era. But people have not. There has been no change in what makes a person masterful, sexy, capable, a leader—or a fool, for that matter.

The qualities that others would describe as sexiness and personal magnetism always come from the inside. Leadership and certainly the essence of excitement in a person are really the psychological results of high-order evolution.

Job opportunities and pivotal roles go to people who are most evolved, who know how to use Will Power!, even though the person doing the hiring may not think in terms of evolution or know what he or she is responding to.

Lovers are naturally attracted to the evolved person. That person exudes force, energy, sexuality, and self-trust, which makes us feel very safe and yet very alive in the person's company.

It has often been observed that we are not as sexually attracted to "nice" people as we are to those who present an enigma or who imply a darker side. This is apt to be true. But what many people call mystery or darkness is in fact the true complexity of a highly evolved person. People who are merely nice may strike us as lacking that complexity; they don't create sparks and we have no desire to go deeper with them. The truly sexual person knows himself or herself, and knows the world.

Even relationships between caring people may sometimes fail when the two people have reached different levels of emotional development. Relationships often fall apart when one person evolves to a higher level, learning and understanding through experience, while the other person stagnates. When two people continue to evolve together, however, relationships tend to last and remain fresh and bright.

This concept of self-improvement, as moving up a scale of emotional development throughout life, is both very old and very new. It is an overall approach that involves all aspects of the psyche. Shakespeare might have thought of it as everyday common sense.

Over the last few decades, many popular books have appeared giving practical advice for solving a wide range of personal problems. A number of these books and the programs that go with them have been very helpful in themselves.

However, working on one kind of sensitivity—for example, learning relationship techniques or how to package yourself as forceful—is not enough. The key is to integrate what you learn and to evolve psychologically. When you do this, "techniques" become natural expressions of who you are.

For instance, many relationship books written for women give advice such as, "Never cancel an appointment if your difficult lover calls and asks you out at the last minute."

This is doubtless good advice, but the ideal would be not to need it. Development from within will enable you to do these things naturally. When you have mastered the Fourth Stage of Evolution, what we shall call Preserving Your "Self" in Relationships you will naturally keep your appointments and your promises. You won't allow people to throw you off-balance, as by summoning you at the last minute.

Forms of therapy differ, but the aim of all therapy is to help people bring out their own truths—to help people discover what is best in them. It is to help people keep their balance. The aim is for the patient to become able to say in the fullest sense, "I have lived. I am whole."

We hope that this book will blend Shakespeare's "humanistic" everyday psychology with the demands of life as we know it in the 1990s. Within the Bard's work are all the keys for breaking loose from the psychic ties that hold us down. Our aim is to give you these keys. If we succeed, you will find yourself using stunning new psychological methods that will greatly improve your life.

Shakespeare doesn't start with any magical beliefs, like the Oedipus complex. Will Power! has no magical words. Nor does Shakespeare bog us down with psychological theories. His simplicity is as much a part of his miracle as are his insights. His truths were set down for audiences to hear at high speed. Remarkably, given the volume of his output, Shakespeare virtually never repeated himself. Each character represents a unique psychological state and each play illustrates many different psychological themes.

How did Shakespeare know so much?

No one on earth can tell. People have speculated about it for centuries. In the end, as with Mozart or Einstein, we can only be thankful that the master existed.

Shakespeare shows the stages of psychological evolution, sometimes by depicting characters who have excelled at one or more of these stages. In other cases, he portrays characters who have obviously failed to evolve at some critical rung. Some of his gigantic characters are striving to evolve, and a defect in one stage becomes the person's tragic flaw.

But ultimately, the reason we are so attracted to Shakespeare's characters is that he knew how to create riveting figures who are at the top of the scale of psychological evolution.

Then, as now, the most highly evolved person was the most attractive.

Then, as now, the demand for truly well-evolved people, for life's central figures, was much greater than the supply of them. As in every other aspect of life, there are fewer people at the top.

Here are the Six Stages of Psychological Evolution—the philosophy of Will Power!—which we have identified in Shakespeare's work:

1. Defining Yourself

2. Understanding Others

3. Self-Reliance

4. Preserving Your "Self" in Relationships

5. Keeping the Demons out of Your Life

6. Nurturing Your Soul

Now let's look at the stages of evolution as they apply to you—and see how you can use them.

THE SIX STAGES OF WILL POWER

1. **The first stage is *Defining Yourself*.** This is the stage of realizing that you are a distinct individual, empowered to act on your own and with your own range of feelings. Defining yourself implies listening to your instincts, knowing what you feel, but holding yourself fully accountable for everything you do. You can not be a hero to anyone without being an individual first.

2. **Next comes *Understanding Others*.** You have not only a conscious impact on people, but an unconscious impact on them. You touch other people continually on levels which they can not even verbalize. Your entire success in relationships depends on whether you stay friends with people's unconscious.

Critical is the aftereffect you have on people—how they feel about you on a subconscious level after spending time with you. For instance, *do they feel you accept them as they are or do they feel that you would like them to be different?* Staying friends with people's unconscious requires that you know how to experience people, to enjoy them for their strengths, and not to change them.

3.   *Self-Reliance* refers to keeping your center even when you are under pressure, to knowing who you are, and to sticking with that knowledge.
Stages one and two are necessary to achieve this level, where you remember that you are the same person no matter how things are going. At this stage you learn from others but are not defeated by them. In fact, you may study adversaries and even strangers in order to improve your own performance. Shakespeare will clearly help you here. Ideally you will always keep your own center.

4.   Now comes *Preserving Your "Self" in Relationships.* This involves not bending yourself out of shape for others, not weighting relationships in favor of the other person to your detriment. It means seeing through your own eyes rather than being dominated by concern over how others see you. It entails being able to identify people who are negative forces in your life and reducing their influence or getting rid of them in some cases.

5.   *Keeping the Demons out of Your Life* means not letting any one single emotion or need dominate you. It implies transcendence over compulsions and irrational fears—or irrational anger, as sometimes accompanies jealousy. It means not distorting yourself to control others, as by adopting poses, but instead keeping the kind of balance that allows you the full range of emotional life.

6.   The culmination of all these stages is *Nurturing Your Soul.*
This is the hardest to define, but it certainly entails a sense of community with all living things, a sense of their frailty, an ability to love, a demotion of acquisitions and celebrity in favor of deeper communion with oneself and others. In spirituality is a sense of wonderment, of beauty, of the sublime.

We are convinced that millions of people familiar with Shakespeare have fashioned themselves with these stages of evolution in mind, though they haven't thought about them as such.

*   *   *

You will benefit from this book in understanding the lasting results of *Will Power!* and how it affects you and your relationships. This is safe to say because Shakespeare's insights can benefit nearly anybody.

Shakespeare has a way of discovering us at different stages of life. As we read him, whether we're in love or in a state of jealousy or worried about getting older or have just been rejected, it's as if Shakespeare has come to us through the wilderness. He finds words for how we feel which have eluded us, and suddenly we see more clearly.

He gives us the comforting sense that long before we were born, others came down a similar path, which means we are not truly lost. No matter that our predecessors dressed differently, were a different age, of a different social class, spoke a different language, or whatever. They stood where we stand now, facing the same indecision. They endured the same crises, suffered as we do. Their soul's journey was the same as ours, and in describing them, Shakespeare is describing us.

Beyond hundreds of specifics, this book's emphasis on psychological evolution will give you principles for living. You can apply these in situations of your own which can't all possibly be covered in any book. You will learn to think in terms of psychological evolution in situations as they arise in your own life.

If you've read some self-help books already, you have perhaps thought about your own stage of psychological evolution.

But in reading the stories that we have illuminated in *Will Power!*, we believe that you cannot help but become more personally enlightened. Perhaps you will discover a tragic flaw, which would be fine since there is always plenty of time to change. Or you will discover some stage of evolution which requires more attention. Or ideally you will confirm that you have reached a high order of evolution—a comprehension of true Will Power!— and that you are already a central figure.

—Dr. George Weinberg and Dianne Rowe
NEW YORK, NEW YORK

Stage One
DEFINING YOURSELF

RECOGNIZING YOUR UNIQUENESS
AS A PERSON

The first stage on the journey to wholeness is to celebrate that you are different from all other human beings.

You needn't live in the shadow of anyone else—celebrity, relative, lover. You doubtless have role models, people you look up to and imitate in certain respects. But even these people are important to you only because you have made them important. You have chosen them and you reserve the right to drop them and choose others.

You alone will determine the roads you take and those you turn your back on. No matter what your natural gifts or lack of them, you have great choice over the sweep of your life. And ultimately you have choice over whether you are happy, contented, fulfilled, or are gnawed at by the feeling that you might be doing more.

Your fate is a result of how you exert your will—not necessarily in big ways but in everyday choices. And your emotional life gives you great power if you listen to your feelings and trust them.

Shakespeare, the ultimate therapist, saw each individual life as a journey. He believed that each person could decide what his or her journey would be. Before Shakespeare, characters tended to be one-dimensional and fell into a few basic types. Shakespeare changed all that. In his thirty-six plays he portrays hundreds of characters, each of whom has taken a very different journey. The body of his work is the greatest existing monument to the process of recognizing your unique individuality.

The Bard tells us that our separateness is our greatest gift, even if it sometimes makes us feel lonely. Nourish your individuality and it will give you Will Power!

Modern psychology has made much of the process that allows us to become whole individuals. The road to maturity is both neurological and psychological. We see it originally in the infant. At first the infant can make only gross motor movements like moving a whole hand. It takes time for the child to individuate, or, in this case, to separate various physical movements, for example, learning how to move one finger without moving the rest.

For a long time after that, the infant still cannot even distinguish himself or herself from the mother. The infant has no concept of being different from another person. Learning that your mother is not simply an extension of your own flesh, usually within the first year of life, is your first great moment of psychological "individuation."

Still later, our individuality takes on all the magic that comes with discovering our own separate existence. As time goes on, the child learns that he or she is different from all other human beings in many ways. The child discovers his or her own uniqueness.

For many people this fascinating journey into our uniqueness goes on for a lifetime. We realize that we are different from others and we accept that fact.

Our own individuality gives us a fuller sense of the richness of others. The person who is highly evolved as an individual has a strong sense of his or her own separateness, and through this feels a full sense of community with all other individuals.

Individuality is the full recognition that you are a sentient being, with your own feelings and reactions, which may or may not coincide with those of others around you. The other side of this is the recognition that you make your own choices, from the smallest to the most significant. This means that no matter what others tell you is right, no matter what others do, regardless of peer pressure, you make all your own decisions in life.

Discovering this—that you are an individual, different from all others on earth, on your own—may be painful at times. It may be tempting not to "individuate" yourself, as it was doubtless tempting for the infant to remain attached to the mother. Accepting your aloneness in life also means accepting responsibility for everything you do; it means at times accepting blame and even punishment.

But the rewards far outstrip these momentary displeasures. Since you are the one who must experience your life, what could be better news than the fact that you are in charge of your life?

Failure to become a whole individual leaves a person subject to peer pressure and lack of identity.

Many adults "individuate" only partially, if at all. As a result, they find it hard to form relationships because, not being defined themselves, they offer no novelty or true support to others. It is hard for other people to trust them because it is never clear what they feel or are going to do in an unusual situation. It is as if they offer no pillar of personality for other people to lean on.

Reaping the full benefit of individuality means taking full responsibility for all your own actions. It also means accepting and enjoying your own feelings without having to express or act out any particular feeling unless you want to. When we understand our feelings, we can decide what to do.

Unlike your voluntary acts, your emotional state is like a radar screen on which many messages play, some originating outside yourself but many coming from within. These emotions contain a steady supply of valuable information about yourself, about how you are faring, and about what other people are doing.

Those who are truly "individuated" enjoy the colorful palette of their own emotions. They see incredible detail and ever-unfolding nuance in themselves and in others.

Of course, the term "individuation" did not exist in Shakespeare's time. But a strong sense of it runs through all of Shakespeare's heroes and all those characters he seems to respect. He clearly sees the hero as a defined person. His heroes and heroines take responsibility for their actions, even when they are wrong. And the best of his characters know precisely what they are feeling. Since they speak through Shakespeare's voice, they describe these feelings eloquently.

Shakespeare and his contemporaries tended to write the stories of "important" people—like kings and queens or great generals or figures from mythology. But more than anyone else before or since, the Bard saw that greatness was possible for anyone—the lowly shepherd or farmer or foot soldier or grave digger. He cherished these people provided that they themselves cherished their own individuality.

The "lowly" person who had clear emotions and who acted in accordance with his or her own beliefs won Shakespeare's heart. He could make immortal a carpenter or shoemaker by giving that person definition and a clear-cut identity—by having that person achieve individuation.

On the other hand, a great mob of people, each undefined (not individuated), was a contemptible, mindless beast to the Bard. He recognized the danger of mob thinking. The Bard saw that individuality is the basis for both identity and dignity. He teaches us that individuality is the great first step of personal evolution.

What is the essence of individuality as Shakespeare taught it and as it will always be?

Let's look now at two major Shakespeare figures, one who didn't have a necessary feature of individuality and one whose individuality makes him great despite a tragic flaw.

1
OTHELLO AS ROLE MODEL

TAKING RESPONSIBILITY FOR EVERY DETAIL OF YOUR LIFE

Certain people have the mark of winner on them. They possess a hard-to-define quality that commands respect. As children they choose the game to be played, and others ask them the rules. As adults, they seem born leaders. We feel excited when they congratulate us or when they ask us to join them in a plan or to take their side in a meeting. If there are two social gatherings, the one that they attend seems like the important one. In a company they take over with a naturalness that makes them seem destined to succeed. They are what Shakespeare's King Henry the Fifth called "the makers of fashion."

Who are these people and what makes them special?

No one is born with magical stuff that makes them masters of others. People become leaders by being responsible in even the smallest moments of their lives. They establish themselves not in major crises, as one might think, but by the cumulative effect of how they act in everyday life. Theirs is the knack of presenting themselves as winners in small moments all through the day. Their "sovereignty of nature" (again to use the Bard's phrase), is something that they have developed, and other people have not.

The Myth of Natural Leadership

We have spent a lot of time studying how certain people create this image of what has wrongly been called "natural" leadership. We have watched the verbalizations of these people, their modes of expression: *They make themselves central characters.*

By the way they talk they indicate that they see themselves as central in their own lives, as heroes in their own scripts. Others then take the cue from them and support this centrality.

In my practice, I consider that I have given a patient an invaluable boost toward success whenever I've enabled that person to act and sound more like a central figure in his or her own life. As patients develop better habits of self-presentation, they fulfill their own wishes for themselves. Soon they are natural leaders.

But how do I achieve this?

I teach the patient how to attain the pivotal character trait that underlies this ideal presentation, namely: *They must take responsibility for every detail of their lives.*

The Heroic Personality

The essence of the hero, whether in mythology or in movies or in real life, is that the hero holds himself, or herself, fully accountable for every act of his life. In even their smallest expressions, such people make it clear that all their decisions are their own—including those that are wrong.

Without realizing it, *everyone is drawn to the person who holds himself responsible for his actions.*

Those around such people are seldom aware of exactly what they're responding to. If asked, "Why do you respect this person so much?" or "What is so special about him or her?", they probably couldn't tell you precisely. They would most likely answer something like, "She just seems very competent," or "I feel comfortable giving the biggest projects to him."

Behind this comfort and automatic respect, subtle forces are at work:

◆ One is that the hero—the person who holds himself accountable—communicates the impression that he has often succeeded in the past.

◆ He or she seems fundamentally unafraid of challenges and of other people.

◆ He or she doesn't make excuses or blame others, and instead puts himself or herself squarely on the line. The hero looks like someone used to getting things right.

Superiors turn to such a person when much is at stake. They know that they will get a square accounting.

The Hero Gains Status from His or Her Mistakes

Ironically, the time that you will score the most points is when you've made a mistake. If you take responsibility for an error that you might otherwise have hidden, you give off an aura of invincibility. The natural leader presents all the information that might be needed to salvage the loss, or at least to avoid repetition of the mistake. Superiors and inferiors alike come to believe that such a person's mistakes are learning opportunities, and not simply blunders.

On the other hand, the person who blames others or invents excuses compounds his or her failure. Others lose trust in such a person, believing that if forces could conspire against him in the one instance, then they could do so again.

The responsible person retains optimism no matter how things go. The person who avoids responsibility communicates hopelessness and helplessness. Such a person is saying, "I am subject to influence." He implies, "I may mislead you again, and it won't be my fault then, either."

As a rule people greatly underrate the rewards of assuming responsibility for mistakes in business or in personal relationships. It is important to realize that those who don't forgive you would not have been on your side in the long run anyway. You would eventually have lost the job, lost the relationship, or paid the price in one way or another.

Othello, the Tragic Hero

Othello is usually regarded as one of Shakespeare's most tragic figures. We admire him for his strength and integrity and we suffer with him as his tragic flaw destroys him.

We have a sense of Othello's magnificence even before meeting him. And when we do meet him, we see what this force is composed of: *an absolute refusal ever to attribute the consequences of his own actions to anyone else.* Othello held himself responsible for every act that he committed, from the smallest to the most significant.

We learn at the beginning of the play that Othello is widely renowned as a great general. But he has not achieved his high military rank easily. He has surmounted powerful prejudices against him for his dark skin color—he is a Moor.

Othello has been hired by the Venetians to help them in a war against Cyprus. It is clear that the Venetians are prejudiced against Othello, but they need him because he is a superb leader. He is also a man of great stature and personal energy.

Shakespeare knew the powerful importance of first impressions, and as we first encounter many of his characters, they reveal their essence to us instantly. So it is with Othello. When we first see him, he is facing a great crisis. Othello has recently married Desdemona, a much younger woman, a

Venetian, with whom he is deeply in love. Desdemona, who returns his passion, has defied her father in order to marry him.

Soon after the play opens, Othello is told that Desdemona's father has pressed charges against him. Others warn him to flee to avoid capture. But Othello refuses, insisting that he must come forth and stand trial; since he has done no wrong he is confident that he will be exonerated. He makes his case boldly and is acquitted by the Venetian state.

Othello's greatness is in his force and personal honesty. His tragedy, however, lies in a pocket of self-hate, which leaves him vulnerable to being taunted into jealousy.

Othello is totally secure in his role as a soldier and military leader, but he is just as insecure about his peacetime manners. Secretly, he fears that he may indeed be too old for Desdemona. He is shaken by the cruel prejudice of those around him, and he fears that he lacks the social graces of the highborn Venetians and the younger men on his staff.

Immediately after their marriage, Othello and Desdemona leave for Cyprus. Once they land there, one of the strangest characters in all of fiction surfaces. Iago is introduced as Othello's right-hand man, his "ancient," who has been with him for some time. Othello trusts Iago and believes him to be a close friend, but the audience learns at once that Iago is out to destroy Othello.

The mystery is why. Scholars have discussed the question for centuries. Everyone agrees that Othello never injured Iago and that, in fact, he had given him his position. Various motives are ascribed to Iago. Some speculate that Iago is enraged about being passed over for a particular promotion. Others contend that Iago has no reason at all for his treachery, except for the pleasure it brings him. Perhaps Iago envies everyone and is a pure representation of jealousy in the play.

Iago sets out to convince Othello that Desdemona is betraying him with a younger and more polished man on Othello's staff.

As the play proceeds, we see Othello become increasingly distressed. Iago, by creating false evidence that Desdemona has betrayed Othello, goads him to intense jealousy. Driven mad, Othello strangles his beloved wife. In the final moments of the play, it becomes evident that Desdemona was innocent and that Iago had invented all the evidence.

Never was anyone so diabolically prompted to violence and, in the end, to self-destruction. But the truly heroic nature of Othello triumphs even over his crime. We retain a great admiration for him, even in his madness. Given the easy choice of blaming Iago, of pleading that he was driven to the act of murder, Othello opts to take the full responsibility for what he has done.

He avoids positioning himself as a victim. He will not blame anyone or anything for what he has done—not Iago, who goaded him, nor temporary insanity, nor the stresses of war.

In talking to those present just before he kills himself, Othello retains and, if anything, elevates his own personal dignity by his handling of the crisis. He blames only himself:

> *When you shall these unlucky deeds relate,*
> *Speak of me as I am; nothing extenuate,*
> *. . . . Then must you speak . . . of one whose hand,*
> *Like the base Indian, threw a pearl away*
> *Richer than all his tribe . . .*

Othello's tragedy, as we've mentioned, was that pocket of self-hate which made him susceptible to a jealousy that reached a fever pitch. As a result of that jealousy, which drove him to murder the woman he loved, his life ended tragically. Indeed, he had thrown a "pearl" away—he had killed his faithful wife.

However, there had to be greatness in Othello to start with, in order to make his fall so tragic. And when he is gone, there must have been some glory in his death to make us mourn him and leave the theatre feeling as sorry for him as we do for poor Desdemona, whom he killed.

"The cause is in my will," wrote the Bard elsewhere. *The winner holds himself responsible even when he is wrong.* When you step forward and make yourself accountable for your actions, others don't feel the need to attack you personally.

HOW CAN YOU BECOME A FORCE, A CENTRAL FIGURE?

1. **Most obviously, never blame other people.**

   - If you've made a mistake, own up to it without excuses, and supply whatever information is needed to correct it.

   - If someone working for you makes a mistake, obey the basic tenet of business, which is that you are responsible for what your employees do. Take the blame when you talk to your superiors, and then discuss your employee's blunder with him or her alone. Your aim should be to improve the person's future performance, not to rub his or her nose in it.

◆ If someone else, a friend or coworker, makes a mistake, let it be. If it's obvious, it needs no comment. If the person has knocked over a drink or forgotten an appointment, the classy approach is to lighten the moment as well as you can.

2.   When you are criticized, don't change the subject. Don't make excuses. Make it clear that you are ready to hear the person out without squirming or breaking in. Acknowledge in words what the person has said to you.

3.   If you're faced with making a tough phone call or appearing at a meeting that you know will be brutal because you've made a mistake, don't hide or shirk from the confrontation in any way. Don't put off the call or abbreviate it. Doing so would only infuriate the other person and make you look like a loser. You'll also make yourself feel like a loser, not simply a person who made a mistake this time.

4.   If you think that someone is accusing you wrongly, let the person finish without comment. Then state your explanation clearly and only once. Don't whine.

Understand that your accuser is upset. Share his concern, and agree that the matter is serious. "I understand your concern. I'm concerned too. But in this case . . ." Then explain why you aren't the one for him to attack.

Unless the implications are potentially serious—your job or a raise or your standing in the company is at stake—don't pursue your defense. Defend yourself only to the degree commensurate with the real threat.

5.   Don't try to wriggle out of responsibility, even if you think you can.

Understand that any arm wrestle you get into with a superior has a price. Winning can be the worst outcome. Getting your boss to admit, "Fine, I get the picture. It was Smith's responsibility and not yours," can cost you dearly. In the process you are conveying that you don't like responsibility and that you can't stand being wrong.

Furthermore, your boss may smart over losing an argument to an employee. You may walk away feeling great because you've convinced him that you didn't "do it." But he walks away feeling that you're a major annoyance for having put him through the trial.

6.   Don't bitch about your job, society in general, or how tough things are all around.

If you constantly talk about the world as crooked and unfair or portray yourself as getting the worst of it, then you are inviting people to see you as a poor victim of forces beyond your control. Soon you will see yourself the same way.

7.   When someone tries to be kind to you after a mishap by saying in effect, "That really wasn't your fault" or "You didn't have the right information," if you really want to be a hero, don't take the handout.

Thank the person for the kindness, but insist that it was your fault. "It was my job to get the information. It was my job not to be misled."

8.   Don't badmouth other people.

Whispering about others and talking behind their backs only makes you look small. It's as if you have nothing better to do, or as if you're afraid to confront them directly. Using any technique to make yourself invisible takes away from your being a central figure.

We often think of people who whine as having a crouching body posture. It is as if they were trying to make themselves as small a target as possible. Hiding or gossiping in corners is not the technique of a force.

9.   Keep *every* promise.

If you have any doubt that you can keep a promise, don't make it. And if you fail to keep a promise for any reason whatsoever, make sure that you acknowledge your failure. Bring up the promise you couldn't keep before the due date and before anyone else does. Explain why you can't meet the deadline or deliver the goods. Never play the possibility that the promise will simply go away. Others won't conveniently forget it. Nor will they forget that you hid from it.

10.   Watch your language. Brevity—the ability to speak briefly—is the sign of a winner.

This applies to discussing what you plan to do, talking about what you have accomplished, or discussing why something went wrong.

- ◆ People who talk too much about what they're going to do sound as if they're trying to get credit in advance because they aren't sure they can do it. They are overcompensating with words for what they haven't yet done.

- ◆ Bragging about past achievements also has a note of pathos. It conveys a sense that you won't follow up with more achievements.

♦   Making lengthy excuses is the mark of a loser. We all admire
the athlete who says in a television interview, "I lost today
because the other guy was better." Or, "We have no excuses.
They just outplayed us."

**11.   Remember to emphasize that you, not outside forces, are
in control.**

When you don't want to do something, say, "I'd rather not," instead of
"I can't."

Convey that you are always making choices, and not being acted upon
by outside forces.

Say, "I chose to leave that job," instead of "I had to get out of that
place." Saying, "The relationship just didn't work out," makes you look
more like a winner than if you complain, "He didn't treat me right."

Fatalism Versus Will

The idea that people have power over their own lives, which is a fun-
damental axiom for modern success, was a startling position to take in the
time of Shakespeare.

The underlying sense of the Middle Ages, just ending in Shakespeare's
period, was one of fatalism. It was believed that people were born to a certain
purpose and to a station in life. It was one's duty to fulfill one's destiny
without trying to change it.

Being fatalistic, people believed in a whole range of forces beyond their
control. They looked to omens, to portents, and to the stars. Life all around
them seemed to bear out their sense of helplessness. A slight infection could
mean death. Poverty was almost insurmountable. Few rose in social status
or even learned to read if they weren't from the right social class. Thousands
of people were burned as witches or hanged as criminals without any real
day in court. The plague struck regularly, and so many women died while
giving birth that a pregnant woman was likely to say that her "death was
upon" her. Many believed that Queen Elizabeth I herself avoided marriage
in order to be on the safe side.

Shakespeare was notable in holding the opposite belief. His personal
rise to celebrity and wealth was fostered by the profound conviction that
people "are masters of their fates," that our difficulties are "not in our stars,"
but in ourselves. Time and again, when a character blames his difficulties
on fate, Shakespeare has another character chide him for his belief in destiny and his disbelief in himself. Among his most interesting characters,

though they often include his villains, are those who announce that the only right way to live is to accept responsibility for their own lives.

Shakespeare is our great teacher of dignity through personal responsibility. Those characters whom we love, as well as those villains whom we grudgingly admire, have the courage to stand alone.

Taking Responsibility Is the Key to Empowerment

Psychotherapy is often virtually synonymous with helping the patient to assume responsibility for his life. This means teaching the patient to recognize his or her contribution to outcomes. Many patients initially tend to blame other people—for their own loss of temper. They blame others for their own failure to go to college, and for their frustrations generally. But the very decision to blame anyone for anything that we ourselves did diminishes us. It limits our options and our sense of our own freedom. We forfeit our birthright, which is freedom itself.

Granted, we are subject to pressures of discrimination, deprivation, and the psychic input already made into our early lives. But modern psychotherapy is coming to realize that the key to empowerment is to see that we alone shape our fortunes. And this requires a stern readiness on our part to be accountable for all our actions, big and small.

That special elixir of the psyche which others feel in us and which gives us a continuous sense of individual importance—to sustain this requires that we hold ourselves alone responsible for whatever we do.

2

CAESAR'S MISTAKE

NEVER LOSE TOUCH WITH YOUR EMOTIONS

Julius Caesar was a self-made emperor. He moved rapidly up through the ranks, becoming the Roman Empire's greatest general. Over a spectacular nine-year period, he drove back the enemies of Rome and extended its power across Western Europe and into Great Britain.

At the height of his triumph, he marched on Rome itself. He subdued the armies of the Roman Senate and, with the acclaim of the common citizens, seized complete power. His person was declared sacred, coins were struck in his honor, his statues were placed in temples across the Empire, the month of July was named for him, and the word Caesar became synonymous with the word emperor.

However, among the aristocrats Caesar was resented and envied. One group of them feared that he would establish a hereditary monarchy. Caesar's chief enemy in Rome was the patrician Gaius Cassius, who persuaded Caesar's closest friend, Brutus, and a group of other aristocrats to assassinate Caesar on the grounds that he was a danger to the commonwealth.

On March 15 (the Ides of March), 44 B.C., a small group led by Cassius and Brutus surrounded Caesar in the Senate and stabbed him to death.

Shakespeare's play *Julius Caesar,* based on an ancient account of his life, portrays the conspiracy and the killing of Caesar, and then depicts the ultimate avenging of Caesar's assassination.

In the play, Shakespeare shows Caesar as having strong feelings, almost a premonition, that Cassius was dangerous to him. But Caesar made a great mistake, one that cost him his life. He did not listen to his rumblings of fear, to the inner voice that told him to beware of Cassius. He dismissed the rumblings, instead of heeding them as a message to take the necessary precautions.

Shakespeare has Caesar comment to his dear friend Marc Antony

> *Let me have men about me that are fat,*
> *Sleek-headed men and such as sleep o' nights.*
> *Yond Cassius has a lean and hungry look.*

Obviously, something more about Cassius than this "look" was troublesome to Caesar. Some as-yet-undefined essence behind that look gave Caesar powerful misgivings. His feeling might have prompted him to pause and examine exactly how he felt, and why.

But Caesar refused to take his own feelings seriously or even to examine his own reaction. Obviously, Caesar, overcome by his own greatness, didn't like feeling afraid. It didn't become a man of his stature, he told himself, admitting only that if he were ever to be afraid of anyone, it would be of Cassius.

> *Yet if my name were liable to fear,*
> *I do not know the man I should avoid*
> *So soon as that spare Cassius.*

Caesar's pretense of not being susceptible to fear or to personal interest of any kind showed itself one last time minutes before he died. On the way to the Senate, a loyal follower thrust a paper into his hand exposing the plot, entreating him to read it at once for his own good. Caesar refused on the ground that

> *What touches us ourself shall be last served.*

Caesar's great mistake was his refusal to listen to his own emotions—at least long enough to investigate what they might be telling him. If Caesar had honored his feelings and looked into the matter, he might have uncovered the conspiracy in time to avoid the fate that Brutus and Cassius had in store for him.

Your Emotions Are Early Warning Signals

Obviously, you're not dealing with the Senate on a daily basis, and we hope you're not facing friends who literally turn out to be murderers with you in mind. Repeated failure to identify emotions won't leave you in a bloody heap on display to the populace.

However, your emotions are natural warning signals put there by nature to give you clues. Are you succeeding in a relationship? Is the other person on your side? Are you going to close the deal? Are you staying too long in a useless endeavor or a hopeless relationship? Your emotions are your guides in all relationships.

Caesar's inability to use his emotions as clues—to trust what he sensed—was part of a broader problem. His loss of access to his own fear prevented him from being truly close to people, from knowing whom to trust and whom to distrust.

Staying Emotionally Alive

In the course of a day you may experience a great range of feelings— such as fear, dependence, confidence, exaltation, love. These feelings come and go, passing through you as flocks of birds might cross the sky.

The inner life of even the least evolved person is extremely rich. At different moments we experience fear, love, rage, exaltation, hatred. There is nothing unnatural in having a kaleidoscope of personal reactions. *To have a wide palate of emotions is to live.*

As forms of experience, your emotions are a blessing, a fact of your birthright. To be without any particular emotion, to stifle any aspect of yourself, is to be diminished, to cheat yourself out of the fullness of being. Without recourse to our range of feelings, even unpleasant feelings, we are unfulfilled.

Your emotions can save your life. They were invented for that purpose and the character who is cut off from his emotions is in a sorry state indeed, like those occasional children we read about who can't feel pain.

You may delight in some of your feelings. You feel strong, competent, young, no matter what your age. In other moments you feel loved and wanted. It doesn't take much—a smile from your lover, a moment of evident joy from your dog glad to see you at the end of the day.

Other encounters leave you with negative feelings. Your lover or boss looks disgruntled. A man or woman you are interested in seems preoccupied when you call. You feel momentarily like a loser.

You may be tempted to shove aside such bad feelings. Don't. Good or bad, your emotions are your guidelines.

Don't Be Afraid of Any Emotion—Even Anger

The main reason for people's systematically cutting themselves off from their own feelings is a fear that if they allow the feeling in, they will do something they will be sorry for. They repress their feelings—especially those of anger and of sexual desire.

People who do this go through life short-circuited, out of touch with themselves, and this proves extremely costly. If we deny having any emotion, we limit the richness of our own experience and our empathy with others. By self-enforced blindness to our emotions, we limit our ability to navigate in the world. We make blunders and repeat them. *We need to use our feelings as cues to stay steady in life, to act rationally.*

If we know, for example, that we feel violent rage toward someone and can admit this to ourselves, we are *less* likely to do violence to the person than if we hadn't acknowledged how we felt.

The denied feeling—for example, the sexual desire toward someone out of bounds—is the feeling most likely to take control of us. Before we know it, we have expressed rage or antipathy toward the person out of bounds to hide our sexual attraction.

Be Your Own Therapist—Tune Up Your Emotions

Your emotions are the very stuff that psychotherapists work with. They are the instruments that therapists want you to tune up for your own sake. The best therapists never give advice, even to the patient who asks for it. Rather they ask the patient innumerable questions to help the patient understand his or her feelings.

Only you can truly know what you feel, and no one else can tell you. When you learn to identify your feelings easily, you will make the everyday decisions that best serve you.

For you to become your own psychotherapist, as we all need to be, it's vital that you have access to the great range of your emotions.

Let us suppose that a particular business client makes you feel that you are boring him all the time. If you don't identify this feeling, you may try to correct for it, as by talking too fast, by becoming flustered, and leaving out important points.

As soon as you identify your feeling—that is, diagnose yourself as anxious and breathless and hurried in this person's presence—you can stop hurrying. Instead, you might make a habit of asking this client, even during a conversation, if you notice him losing interest, "Is this a good time for us to talk?" That seemingly simple question will put the person on notice to listen and it will earn you instant respect. Now you can make your best pitch slowly and fully, and you have ten times the chance of closing the deal.

Once you know what you're feeling, you are in control.

Therapists themselves depend greatly on their own emotions as a tool for diagnosing patients. For example, if a certain patient always makes me feel heavy and burdened, I have to know it. He is almost surely doing the same thing to other people, which could explain why his boss didn't give him a promotion or why his wife left him. Identifying my feelings cues me in to the kind of questions I can ask to discover what is really going on.

You Need a Healthy Blend of Emotions

Some people seem overflowing with emotions. For these people the challenge is to regulate how they express these emotions to the world.

The deeply emotional person has intense reactions to a great number of events in a day, including his or her own thoughts.

If you are this kind of person, you see importance in everything around you, in what people do and say, in events that have nothing to do with you. That's the good side—you live richly. The bad side is that you're prone to say all kinds of things you're sorry for. If you're not careful you can become irritating, and if you are with a low-intensity person, you will drive him half mad.

Ideally, understand your emotions and enjoy them. But be careful about expressing all your feelings to people who don't care or who will hold them against you. If you express strong emotions, even though they are temporary for you, other people may hold you to them later.

For instance, if you express intense excitement over a project that fails, people may see you as gullible. Or if you show wild exuberance over a new person at the office, people may mistakenly think that you are endorsing that person when you are merely excited over the prospect of a new associate. In these cases, your enthusiasm was just your typical way of getting into a project or of bonding with a new person. But low-key people will remember you as "weird" or "off center" if the thing fails or the person doesn't work out. In other cases, if you show momentary anger, even though you calm down instantly, others may think of you as irascible or difficult. What is a momentary reaction for you is more durable for them.

It is important for the deeply emotional person to guard against any one emotion dominating at the expense of the rest.

If you always feel weighed down by some particular unpleasant emotion—for example, you are regularly furious with people for neglecting you, or envious of your friends, or impatient with the slowness of others, then you probably are "overdosed" with a particular emotion.

Examine that emotion—say feeling put upon, or feeling frustrated, and ask, "What do I expect of the world?" You may begin to see that you feel put upon because you have a lazy streak. Or you feel frustrated because you are counting on others too much. The next time that emotion pops up, use it as a clue that you are falling into your old trap. In every case, the emotion tells you something about yourself.

Why Should You Encourage a Rich Emotional Life in Others?

Give other people's emotions the same respect that you give your own. As important as encouraging your own emotional life is showing ready acceptance when other people talk about how they feel.

As soon as you criticize a friend for liking a certain person or for being sexually attracted to someone, as soon as you criticize him for being angry at something that seems insignificant to you, you create distance from that friend. Your friend may not recognize your effect on him, but he or she will confide in you less, saving truly intimate disclosures for people who accept him as he is.

If you want people to like you and feel close to you, don't censor their expressions of feeling.

We've all had "friends" who don't get angry along with us when we have been hurt or mistreated by someone. This kind of "friend" may instantly try to shut us down when we seem angry, as by implying that we are immature or juvenile or cruel.

The person does this because our anger frightens him. Our seeming loss of composure is more threatening to this person than the assault on us. Such a "friend" is incapable of the emotional loyalty required for solid identification with us.

♦ Censorship of any kind will interfere with friendship.

♦ It is a mistake to imagine that maturity implies reduced emotional range. Maturity merely implies the ability to act with discretion, to select from among the many promptings of a rich emotional life.

Deepening Communication with Your Emotional Life

How we tune up our emotional lives is best grasped when we understand how we have compromised them in the first place. Essentially we forfeit our true individuality through censorship of ourselves—by condemning our own reactions. By stamping them out when they occur quite naturally.

There are sound psychological principles for recovering our emotional lives, some of them well represented by Shakespearean characters. Here are seven principles taken from Shakespeare that I have found helpful with my patients:

1.   Decide if you are truly an emotionally "cut-off" person or not.

You are cut off emotionally if you are frightened by the idea of strong feelings, yours or another person's. Perhaps you don't even want to be loved too much.

Suppose you find yourself thinking all the time, "Oh no, I shouldn't really feel that." In this case, you are probably underexposed to your own feelings. Some corroboration would be if people consider you stolid, a silent type, or secretive. The real problem is that you are keeping your emotions a secret from yourself.

Begin by asking yourself, "What am I afraid will happen if I have the feeling full blast?" For instance, if you admit that you don't like your boss or that you're furious at someone you love? No feeling in itself can force you to do something destructive. Nor does having any particular feeling mean that you are an evil or immoral person. However bizarre or inappropriate a feeling may seem to you, you can be certain that millions of other people have had feelings just like it. Most people have much stronger feelings than they express, but this doesn't mean that they are out of control.

You can judge that you are generally in touch with your emotions if you have a wide variety of strong feelings only some of which you act upon. The healthy person is able to hate and then love in quick succession. He or she retains his emotional life, and in this sense understands his own essence—without having to act in accordance with every feeling.

2.   Learn to process your emotions.

Stop and permit yourself to experience emotions before you act upon them. Prove to yourself that you are not an impulse person. If you're angry or terrified or in love, don't always immediately act in accordance with those feelings. You will be far more likely to embrace all your emotions, to get them to work for you, once you realize that having an emotion does not require that you act upon it.

A major reason why many people pretend that they don't have some feeling is the fear that if they do acknowledge it, they will act rashly. For instance, they worry that if they hate someone or are attracted to someone, they will show it. The truth is just the opposite: we are less likely to involuntarily show a feeling if we know we have it. When you know what you're feeling, you are least apt to do something foolish.

Even if you plan to act on an emotion, it is still important to give yourself time to experience the emotion first.

For example, you realize that you've been forced into making an appointment with someone you really don't like and don't want to see. You decide to call and break the appointment. Allow yourself to experience what you're feeling—"This guy just talks about his troubles and I don't want to be around him."—while you rehearse exactly what you're going to tell him.

Identifying your feelings frankly to yourself will stop any urge you have to tell him off, which you may not want to do because you don't want to get into a long discussion with him. You can decide just how discouraging you want to be. You can be polite with an excuse that will hold him for a while. Or you can cover the whole future—for instance, by saying you're too involved in your career for a relationship right now. This, too, you can do without damaging his ego. If you'd still rather tell him off, go ahead. But at least recognize that you have a choice.

Much has been said about taking the time to mourn a death or a loss.

When Macduff, a character in *Macbeth*, learns that his wife and children have just been slain, a friend urges him to dispute it like a man. But Macduff replies,

> *I shall do so,*
> *But I must also feel it as a man.*

A processing of the experience goes on, and presumably Macduff feels the need for that process. And this processing time is needed for many other emotions, too.

Experiencing romantic emotions is just as important.

The best way to fully experience warm emotions is to state them in words. By immediately *doing* something instead of allowing yourself to feel the emotion and state it, you cheat yourself and the other person out of the shared experience.

It is always hurtful when a romantic partner says, "Why should I have to tell you I love you when I show it in a million ways?" Such people are nearly always inhibited about their true feelings. They don't want to acknowledge them, even to themselves. At best, these people miss the point and live more shallowly than they might. By never expressing their feelings in words, they themselves may lose touch with their feelings for the other person, substituting repetitive actions for those feelings.

Our feelings need space and direct expression in words.

3.   Don't condemn yourself for any emotion.

If you despise yourself for feeling afraid or homesick or jealous, you will teach yourself to repress these feelings.

Repressed feelings will often come back to haunt you. You may never actually admit to yourself that you're lonely or homesick, but you will still have nightmares about homelessness and will feel an inexplicable emptiness during the day. It is far better to know what you are feeing than not to know. If you know, even if you can't solve the problem, you will feel less helpless.

The value of recognizing an experience, even a monstrous one, arises in the contrast between Macbeth and his wife, who share the guilt of killing King Duncan. Macbeth experiences his guilt and talks about it, sobbing inconsolably for a while. But he deals with it, recovers, and fights valiantly for his life in spite of it. Lady Macbeth never acknowledges her guilt and mocks her husband as a coward; later, however, she goes psychotic as a result of it.

Macbeth actually describes the danger of losing touch with oneself, of going mad, as a result of guilt. He comments on what he has done:

To know my deed, 'twere best not know myself.

This is a perfect statement of the alienation of self which present-day psychology considers a cause of psychosis: losing touch with one's own experience.

4.   Don't mock an emotion in others.

If you do, it becomes awfully hard to admit it when you have the feeling yourself.

People who make fun of their own initial warm feelings for others are likely to obscure and stifle those feelings. They make it hard for themselves to form attachments. If you make fun of commitment, it's hard for you to admit it if you fall in love. If you think that being fearful is ridiculous, you will be brutal on yourself if you catch yourself being nervous. Mocking any emotion in another person is virtually equivalent to mocking it in oneself.

5.   Don't expect yourself to be perfectly emotionally consistent.

From time to time, you will surely feel angry at those you love, and you will enjoy things about people whose values you abhor.

Your emotions are in constant flow, and if you pretend to yourself that you always feel positively about friends or that you never admire someone you dislike, you are only fooling yourself. Even your worst enemy can tell a funny joke, and you may laugh with him. To deny this is like telling yourself that you never had a sexual feeling toward someone outside your primary relationship. That certainly isn't true.

Don't try for absolute consistency in how you feel about anyone, or you will obscure your real feelings. The demand for such inner consistency is an unfair censorship of your own emotional life.

6.   Treasure your feelings more than any device that might eliminate them.

If you take a drink or two, it should be for pleasure or relaxation, not to get rid of fear or anger or any other feeling. It's rare that I want a patient to seek medications in order to change his or her mood. If you're depressed or anxious, there's a reason, and simply knocking out those feelings won't help you discover what they are.

We've all seen relationships that were made possible only because the participants regularly got drunk or stoned together in order to mask the real trouble between them. If one or both of them hadn't tried to blank out their consciousness, things would have become clearer a long time ago. If there's trouble, keep your mind and feelings clear so that you can find it.

7.   Cherish every emotion, even if it is one that causes you pain.

The true stimulus for your pain is not the feeling itself. Your feelings are like eyes which are seeing something unpleasant. Use your feelings as you use your other senses, to avert danger outside you or within you.

Be especially alert to repeated danger signals—as an example, if you always feel bad about yourself when you are with certain individuals. Perhaps those people, though seemingly friendly, are acting in some way that hurts you. You hadn't thought about it, but the feeling is telling you something.

For instance, a friend talks but doesn't truly listen to you or doesn't remember what you say. Or the person subtly brags that he is doing better than you are and you feel empty and a bit depressed. Or you have started to do well in the world and the other person isn't happy. It's upsetting to recognize these discordant notes in a friend or in someone you've known for a long time. But your feelings are always telling you some truth, and it's up to you to listen. Our reactions, unpleasant as they may be, are often our last directives toward honest assessment and repair. They provide the latitude and longitude needed to direct us toward positive actions. To be proud of our ability to feel is to remove the temptation to dull ourselves.

*   *   *

That Shakespeare was so conscious of himself, was so accepting of his own feelings, may actually have saved his life. He lived in a dangerous underground world populated by playwrights, actors, and political activists.

From what we can tell, Shakespeare's life was steadier and more secure than those of his rival playwrights. Ben Jonson, a fellow playwright, killed two men in duels and was himself imprisoned and nearly executed. Christopher Marlowe, Shakespeare's greatest rival, was also in knife fights, and was murdered at twenty-nine. Playwrights also ran the risk of offending powerful people by what they said or what they wrote.

How did Shakespeare manage to survive, finding favor not only in his theatre world but with royalty?

Almost surely, his knowing precisely what he was feeling at all times, as well as his canny sense of his terrain and of what was possible, helped him make successful decisions. Being cognizant of any strong feelings he had, he could choose what he expressed, and could avoid being overcome by impulsive needs that might have jeopardized him. He was enough aware of his own impulses to fight them when necessary and go with them most of the time.

Stage Two
UNDERSTANDING OTHERS

DEVELOPING THE FORCE OF EMPATHY

Empathy was of the greatest importance to Shakespeare. He saw empathy or the lack of it as decisive in all human dealings. People who understood others found success in love and in the world. Those who were blind to others, who had no empathy, often paid the price. In this, Shakespeare again anticipated a goal of modern therapy, that of helping people develop empathy.

Empathy has been defined in many ways, but the actual mechanics of how it works have been less discussed. Empathy is the sense of feeling what others feel. It is also the willingness to experience those feelings.

But how do we actually express empathy in the real world? The foundation for empathy is understanding that whenever we speak to someone, we are addressing not only the person's conscious mind, but also his or her unconscious mind. In a sense we are speaking not just to the person's intelligence but to his or her spirit.

The unconscious mind—the spirit—understands many levels of what is said and it remembers everything. The person who is sensitive to these unspoken levels of communication is the one whom other people go toward and favor. You possibly have such people in your life—a friend who always seems to say "the right thing," a mentor at work whom everyone feels free to talk to, an intimate who knows what your day was like before you open your mouth.

You may think of these people as being masters of empathy, and perhaps they are. They are masters at staying friends with the spirits of other people—with other people's unconscious minds.

As you strive to draw people close to you and stay friends with their unconscious, you will learn progressively more about them. You will grasp them in their great diversity. Empathy will be a seemingly natural outgrowth of your efforts, and other people will feel that empathy and will repay you in kind.

*　　*　　*

Every time you deal with someone, you are affecting the person on two levels. The exchange that you and the other person could describe is that on the surface level. You may have worked hard on presenting yourself well and on making a good impression. You have succeeded on this level.

But though this surface level of dealings is important, it must be supported by your making a good impression on the second level—on the unconscious level. People register far more in this deep unconscious realm.

The other person will not verbalize how you affect him or her on this second level. He won't be able to pinpoint it or put it into words because it is unconscious. But it will deeply color his attitude toward you.

Even if you are very well balanced with a fine sense of self, and in fact do well at other stages of development, your efforts will be in vain if people unconsciously react to you as an injurious person or a neglectful one. If you attend only to the surface level in your dealings with people, they will feel that you are "handling" them instead of genuinely interacting with them. Or they may like you and dislike themselves in your company, in which case you will pay the price in the future.

By your impact on others—whether they are your intimates or you meet them only once—you cause them to feel proud, intelligent, young, and bright—or neglected, demoralized, aged, and past their prime.

They translate your effect on them into their treatment of you. Often, without even knowing it, they decide not to see you again or not to offer you a raise or not to introduce you to someone you might have loved.

If your impact on their unconscious is favorable, they may not even recognize consciously that they like themselves better with you in their lives. But you reap the benefits. When the right job opens up, you come to their minds. You may be short on qualifications, but something in their unconscious tells them that you can surmount this drawback. Their unconscious likes you or loves you.

You go through life making friends or enemies of people's unconscious. If you make enemies, even if you are great to look at, charming and bright, you will be an underachiever and find yourself curiously unwelcome in many places. At best you will be like the proverbial guest who found himself invited to each of the finest homes in London *once*.

You will suffer in love relationships in ways that seem unfathomable to you and unfair. Your partner may start out infatuated with you, adoring you. You won't realize it but if he unconsciously feels inadequate—say because you constantly tell him that he's too emotional, or you give him a sense that he'd be nowhere without you—his unconscious will perceive you as an enemy even if he loves you. Let his love diminish a little during a bad period and you will pay the price.

In most cases, the unconscious becomes conscious over time. A psychologist, Wilhelm Wundt, who lived before Freud, described the unconscious as having a life of its own, constantly trying to thrust its truths into consciousness.

Your entire fate in relationships relies on how you affect people's unconscious. You need to think of other people's unconscious minds as the unseen deities that influence your fate.

Although Shakespeare never used the word, he was the first person to define by his body of work what the unconscious was. He often used it to show hidden motivation, but in large part he showed its operation by portraying people who were making friends or enemies of other people's unconscious minds.

In Shakespeare's time, this second stage of psychological evolution might have been summarized as, "Do unto others what you would have them do unto you." The psychological extension of this universal truth would be, "Remember that other people react unconsciously, just the way you do. Thousands of impressions cross your mind every day. Why should others be any less perceptive or sensitive than you?"

For instance, we might say, don't be late for appointments because it inconveniences others. Someone may hate to be kept waiting, partially because of surface reasons. It's cold outside and it's annoying to wait.

But they may also hate to be kept waiting because of deeper messages that are being delivered to their subconscious. The other person is in some sense saying to them, "You aren't as important to me as something or someone else." Or, "It's not worth it to me to watch the clock for your sake."

The other person's unconscious experiences neglect and, perhaps, humiliation. Being demoted in dignity, even without knowing that this is happening, he or she draws closer to mistreating you as a defensive act.

This second stage of psychological evolution—staying friends with people's unconscious—springs very much out of the first one. The fully balanced person values the individuality of others. This person respects the feelings of others, whatever they are. And, he or she respects the need that other people have to be recognized, to be acknowledged.

He or she understands the concept of aftereffect, the idea that much of what people feel about you comes from the effect that settles in *after* you have gone. An hour or a day later they realize that they feel calm, having been in your presence or, conversely, they feel suddenly panicky or inadequate. Being with you has made them feel that they aren't doing well enough in the world or that they aren't looking after their appearances well enough.

These aftereffects determine the course of relationships as surely as experiences that two people have when together.

Being friends with people's unconscious involves realizing that you are no longer a child at school. Your world is far from being composed of people who root for you and are waiting for you to succeed, like teachers or loving parents. With perhaps a few exceptions, people are not looking forward to your next success. Shoving your successes at them or flaunting your greatness is not enough to make others happy. Enhancing *them* will do a lot more.

The art of befriending people's unconscious is also that of helping them to feel comfortable in their own skin. People instantly sense, though often unconsciously, when you want them as admirers, when you feel that their main function is to glorify you.

Just as surely, people will shy away from you if they feel that you are not experiencing them and enjoying them as they are. They will sense it when you wish that they were different—for example, if you wish that they took more of your advice. A major part of staying friends with people's unconscious is learning to experience people and enjoy them instead of trying to change them.

Your very appreciation of the need to make friends with people's unconscious is a start toward doing so. You realize that people are smarter than they may seem and certainly smarter than they typically let on or even know themselves.

The next chapters present and illustrate the basic keys to staying friends with people's unconscious. Giving people the freedom of their own feelings, acknowledging them and enjoying who they are, and understanding how to present ideas in ways that will ingratiate the unconscious minds of others—Shakespeare has a great deal to say about all of this.

3

ANTONIO'S VIRTUE

NEVER REMIND PEOPLE OF WHAT YOU'VE DONE FOR THEM

As a psychotherapist, I've often had couples sit in my office with a wide chasm between them. Sometimes they've just started to make progress toward understanding one another, and I begin to feel hopeful, when one of them ends the communication by suddenly listing to the other "all the things I've done for you over the years."

Recently a patient of mine told her husband, "I put off my career the whole time you were in medical school, and now I'm too old to get into an executive training program."

Another patient, a man, regularly complained to his wife, "What credit do I get, after all the time I poured into those rotten friends of yours who came over and never gave a damn about me?"

Once the catalogue of past good deeds starts unfolding, I know that the other person will simply stop trying to reach out.

The person delivering the invoice may be snarling or crying. It doesn't matter. The other person inevitably feels assaulted and hopeless.

The one with the catalogue may imagine that he or she is making a case for being loved, explaining why he is lovable. But the listener always feels pummeled, and instinctively knows that any tears being shed aren't for him or her. They are tears of self-pity.

If the listener has a personality as intense as that of the speaker, he or she will break in before long with his own list. "You put up with my friends? And what about all the years I put in dealing with your hysterical mother and her imagined illnesses?"

More often, however, the listener expresses his rage by falling silent, by going dead, as if unmoved by this plea for "justice."

The Temptation to Indebt People

These days, a seldom-examined speech by a minor Shakespeare character has been coming to my mind when people go into these little speeches.

The character, in the play *Twelfth Night,* is a man named Antonio, an old sea captain who has a shady past. We learn that Antonio has done a good deed. He has saved the life of Sebastian, a youth who nearly drowned in a shipwreck. And after that, he lent the boy money so that Sebastian could make his way on shore.

Later in the play, Antonio is recognized as a pirate and arrested. At this point he begs Sebastian to return his money. However, *Twelfth Night* is one of those plays whose plot hinges on mistaken identities. Antonio is mistaken in thinking that he is talking to Sebastian. He is actually talking to Sebastian's twin, who has never seen him before. This twin, understandably, will not repay the debt because, from his point of view, there is none.

Most people in Antonio's situation, shocked by what appears to be extreme ingratitude, would immediately list for the other person everything they'd done for him. But Antonio rises to greatness in resisting the impulse. He decides that if his good deeds aren't persuasive, his words won't add a thing. He merely mutters, half to himself,

> *Do not tempt my misery,*
> *Lest that it make me so unsound a man*
> *As to upbraid you with those kindnesses*
> *That I have done for you.*

I would like my patients to reason as Antonio did, that it is always unsound to list for other people whatever kindnesses they have done for them.

But it is sometimes very hard to convince people that this is always a useless tactic.

Obviously, once a person starts doing this in my office, I can't stop him in his tracks. But I make a mental note to bring up his approach with him, ideally when his partner isn't there, and help the person see that such an approach never accomplishes what it's supposed to.

Fear of Disappearing

There's a growing tendency for people in our culture to crave visibility. So much attention is lavished on media figures and athletes that the great majority of people fear that they are lost and unseen. Many develop what we call a fear of disappearing. This dread of being overlooked is heightened because in so many contexts people are reduced to statistics. More than ever, individuals want credit for every little thing they do, as if being noticed were everything.

I was recently in a hospital for the aged, and on the ward, there were forty wheelchairs. Each one had a little plaque on it, "Donated by . . ." so that when one of the elderly people leaned back, the name of the donor got engraved on his or her back.

This fear of disappearing becomes most acute when we feel unappreciated by people we're close to.

We've nearly all felt stung by people's ingratitude from time to time. When someone takes us for granted or criticizes us after we've extended ourselves, it's a natural impulse to want to shout into the person's ear and enumerate everything we've done for him.

Thankless people make us feel as if we can make no mark, even when we do our best.

A female patient was furious with her mother. She had bought her mother a dozen thoughtfully chosen items over the year, not very expensive but luxuries that her mother couldn't otherwise afford. She received hardly a perfunctory thank-you.

Besides being thankless, her mother was critical of how the woman ran her life and how she spent her money.

My patient understandably felt a profound temptation to bellow into her mother's ear a list of sacrifices she had made for her. She arrived in my office with a long letter written to her mother but not yet mailed, listing the donations of money and time that she had made to her.

I asked her to delay sending the letter while we discussed her need to send it, and in the next few sessions I helped her see the adverse effect that sending it would have on her psyche.

- ◆ No matter how abused we feel by someone for whom we have done a great deal, we will only end up feeling worse if we succumb to listing the favors that we have done for the person.

- ◆ We may get some immediate gratification out of swamping the person this way, but hours later we'll feel unhinged.

As we saw, Shakespeare called the behavior "unsound." And, indeed, even if our list is accurate, we often present it hysterically. The feeling of our having been a bit crazy tends to linger.

Essentially, we've been pleading for the person's gratitude and we'll feel reduced by having done so. It's a form of begging for recognition and love, and doing this never makes us feel good afterwards.

At worst, we'll feel hollow and somewhat second-rate. Such a diatribe will make our kind acts feel manipulative even if they really weren't. It starts to appear, even to us, as if we wanted credit or expected something back.

Citing what we've done for a person in the past nearly always implies that we feel helpless in the present. Our drawing on favors that we've done is a way of arming ourselves when we feel weak.

If you stoop to listing what you've done for someone, you will certainly not elicit gratitude at that moment, even if it might have been there at another time.

After examining the pros and cons of sending that letter, the woman in my office came to see that the letter would not goad her mother into giving her any satisfaction. Originally, she had pictured her mother receiving the letter, being moved to tears by a recognition of her daughter's kindnesses, and hating herself for her own ingratitude.

I convinced my patient, however, that instead her mother would only see the letter as a frontal attack. The "kindnesses" would disappear, and instead of hating herself for her ingratitude, the woman would hate her daughter for calling her on an ugly trait and putting her behavior in the spotlight.

Rather than thanks, such a letter would reap only resentment.

Which Do You Want: Victory or Love?

In many cases you may be so angry that you think you don't care what the other person feels. Reciting your list is all that matters to you. However, you must look deeply into yourself and understand that your very recitation means that you are begging. You are desperate to elicit gratitude and, possibly, love.

If this were not the case, and you really were as angry as you believed, you would simply walk away and attribute your losses to poor luck or poor judgment.

More often, though, we have to admit to ourselves that we do care deeply about the other person's reaction. We understandably want our loved one or some associate to recognize us and acknowledge us.

At work it may be a matter of survival. Our job may depend on our boss's giving us the credit we deserve.

In all cases it is important for us to diagnose how we affect the other person when we tell him what we've done for him.

On the most basic level, you are always humiliating that person. For this reason, introducing catalogues into any argument escalates it to an ugly level. People instantly want to back away from you. You make them feel beholden and dependent. You cheat them out of their sense that they are of good character and you generally undo many of the benefits of what you've done for them.

By definition you are saying that the other person has been in need of you and that he is less of a person than you are. You assault his or her pride and status. You are attempting to make him appear indebted to you and obligated to you. You are as much as saying that he couldn't be where he is without you.

Don't Let the Helpless Child in You Talk

Telling someone what you did for him is the last resort of a person feeling utterly helpless.

If your desirability, your maturity, your inherent worth, can't move the other person, then all you have left is to indebt people to you. You are preying on their guilt. This is a ploy that certain children use, exploiting the guilt of a parent who loves them and worries that he or she may not be doing enough for them.

Often as I watch the faces of people as they rattle off the list of how much they've suffered and how much they've given, I see a very infantile expression come over them. Some close their eyes tightly as they contrast the irony of how much they give and how little they get back.

COPING WITH THE "WHAT ABOUT EVERYTHING I'VE DONE FOR YOU?" URGE

1.   In the office.

In business, it is vital that you understand the difference between taking proper credit for your achievements and telling others what you've done for them.

Part of being responsible in a job is being able to step up aggressively and take credit, just as you must step up and take blame when you've made a mistake. Women often find it especially hard to seize the credit they deserve. Your tone of voice will tell you, and will tell others, if you are taking due credit or speaking out of infantile injury.

Some people find themselves faced with a chronic problem—namely, their boss. If your boss is taking credit for your ideas or for your contacts, there is, unfortunately, very little you can do. Hundreds of guidebooks will offer you nuances of what to say or do in such a situation. But the bottom line may be that if you do anything to directly confront the boss, he or she will feel either betrayed or caught.

Obviously, you never contradict the boss in public, but you may feel tempted to say after a meeting, "How could you say that was your idea when I worked overtime all summer researching the concept?" He or she may agree with you in private and even give you credit publicly. But the boss will feel that you are not a "team player," meaning that you won't obliterate yourself after you've done a good job.

Whether or not you win this battle, you are on your way to losing the war. Your boss may now feel that you are not a good repository of his secrets, which may range from real business matters to the "secret" of his own incompetence.

Many successful patients of mine in this situation have opted to put in their time quietly, but with an eye to a better future elsewhere. If you log the time on your résumé and suppress your open ambitions as the boss requires, you will probably leave a winner. You will get a good recommendation and have a business friend for life, provided your boss is able to keep his job without you.

2.   Parents feel the urge more than most.

Parents often feel a strong urge to give children a catalogue. When they feel they're being defied, or when the children aren't behaving as the parents hoped they would, there may be an urge on the parents' part to control them by indebting them, particularly with money. Out come the lists of "all the sacrifices we've made for you."

Any parent may be prone to do this, but I've noticed that it is especially tempting to the more hardworking but less glamorous member of a divorced couple. Nearly always it's the wife. The husband comes by on custody day, gives the child more freedom, buys a few luxuries, and takes the kid on a desirable outing.

Many men in this position play it to the hilt, for instance, by keeping the child out too long and joining the child in seeing the mother as a worrier or as a warrior.

Young children obviously aren't in position to appreciate that the mother agonizes over survival details. Perhaps the mother alone worries about the child's sleep schedule, about the child's having warm clothes. The mother is by necessity the disciplinarian and the one who arranges to bring positive adult figures into the child's life. From the eight-year-old's point of view, Daddy's willingness to buy extra candy bars on custody day counts far more than these things.

Perhaps no one ever feels more tempted to rattle off an "all I've done for you" list than such a mother, up against a father who counts himself a luxury. But don't succumb even here. Your child almost surely loves you even if it doesn't show right now. Your list won't help; it will simply upset the child and make you look hysterical. But if you stay responsible, it is virtually guaranteed that your child will some day appreciate what you've done. Your caring will win out in the end.

3.   Love and lists don't go together.

Any impulse to recount your virtues to a lover is a sure sign that you feel neglected. At worst, you may feel that the person is falling out of love with you.

If he is seeing beauty in someone else or is actually having an affair, it won't help at all to remind him that he wouldn't have gotten half as far without you. We've nearly all had the infantile impulse to remind someone we love of how indispensable we have been—and still are. But doing this will make your rival look better, not worse.

No one wants to be with a lover out of obligation. The very essence of love is freedom and the enjoyment of one's own greatness in the lover's eyes.

If, sadly, the other person no longer loves you, then your recounting all that you have done for him will only demoralize you more. Even if the person took your list to heart, and said, "You're right. You have done more for me than I realized. I will stay with you," you would know that you hadn't really won the person back. He would be staying with you only out of guilt. Bad as it might seem for him to leave, this would be worse because you would subconsciously feel unwanted and would be waiting for him to leave.

On the other hand, there are bad days in every love relationship, days when you don't feel loved, but days that pass and lead to better ones. Reminding your lover on one of those days of how much you've done for him will only prolong his or her bad mood. By not allowing her the spontaneity of her feelings, you are pushing her away.

Finally, if you are unlucky enough to be in love with a born detractor, forget it. Born detractors will never give you credit, and your asking for it can only demoralize you.

4.   When the urge to confront the person with a list comes over you, ask yourself, "Why do I need this credit?"

If it's a business matter, and the credit is absolutely necessary for survival, then make your presentation. But do it carefully, and with no hint of accusation toward anyone else. It will help to rehearse to be sure that you don't allow any whimpering or self-pity to invade your tone. And remember, *forcing* your boss to credit you may leave her smarting.

If you feel the urge with a family member or lover, refrain. Then study how you feel. What is prompting you to want to present this data?

5. If you're dealing with an ingrate, cut your losses.

If, when you're with a particular person, you chronically feel the need to give a list, consider the possibility that you are overgiving in this case.

If it's not a business situation in which you have to bite the bullet, then the cure may very well be to cut back on what you give.

Your continuous impulse to tell the person what you've done for him probably means either that he's an ingrate or that he truly doesn't want all your "good deeds." In either case, your telling him what you've done for him is a pure waste of time. Stop making some or all of your unappreciated contributions.

And resist the impulse to announce that you're going to cut down. Confronting him with that information would be just another attempt to make yourself heard and to elicit thanks.

6. Learn how to argue without citing your donations to people.

Keep your argument on the topic where it began. In general it's not good to load any argument with irrelevancies, and telling people they're obligated to you is the worst form of name-calling. With some people, it can become a way of life. Don't do this even if the other person does.

Certain family and office crowds engage in harping on what they've done as their main form of communication. See this tactic for what it is, and don't fall into the practice just because others do.

Stay in the present tense. Rehashing the past never works. If the basic issue of the argument is the other person's ingratitude, tell the person that he's an ingrate and forget the list.

Remember Antonio's approach. Keep the list to yourself, and you will feel more sound and surer of yourself, no matter what the other person does.

4
FALSTAFF'S GENIUS

MAKING OTHERS LOOK GOOD

One of Shakespeare's most miraculous characters is fat, elderly Sir John Falstaff. Shakespeare portrays Falstaff as a boastful man, a liar and a drinker, but still as one of the most likable characters in all the plays. Shakespeare must himself have loved Falstaff. He is one of the Bard's true creations, being at most loosely modeled after a nobleman whom Shakespeare must have known about.

Falstaff suddenly appears in *Henry IV, Part One,* as a fun-loving, roving, irresponsible character. We see Prince Hal, the son of Henry the Fourth and the heir to the throne, spending a great deal of time drinking with Falstaff. Though it is hardly possible to find a greater contrast in social status between two characters, they delight in one another and are quite intimate. Throughout the play, we see Falstaff misleading people, playing pranks, being caught out in them, and being enjoyed.

In *Henry IV, Part Two,* Falstaff appears again, full of life and joviality. The character seems to have grown in Shakespeare's own mind just as he grew in the public fantasy. Queen Elizabeth the First herself commissioned the Bard to write a play solely about Falstaff, and thus came *The Merry Wives of Windsor,* in which Falstaff rose to be the central figure. The death of Falstaff, mentioned in *Henry V,* is a real tragedy.

Why does the personality of Falstaff, this man who never actually lived, run through four separate plays? Why does he have this extraordinary status in Shakespeare's collected works? Why did Verdi, in fact, choose Falstaff to be the subject of one of his greatest operas?

One reason is that we see ourselves in Falstaff. But more than that, we *like ourselves* when we are in his presence. Always he creates an atmosphere of ebullience, making us, his audience, feel warm and perhaps a little superior to this very charming man. We are proud to be taken into his confidence and we sense that he likes us.

Falstaff himself knows that he has this talent for making others feel smart in his company. He knows how precious it is to do this. He announces, quite correctly,

> *I am not only witty*
> *in myself, but the cause that wit is in other men.*

He was the cause of wit in women, too, we might add. He brings out the best in us. We love ourselves when he is present. Falstaff knew the secret of success with other people.

The Art of Pleasing Is to Be Pleased

It's a common mistake to believe that if you impress people, they will advance you in life. Intelligence and polish certainly do count. But the criterion that many use to judge whether or not they have left a successful impression is dead wrong.

Dazzling others with your accomplishments and insights may seem the obvious way to win people over and achieve status. Certainly that's what you've been told to do all your life—to shine. In school you learned to compete with other kids and the idea was for you to be at the top of the class and for everyone else to know it. That was how you got accolades.

A very subtle factor had not yet entered the equation of your life. In the very narrow world of school and neighborhood you didn't need any of the people you beat out. The losing kids didn't matter. The people who counted—your parents and the authorities—were for the most part on your side if you excelled. However, in the real world, things aren't so simple. Excelling isn't all good; there's the real risk that you'll make other people feel diminished. When you are an adult, the people you beat out can hurt you.

As an adult you can be in serious trouble if your female boss acutely feels that you're much more attractive than she is or if your boss, male or female, feels that you deserve his job more than he or she does.

The Pie Concept

Many people hold a "pie concept" of life—that good things add up to one pie, and if you get a bigger piece they get a smaller one. These people automatically feel diminished when something good happens to you that doesn't happen to them. They feel as if your losing twenty pounds makes them fatter or your getting a big raise makes them poorer.

But it doesn't take a pie neurosis for others to feel overshadowed in the presence of someone who shines too much too often. You can make even the healthiest person feel invisible by besting them in small ways in conversation or in an interchange.

Remember, the key questions you should ask yourself after any meeting are not, "How well did I do?" "How did I sound?" "How did I look?" More important is how you made others feel in your presence. Though those questions should matter, the successful person also looks at the second, much deeper level.

The highly successful person asks, "Did the group, and in particular the key people there, feel that I respected them?" "Did I leave them feeling good about themselves or did I take away from their feeling of completeness?" "If they wanted to come across a certain way, did I let them?" For instance, if I was making a presentation to an older man, did I allow him to feel that he was young? If I was talking to someone without a college education, did I allow him to feel educated?

Don't succumb to a "pie concept" of the world that implies that for you to be great, others must be *less* great.

Make Even Your Interviewers Look Good

From time to time a patient of mine will call me just to talk about an upcoming interview for a job or an account that he or she is trying to get. "Have you any last-minute words of wisdom?" the person asks, knowing that there's little I can say at such a time and that psychotherapists don't really give advice.

I usually tell them, "Make the interviewer look good, that's the important thing. Give him the impression that he asked good questions and did a good job."

I assume that my patient has prepared thoroughly for the meeting. If he hasn't it's too late anyhow. But I also know that a great many very well-prepared people miss their chances at the last minute by not understanding that the interviewer, being only human, needs to feel competent too. Don't talk fast as if he's not a human being and you're just there to prove your worth. If you can, enjoy the interviewer's questions. Convey that they're interesting. Don't bury him or her under technical language. And if the interviewer mentions his own accomplishments or experience, take time to appreciate them.

Understanding the "Aftereffect"

The real impact of every meeting occurs in what we call its "aftereffect."

That aftereffect, the collection of feelings and impressions that materialize in the other person's unconscious after you have gone, is what determines your success or failure. It is this impression, resounding in your listener's unconscious, that determines whether another person likes you, respects you, whether he or she will give you the contract, whether he or she will want to go out on a second date with you.

Far more important than stamping your own intelligence and charm into the consciousness of onlookers is to touch their *unconscious* mind by making them feeling charming, young, brilliant, and vital in your company. If you can make people love themselves without their even considering it, they'll want you back again.

Leave a good aftereffect, and others will come toward you and cherish you. Leave a negative aftereffect, and the door will remain forever closed. Someone who was at first impressed by you may later realize that he feels put down. The darkness sets in as he senses that you didn't ask him a single question about himself, or that you didn't listen to her when she spoke.

The idea that a racy wit and quick answers will make you likable is as wrong as thinking that people will like you better if you one-up them in any other realm.

HOW CAN YOU MAKE OTHERS LIKE THEMSELVES IN YOUR PRESENCE? HERE ARE A FEW SIMPLE RULES:

1.   Stay visibly involved when other people talk.

Don't be animated when you talk and then use the time when others are speaking to rest. There are people who look animated when they're on, and glum when the other person is on. No matter how bright they are, they demoralize everyone with them.

2.   Be interested.

Ask people questions about themselves, their accomplishments, and their interests.

3.   Avoid asking demographic questions.

Demographic questions are those that you would find on a census form. They include, "How old are you?" "What do you do for a living?" "Do you own your apartment or home?" "Is it fully paid for?" "How many rooms do you have?" "Do you have any people reporting to you?"

Some of these questions might instantly appear vulgar or gross to you, and the more refined speaker might not use them. But many of the questions that fall into this category pass as the first things you should ask another person. They seem like icebreakers, and you can expect a battery of them at most cocktail parties or social gatherings where you are meeting new people.

However, if you think about it, these questions may bother you more than you imagine. In fact, they may be one of the reasons why you have some dread about going to certain parties that you think you should attend and even like. These questions are *not* the best way to present yourself to a new person. They are basically invasive, disturbing to many, and they put people on the spot to give a direct, factual answer.

At best, your listener will consider your question routine and answer it as he or she has a thousand times before, with resignation or boredom. At worst they will consider the question intrusive. And suppose they don't like the answer they feel forced to give, that they're older than you or that they live in a worse neighborhood or aren't proud of their job. Now they like themselves less than before they met you. They feel uncomfortable around you even if they don't know why.

If they give in to any urge to lie to you, as a way of upgrading their image, saying that they make more money than they do or implying that they come from a wealthier family than they do, then they will like you even less for forcing them into telling an untruth.

Try instead to talk about common third-person subjects. These could be common interests, news events, sports, or social facts that you both know. The ideal Falstaff would talk about everybody's subject so that other people can shine.

The demographic facts may well come out on their own; they surely will if you get to know the person over time. But you are giving the person the freedom to bring them up or not, as he or she pleases.

4. Stay on people's topics.

Switching people off their subject will give them a sense of breathlessness. Don't abruptly shift the focus of conversation when someone is speaking.

For example, if someone is discussing a new tax proposal and you don't follow those matters, don't wonder aloud why people discuss issues they have no control over. Even if you break into the conversation to say how impressed you are by how much the speaker knows, you are stopping the flow of conversation.

If you're not versed in a subject that people are talking about, just be quiet. A new subject will come up. Don't break up the flow with a new topic of your own, even if you can make it seem relevant.

5.   Convey a sense of having infinite time even when you don't have much.

When you are with people, give them the sense that you are completely with them. Don't give them the sense that you're half there and half looking ahead to your next appointment.

If you have a very limited time to be with them, let them know early. "Ken, I wanted to call you right back, but I only have a few minutes to talk. I'm due at a meeting."

By saying this in advance, you are alerting the person to get his message across quickly if he has one.

But more importantly, you are letting him know that a time constraint is your reason for being brief with him or her. If you tell the person this directly, then it is just a fact, but if the person senses this from your hasty manner, then all sorts of uncontrollable feelings may come over him. He may feel insignificant or think that you don't like him and have someone better to talk to. The other person, not knowing why you're in a rush, may feel that he's boring you. Don't risk the person's disliking himself because he thinks you're eager to finish up with him.

6.   Don't free-associate using your own stories.

If someone is telling you about his flight that was delayed, don't follow up with a delay story of your own, or worse yet interrupt with such a story. Doing so takes the focus solidly off him and puts it on you. Allow the person to regale you with his own tale.

When people tell jokes, resist the temptation to follow up with one of your own.

7.   If someone gets interrupted, as by a waiter or someone else in the group, reintroduce what he was saying.

Remind the person of where he was and ask him to continue. The person in the party who does this is the master of conveying that the speaker has something interesting or important to say.

8.   Finally, be ready to compliment people when you are genuinely impressed by their learning or by an insight.

And always be ready to say, "I never thought of that."

Falstaff and his gift have very special meaning to me as a therapist. My parents could not have been more unlike in social status and in the start they got in life. My father was educated and from a wealthy family, but my mother was a seventh-grade graduate who went to work to help her parents pay the rent. Doubtless Fred, my own father, had looked like a great catch to my mother's ten brothers and sisters. But my father was cynical, a wise guy, contemptuous, always using big words—the ultimate *poseur*.

Before I could form any recollection of him, he was gone. He never sent a penny home to help my mother, who for a time labored in menial jobs. My father's specialty was in making others look bad while my mother devoted herself to making others look good. Though my father had been sent through Columbia, and later through Yale Law School, he soon so estranged himself from his family by trying to look smart that they removed themselves and their assets from him, relative by relative.

When I was eighteen years old and found him, he was living in a fleabag hotel on Broadway in midtown Manhattan, a mile away from me. Over all those seventeen years, he had never troubled to contact me or even come to watch me playing in the street. By this time he had been cut off on all sides. Poor judgment had cost him his inheritance and his law practice had failed because he was smug and superior.

In his room he tried to impress me with fine words, saying that I was immature and stupid and implying that he was a genius, with vast knowledge. He told me that he read books, one after the other, and explained his poverty by saying that people didn't appreciate his talent. My mother certainly didn't, I thought.

She, by that time, had gone from typing in a secretarial pool to being the full-time secretary of a successful lawyer. She served him utterly without ostentation in so many ways that she was continually rewarded with raises. She was still with him thirty years later when he ran for mayor of New York City.

Guess which parent I was closer to?

Since those days, I have come upon many of these "smartest man in the world" types. I have watched them disqualify themselves, even as they felt sure that they were impressing everyone they met. I have watched others, some perhaps with less natural talent, who enjoyed other people openly and who were always ready to laugh or to say to a friend, "I never thought of that." These people who were openly receptive and never boastful, who, like our beloved Falstaff, made others look good, have risen slowly but surely, like great trees that canopy the forest.

In a race between wit and decency, as the Bard implies, wit will come out a distant second.

5

POLONIUS'S DOWNFALL

DON'T GIVE ADVICE

Shakespeare's name too often evokes mixed feelings in today's mass-market media age. Many people back away the minute they hear it. In childhood they developed a strong resistance to Shakespeare when his plays, along with other "great" works, were shoved at them.

Some of us later came to love Shakespeare or Beethoven or Mark Twain. But often this was no thanks to our teachers. In many cases they seemed to conspire against our ever genuinely liking the "masters." There were exceptions, of course, but most instructors presented the great artists to us stiffly, with reverence and a high moral tone. These teachers often implied that we were stupid if we couldn't grasp what, indeed, was over our heads at the time.

We began to equate Shakespeare and the others with those adults who were out of touch with the everyday world. To many it was as if Shakespeare and our English teachers were colleagues who never took their jackets off or laughed or went outdoors.

Of course we didn't see the teaching as defective. We saw ourselves as defective. And we began to see Shakespeare as a heavy, boring academic challenge—an alternative to going out and having a good time. A friend of mine likes to say, "No one looks forward to being good."

This presentation of Shakespeare was exactly the opposite of what the Bard would have wanted. Shakespeare was at times a rowdy who talked a lot, spent his share of time in the taverns, and was once haled into court and charged, along with his buddies, with threatening a man's life. His only purpose in writing the plays was to entertain, and the people who attended them looked forward to them the way we might look forward to going to a hockey game or to a spectacular film.

Unlike other playwrights of his time, who still held the medieval view that the purpose of a play was to teach morality, Shakespeare held the modern viewpoint. The aim of his plays was to pack them in and give the audience a big experience. He was more a Steven Spielberg than a director of subtle French art films. He wanted to give his audience action and characters they could root for and against. When his plays were performed for the people of London, there was plenty of noise and drinking in the theatre. As with modern sports events, precautions had to be taken to keep troublemakers off the stage.

Even when the plays were performed at Queen Elizabeth the First's court, we can picture a loose atmosphere with flirtations taking place and food being served. Nothing like a stiff, required English class.

Like Any Good Psychologist, Shakespeare Avoided Giving Direct Advice

The aim of psychology is to help people discover themselves and then make their own choices. Young, eager practitioners often overestimate how much they can do for a patient by giving him or her "parental" direction. But if the patient has distorted perceptions, a right decision here or there won't help. As with vision, it's the eye itself that may need correction. Pointing things out won't help.

Shakespeare knew this, as he seemed to know so many of the human truths. He was in many senses the first public psychologist. He used the concept of the unconscious; he understood repression, sublimation, overcompensation—though he probably would have denied that he was any more sensitive than the people he was writing for.

The power of his insights is evident. But he had no desire to shove them at us, and therefore it takes scrutiny of his lines and familiarity with repeated themes to distill his insights and use them. He simply leaves truths in our path for us to consider. From a chance comment by one person, from the way another faces a crisis or reacts to it, we gain insights of inestimable value.

None of this, however, is given to us in the form of direct advice. Shakespeare, in fact, seems repulsed by people who give advice. From his earliest plays to those he wrote near the end of his career, he presents advice givers as fools. In his plays, those who tell other people how to live fare badly in their own lives, while people who are given advice listen to it with varying degrees of boredom and inevitably ignore it.

Therefore, it is a great shame that of all the Shakespeare passages that were forced on us, one of those that we were subjected to most reverently was a famous advice speech. While the speech, like much else in Shakespeare, contains remarkable insights, it was written primarily to portray a pompous, obnoxious advice giver, a man people couldn't stand.

Everyday Lecturers Aren't Sexy, Interesting, or Fun

No one likes to be subjected to a long, unasked-for lecture, whether or not it contains good information. It seems like one of the trials of childhood to be taught such a speech as if we're supposed to love it and can't live without it.

By using the speech in the same way the character did, to impart unasked-for advice, teachers ironically put Shakespeare in the position of being the very advice giver that he wrote the speech to mock. And we are in the unfortunate position of having to hold still for the speech when the Bard expected his audience to laugh in the face of the actor giving it.

Some of the speech is quite familiar:

> *Neither a borrower nor a lender be,*
> *For loan oft loses both itself and friend*
> *And borrowing dulleth the edge of husbandry.*
> *This above all: To thine own self be true,*
> *And it must follow, as the night the day,*
> *Thou canst not then be false to any man.*

Doubtless, good advice. But if you read the whole thing you'll see that it is all an admonition to be fine, to behave, to be sober. Another one of those "nobody looks forward to being good" experiences. And it is also a prime example of "Do as I say, not as I do." Polonius, the man who gives the speech in the play *Hamlet,* is no sterling character.

He commends to his son the ideal of considering friendship an end in itself; however, Polonius exploits all his own relationships. He deals with no one unless they are of use to him. And in any case, the advice that Polonius is trying to give is not the sort of stuff a parent can simply explain.

Polonius: Many Respect Him, but Nobody Wants to Know Him

Polonius is a lord who serves the Crown of Denmark. He is a character afflicted with the need to advise people. He is an advisor by nature, an advisor to his children, and by profession an advisor to the King and Queen of Denmark. We get the sense that he will advise anyone willing to listen.

No one heeds him, of course, though people hear him out. Hamlet calls him a "tedious old fool," and later kills him by accident, not to the regret of the audience.

Like hundreds of Shakespeare's characters, Polonius is extremely complex. Shakespeare has imbued this pompous, purely self-serving lecturer with a great many cogent insights. And it isn't simply that Shakespeare himself had those insights and couldn't resist imparting them to us at every chance. Polonius was, after all, a man who lived by his wits in a royal court, whose rise in favor required that he constantly observe other people and calculate the success and failure of his devices and techniques. Such a man would certainly have acquired a real body of useful knowledge as he grew older, and Polonius has more than his share.

Polonius's speech is one of the best-known runs in Shakespeare. Actors playing Polonius are typically judged by how they deliver this block of advice to Polonius's son Laertes, and many want to play the part because of the speech. Reviewers often comment on the delivery of this speech as if it were itself a character in the play.

The speech is foolish in its totality because it is bound to fall on deaf ears. This was one of Shakespeare's messages, that even the best of advice, given unsought, is pointless and burdensome. The father is talking to his son when the boy is about to depart for France; the audience realizes that if the youth could restrain himself, could listen and learn, could resist borrowing money and could be true to himself, he would hardly need such a speech. And if he couldn't, if he were a mere mortal like the rest of us, and young at that, Polonius could obviously not do him much good with such a going-away speech. It would have been far better for Polonius to embrace the boy, wish him luck, and say that he was going to miss him than to pontificate as he did.

The Key to Relationships Is: *Experience People but Don't Change Them*

I grew up in a neighborhood where everybody gave everybody else advice. You could hardly go down the street without being stopped by an adult who told you what you ought to be doing that you weren't doing. Mine was a post-Depression neighborhood of hardworking people, mainly second-generation immigrants. Families had a fear of going under financially and a fear of authority. Landing a secure job was the highest goal, and the highest value was keeping your nose clean. Though Washington Heights in Manhattan was a congested neighborhood, it wasn't dangerous (unless you consider advice dangerous).

As kids, we didn't think about the future very much, but our parents worried constantly. They wanted more for us than they'd been able to achieve. I almost never made it through a day without having to stand still for advice from all kinds of adults who towered over me. They would ask me what I had done that day, lecture me on what I ought to do, and if they lacked subject matter, would tell me to be a good boy.

Before we were in our teens, most of the kids had picked up their parents' anxiety and become advice givers, too. Some of my friends began to lecture me freely on whatever came to their minds. If I sat behind third base in Yankee Stadium, it would have been better to sit behind first. If I had worked turning the turnstile, been what we called "a stile boy," in order to get in, it would have been better to sell frankfurters. You couldn't see the game that way but you made more money. And if I sold frankfurters, it would have been better to sell scorecards.

Like many children, I naturally migrated toward those who had a live-and-let-live attitude, who welcomed me without telling me what I ought to be doing. It seemed better to be an outcast if necessary than to be in the center of things and be constantly told what to wear, when to get up in the morning, and how to be a good boy.

I never pictured an adult world in which I could someday have friends, acquaintances, colleagues who accepted me without telling me that I was doing something wrong.

I remember all my uncles and aunts at family gatherings asking me how I did in school, whether I was studying hard enough, how long I studied, whether I was being sure to read under a bright lamp because otherwise it would be bad for my eyes.

Only one of that crowd, an uncle, simply welcomed me; on occasion we went for walks, and those interludes had the serenity of his giving me no advice but of accepting me as I was, and still am—as me. He stands out in my memory, because for him I was good enough. With the others, I always felt I needed correction.

I couldn't articulate back then what seems very clear to me now—that *people all want to be experienced and not advised.* Without thinking about it, I grew up phobic about advice givers. To this day, when I see seasoned therapists telling their patients how to live or suggesting by innuendo who they ought to date or marry or how they ought to treat their mates, I feel revolted. I am convinced that the art of sustaining good relationships is *to experience people, not to change them.*

*   *   *

When I got to City College, I found a mass of highly intelligent and competitive people who were reluctant to help one another toward the few scholarships or jobs around. Advice dropped out of the picture, though not for the ideal reasons. At least people weren't relating to one another by the medium of telling each other how to live.

By then I was unconsciously seeking out people who simply enjoyed me, and whom I enjoyed. These were friends who shared my interests, but didn't steer me in any direction; and I didn't steer them. It seemed much better to be lost with them in a world where some good advice might have helped than to be among people who barraged me with unasked-for directions.

A few years later I was at Columbia University working for my doctorate. People there refrained from giving advice but it wasn't because they were competing with one another. They simply had less urge to give it. Most had come from more secure households than the ones I knew. They hadn't inherited the same urge to prove themselves, and were on the whole more quiet. They seemed less energetic in some ways but were also more patient with others and with themselves. They didn't compete openly and didn't advise each other much either.

Nor did they boast as the kids in my neighborhood were prone to do. It was as if they were accustomed to success and accustomed to seeing others handle themselves well, which in their case meant not having to be center-stage.

After graduating and working in a few hospitals, I started in private practice and became privy to the lives of people from many walks of life. It was then that I saw the real correlation between people who quietly go about their way and those who feel compelled to give advice. I saw a number of successful people who never squandered their energy correcting others. They were determined, planful, often generous. Even when uncertain of their own productivity and their own future, they kept a steady focus on what they needed to improve in their *own* lives.

I was often surprised when in the tenth session one of my quiet patients would tell me that he had built a business from scratch. When I worked with creative people—actors, sculptors, directors, artists, writers—I found that the more successful of them had very little advice for others in their field. They were too busy improving themselves, perfecting their skills and finding out what was missing in their own performance. These people were quite different from those I had grown up with, who, as rampant advice givers, made more enemies than friends and didn't seem to care as long as they could talk.

I soon developed an invaluable diagnostic tool from these observations. There is a strong negative correlation between succeeding in the world and being an advice giver.

Losers Tend to Give Unasked-for Advice. Winners Do Not

Compulsive advice givers are uncomfortable in their own skin. They know that something is wrong in their lives but can't identify it, so they constantly regulate other people—a solution which serves to pass along their discomfort.

The biggest advice givers are those least satisfied with their own progress. Their need to tell others how to live is a giveaway that they are unhappy. They try to manage others because they can't manage themselves.

When someone regularly gives unwanted advice, I conclude that no matter how much he has bragged to me (bragging is a trait that typically goes with advice giving), he is far less successful than he lets on.

Conversely, when capable people are slow to give advice, I suspect that they are even more successful than they are willing to admit.

Their secret is that they have understood the rule that the key to relationships is to convey that you are responsive and not critical.

Advice Is Always Implied Criticism

Successful people attain their status in part because they resist any impulse to tell others how to live, what to do, or to regulate people in social situations. If another person lives differently from them, they regard him or her without passing judgment. Perhaps what is right for them is not right for the other person.

When we leave such people, we feel that we were with someone who has enhanced us, not someone who leaves us feeling less than we were before we met them.

Another person's very need to give us advice implies that he thinks there is something deficient about us. There is something going on in our lives, something about us, that cries for correcting so loudly that this person is honor-bound to try to fix it. We might have met the person feeling pretty good about ourselves. We leave wondering what else is wrong with us and what shortcomings other people see in us but are too polite to mention.

Advice Givers Fall into Two Categories:

♦ Blatant ones and

♦ Insinuators.

Blatant advice givers lecture us as if we should take notes, implying that they know how life should be lived and that if we don't follow their recommendations we will surely go under.

For instance, a patient of mine, who frequented four-star restaurants known for their romantic atmosphere, would often complain to the maître d' brusquely and in a loud voice: "You should have brighter lights. People can't see what they're eating." He wondered why the owners seemingly never remembered his name or greeted him warmly as they did the other patrons. Blatant advice givers never stop to ask how they are going over.

Whenever someone tells you what you ought to be doing, the person is telling you in effect that you're not doing things right, that you've missed the essence of life, that you've squandered your chances. And he's saying that he knows better.

Insinuators are far more harmful because their poison enters insidiously. Unless we spot them we can't avoid them or even discount what they do. We will end up feeling that we are awkward and wrong ourselves.

They say such things as, "Don't you worry that you'll be sorry one day if you don't have children?" (This means you had better have children, as I did, or there is something wrong with you.)

Or, "It's not so easy to find jobs nowadays. Maybe your boss isn't so bad." (This is saying, No matter what your vicious boss does to you, you had better keep your job. Sensible people don't move around and try to upgrade their careers.)

Or, "Gee, those taco chips you're eating really have a lot of fat grams." This is great to hear when you're out to dinner with friends. (Translation: If you eat that you'll be a fat pig. I'm suffering to be thin, so should you.)

Always—and we feel it—it's not merely our behavior that's being addressed. The person is telling us that we have generally poor judgment, no class, no sophistication, or no morals, as the case may be.

Our first reaction to the advice giver, blatant or subtle, may be to hate ourselves and shrink back.

Next, if we can identify what's being done to us, it might be anger at the other person. "Who is this person to run us down?"

What Should You Do?

If the person is necessary to you, for example, if he is a client or your boss, there may be nothing you can say.

But there are vital steps that you can take to nullify the effect.

- Identify to yourself in words what the advice giver is doing, and then, in your own mind, discount the assault.

- Realize that giving advice is the other person's compulsive need and is not a response to anything that you've done wrong.

- Minimize contact with such people as gracefully as you can.

- If the offender is someone you love, like a parent, talk about it. Tell the person what he or she is doing, as lightly as you can. Acknowledge that the person loves you and is trying to help. But make clear that you're not in the market for help. You just want to enjoy your time with the person.

- The same goes for those innumerable people who give advice by innuendo. You may elect silence, which is fine so long as you are clear that the problem is theirs and not yours.

- Above all, remember that the key is to identify for yourself what the person is doing.

- Don't succumb to the pressure of advice just because it sounds soft and sincere.

Innuendo people, by appearing to state gently only what is obvious, put more pressure on you than do blatant people. By their whispering tones they imply that if you don't go along with them, you really are throwing everything away.

If you can speak freely to these insinuators, you must bring to the surface what they are really saying, to make them aware of the message they are trying to impart.

"John, we all have to live our own way." Or, "John, so far you've told me four ways to improve my life and we've only been together a half hour. What's going on?"

Or you can use a technique known as joining the other person in order to make clear what he or she is doing. "With all the mistakes I seem to be making, it's amazing I'm still alive."

The favorite technique of Shakespeare's characters when subjected to advice is to listen as politely as possible and then do exactly what they wanted to do in the first place. Polonius's son did this. And in one of Shakespeare's late plays, *Troilus and Cressida,* a set of aging kings seems addicted to giving advice while their listeners nod off. When these veterans are treated seriously by the director (and by the actors on stage) the play is slow. When their windy advice is considered a symptom of their decline, they come across as realistic and the play works much better on stage.

A Fatal Case of Advice Giving

A patient of mine used this method, portrayed by Shakespeare, when given unwanted advice some years ago.

The man, who later became a world-famous restaurateur, began his career early. As a twenty-three-year-old private during the Korean War, he was stationed on a small island a thousand miles from the fighting, and was already in charge of an elegant officers' restaurant to which General MacArthur was coming the following Friday. My patient's commanding officer, a colonel, was giving a sumptuous dinner in honor of the general. My patient had to plan the dinner in its every detail, utilizing what was available in the area and what he could arrange to have flown in.

The colonel, who himself was something of a gourmet, had recognized the youth's expertise; when my patient had gone to him with a detailed proposal for the dinner, including the decor, the seating arrangements, and a marvelous menu, he had given him his enthusiastic approval.

Three days before the visit, while the restaurant was buzzing with preparations, a woman well known on the base came in and demanded to know who was in charge of the dinner. The youth replied that he was. The woman, the wife of a senior officer, viewed herself as the island's arbiter of social graces. She told my patient that he was doing everything wrong. She then went through the menu disdainfully, disapproving of his very sophisticated choice to serve a certain red wine with the fish; she doubted that the quenelles would be a substantial enough appetizer for military men who had flown for many hours. On and on she went for twenty minutes about the seating arrangement, the flowers, and where the waiters should stand.

The youth listened politely to all this unsolicited advice. But he changed nothing, not the fold of a napkin.

The meal went spectacularly. MacArthur congratulated the colonel, saying that it was a miracle to find such a perfect repast in the middle of the Pacific.

The next day the colonel called in the youth and passed along the praise.

My patient then told him about the woman who had given him twenty minutes worth of unsolicited advice which he'd had the guts to listen to and not to take. He didn't identify her, but the colonel knew at once who she was. It turned out that she had been giving advice all over the island to people who were understandably quite tense to begin with. No one liked it.

Three weeks later, the woman was sent home and her husband was shipped off to battle in Korea, where he was killed before the end of the year.

Obviously, the outcome of giving advice is seldom lethal, as it was here. But the amount of harm that people do to themselves and others when they give unsolicited advice is immense. It is underestimated because those who receive the advice typically shrug it off and distance themselves from their would-be mentors, and the advice givers themselves never see how much damage their behavior does to them in relationships.

HERE ARE A FEW POINTS TO THINK ABOUT ON THE SUBJECT OF ADVICE

1.   Give advice sparingly if you must give it at all.

We all offer advice on occasion, even when it's not asked for. But we should give it very sparingly. Successful people scruple at giving advice even when they're asked for it. If someone asks them what they ought to do, the successful person will generally try to offset the superiority that automatically goes to anyone who gives advice. He or she will say something like, "I'm sure you know best." Or, "You probably have a workable system, but if it were me, I might . . ."

- When someone comes to you with a problem, it is vital to remember that responding at once by giving the person advice is the wrong thing to do.

- Remember, the aim is to experience the person, not to change him.

- Hear the person and let him know that you are hearing him. Try to experience his conflict as he does. Maybe you don't have a solution either, and maybe he doesn't really want your solution even if you have one. He wants you in his corner.

- Don't step on someone's pain by supplying a "to-do" list.

It is crushing for someone who comes to you expecting a sympathetic ear to be given a list of instructions. The person is already in pain, and is probably hoping that you will say something supportive, such as, "I'm with you whatever happens." Or reassuring, along the lines of "I'm sure you'll make the right decision. You usually do."

This particular need to give advice when someone comes for love and support in a dilemma causes a great deal of trouble between husbands and wives and between parents and children.

Your child or mate comes to you with a problem, wanting sympathy and support. Your aim should be to experience their isolation and their struggle. The child especially is often saying, "Tell me you love me even though I have messed up or am about to." Giving advice, telling people how to change, is the opposite of saying, "I love you as you are."

Learn to live with other people's uncertainty. Unfortunately, many people find it almost impossible to live with the other person's uncertainty. They can't resist letting loose with a barrage of "Here's what you should do," or "Here's what you should have done."

The impulse to give unsolicited advice is especially powerful for a parent with a child. It's hard to see someone we love, someone more helpless than we are, about to make a mistake, when we feel sure we could help. The urge to rush in, to fill the vacuum, is strong. But to do this is to miss the point entirely. You are trying to change something about the person or his behavior, and you are simply refusing to share his experience.

If you cannot control yourself, the other person may end up feeling unheard, overregulated, and sorry that he told you anything. Often, the strongest vote of confidence is to sympathize, to make clear that errors are part of existence, and then to step back and allow your child to live his or her own life.

2. Hear the person out.

Even if you plan to give the person the benefit of your experience, namely your insights, be sure to sympathize first and then to present no more than is requested of you very directly.

3. Make your advice easy to reject.

If possible, give advice in the form of a menu from which people can choose their own options.

This book, like many self-help books, presents advice in this menu form. Some of it may be useful to you. Some may not.

Credit the other person with having as much judgment as you have. It may be that you have seen something that he hasn't, that's all. Think of yourself as a consultant whom the person might employ for a particular purpose. The best doctors, lawyers, psychologists, consultants in any field, do this. They are speaking because they have gone down a particular road and the other person has not. The person has come to them for a menu of options in their domain of specialization. But they are not presenting themselves as "better" than the other person.

4.   Bear in mind that whenever you volunteer advice, you face the other person with a choice.

The person must make a decision whether to go with you or against you. He can follow your advice and stay in your good graces. But if he does so, and the advice is wrong, he may blame you and shun you. His other choice is to "disobey" you.

If he chooses this path of resisting your advice, whether or not he reports to you what he has done, distance has been created. You have become an authority figure. You have either demeaned the other person by placing him in the subservient position of doing as he is told or you have made him an adversary.

5.   Be aware that all advice places the other person in a subservient position, if only temporarily.

In the normal flow of life we exchange positions quickly, and often no harm is done. But those who are advice givers by nature retain an arrogant stance. No matter how much they convey that they are only trying to help, they are creating distance from those they advise.

Advice masquerades as an act of love, but refraining from giving advice is the true act of love. The essence of relationships is to experience people. Don't change them.

6
VALENTINE'S VALENTINE

MOVING AHEAD BY FLATTERY

The other night a friend stopped by my office to look at my computer. I had just added a new feature, a scanner, and he was thinking of buying one. I knew in advance that no matter how much he liked it, he would find a flaw. He would never compliment me on my judgment or put his seal of approval on my setup. He's a generous and decent person but seems emotionally opposed to flattery.

Other people embarrass us by their tendency to flatter excessively, predictably, almost compulsively.

"How marvelous that sofa is! Is it new?"

"No, I've had it for seven years."

"We were just talking about you yesterday and saying how handsome you've become in the last few years." You feel that your emotions are being played with, especially when the flattery is general and could apply to anybody.

You are going to be flattered from time to time. And you yourself will have to decide whether to compliment people or not and how it will sound if you do—in the office, in a love relationship, and even in the most casual friendships.

The position you take in relation to flattery will affect your life profoundly. To err on the side of not complimenting people enough will cost you dearly. Others will feel cheated and will feel distant from you. To overdo can be just as costly. People soon come to feel that you're manipulating them or even mocking them, and this way, too, you may create great distance from them.

Flattery as a Courtly Skill

Flattery is not simply a sixteenth-century skill that was used by the folks who surrounded Queen Elizabeth I in the time of Shakespeare. Most successful people are still courtiers in much of their lives. The Renaissance professionals were correct in assuming that flattery is a complex study. Whether we like to admit it or not, it is evident that those around us who have mastered the subtleties of the art use it to great advantage.

Is it manipulative to tell your mate that he or she looks well when the person really looks tired? Yes and no. You are choosing to be less than honest. But probably no one is harmed by the statement, and a bad scene might be avoided.

In a perfect world we might never have to flatter a boss or a coworker. But this is not a perfect world, and those who learn this early do a great deal better than those who don't.

Think of those people you know who always seem to say the right thing. They are probably the sort of people who seldom act without some overview in mind. Doubtless at some point in their lives, they formulated their own approach to flattery, made decisions about how to do it and when.

But flattery is by its very nature a secret skill. Masters of it almost never acknowledge that they are using a technique; they convey a sense of absolute spontaneity and ingenuousness.

Shakespearean Flattery

With his typical genius, Shakespeare saw subtle differences between kinds of flattery. He was allergic to some of its more overblown forms. But careful study of his work shows that he himself had carefully thought through the role of flattery. He divided the use of flattery up into several categories that still serve as a primer for our use in everyday life.

Shakespeare portrays three kinds of flattery which we find important to distinguish, and you may, too.

Let's call them:

◆ expedient flattery

◆ cavalier flattery

◆ flattery of genuine delight

Expedient flattery is the kind we traditionally think of. It is the most unsavory form of flattery. It is designed to get something from a person which you don't think you deserve or might not be given without it.

Obviously, no one is truthful all the time, especially in competitive situations, such as business dealings. But if you do flatter people for advantage, realize that you are being basically dishonest. Pushing the flattery button amounts to concealing your purpose in order to get another person to shell out what you want.

Should you adopt a policy of never flattering anyone for sheer expediency?

This would mean living with impeccable purity at great cost to yourself. Shakespeare's *Coriolanus* is the story of an ancient Roman warrior, who was so averse to this kind of flattery that he would never engage in it. In the end Coriolanus paid with his life for his refusal ever to say anything untrue or to flatter anyone in Rome.

Shakespeare has a friend say about Coriolanus:

> *His nature is too noble for the world;*
> *He would not flatter Neptune for his trident,*
> *Or Jove for's power to thunder. His heart's his mouth;*
> *What his breast forges, that his tongue must vent . . .*

Coriolanus was a real-life person, and Shakespeare took his story from the account of the ancient historian Plutarch. Shakespeare's description of Coriolanus, if we are to judge by Plutarch, was very accurate.

Few of us are Coriolanuses in life. We don't make a habit of expedient flattery but we do engage in it from time to time. If you do engage in it, as ninety-nine percent of us do on occasion, you would do well to own up to the fact that you are using it.

Let's face it. Expedient flattery is an art form.

◆ The key to successful expedient flattery is to stay as close to the truth as possible. Always be aware that you are entering a region that borders on mockery. Don't go too far.

◆ Make sure that your statements are basically accurate, or at least could pass as accurate. Most people know what their shortcomings are. Never say things that are obviously untrue.

◆ At best, find a way to give the truth a novel twist.
   If a woman says, "I hate myself; I'm too short," don't say, "No you aren't," as if implying that the woman is really tall. She knows she isn't. Instead, join her premise but interpret it in a better light. For example, say, "It's really feminine to be so delicately boned."

A few months ago, a woman who was getting on in years came with her new husband to a gathering I attended. She wondered aloud to the group what the younger man she had just married and who evidently loved her saw in "me, an old wreck." I will always remember a certain man, a very gracious employee of hers, responding, "There's a lot of gold in wrecks." He didn't mean it in the monetary sense, and everyone recognized that there was gold in the woman, who was extremely humane and gracious herself.

- ◆ **Try not to say anything that has probably been said to the person many times before.**
  If you say to a secretary, "Your boss couldn't do without you," it sounds like a line, a worn cliché. It would be better to say that you appreciate something in particular that he or she did for you. If a person says something well, it's hardly a stretch to say that he said it eloquently.

- ◆ **Don't cover up for people or flatter them when they are clearly in the wrong.**
  If you're a baseball fan you may have noticed that no one says anything in the dugout to a batter who has just struck out. There's nothing positive you can say to the player who probably feels terrible, and almost any comment at that time would simply infuriate him.

- ◆ **Don't let someone you have just flattered find you in the hall flattering someone else similarly.**
  I vividly recall being praised by a French woman for how well I spoke French. I was feeling great, since I always prided myself on how good my French was. A day or two later, I heard the same woman saying to a friend of mine that he spoke French beautifully. My friend had one of the worst accents I ever heard and had almost no vocabulary. I felt quite embarrassed at myself for believing the compliment and very annoyed at the woman, who left me feeling like a fool.

Remember that expedient flattery is basically dishonest. At worst, it is an act of contempt in that it treats the other person as if he or she were a moron. For this reason, you should engage in it as little as possible.

Cavalier flattery. Since you are going to flatter people throughout your life, take care to avoid the second kind of flattery, too—cavalier flattery.

This kind of flattery is for recreational purposes only; it's a form of laughing at people, so realize that if you get caught, you've had it.

Cavalier flattery is overtly excessive praise, which is often expressed with conscious contempt. Its aim is not to extract something from the other person, but to mock the person by the exaggeration—to show the person up as vulnerable and foolish. It is a hostile form of camp.

In using cavalier flattery, you are offering some compliment which no one in his right mind would really believe. The aim is to insult the other person, but by an evident compliment, so that you give that person nothing solid to complain about. The person knows that you are over-stating, but there is a certain graciousness to your style, making it hard for him to accuse you of an outright insult. The uncertainty that you arouse with cavalier flattery is part of your game. You may even want your flattery to be transparent. The aim of cavalier flattery is to impart pain, not pleasure.

In *The Merchant of Venice*, Portia has contempt for a wide range of men; she revels in mocking them behind their backs—all except Bassanio, who has cynically become a suitor primarily because Portia is a renowned heiress. Portia is merciless in laughing at those who have come to compete for her hand in marriage.

One of the suitors whom she mocks, the Duke of Morocco, is no fool. He knows that she despises him for being black. He makes a proud statement:

> *Mislike me not for my complexion,*
> *The shadowed livery of the burnish'd sun,*
> *To whom I am a neighbor and near bred.*

Then the Duke of Morocco uses cavalier flattery to mock Portia. He praises Portia with such deliberate exaggeration that no woman in her right mind could believe him.

> *I tell thee, lady, this aspect of mine*
> *Hath fear'd the valiant . . .*
> *. . . I would not change this hue,*
> *Except to steal your thoughts, my gentle queen.*

Is Portia worth that much to him? Obviously this respected and wealthy duke would not turn his skin white to win the love of a rich woman whom he had just met. An outright lie, and one that I think the Duke offers purposely to be seen through.

♦   Cavalier flattery is a way of praising someone without praising
that person at all.
It is saying in effect, "Take this ludicrous statement as a
compliment if you will; it is the most that I will offer you."

Cavalier flattery is still very popular. Salespeople engage in it with rich patrons every day. Their intention with this flattery may be less to make the sale than to turn their subservient role into a parody, by exaggerating it.

Flattery of delight. There is one form of flattery, however, that you ought to use and that people don't use nearly enough.

They're afraid of it, and yet if they could overcome their fear of it, it would make them happy and the other person happy, too. We are talking about the flattery of delight. Flattery of this kind is a natural overflow of your enthusiasm, of your sheer joy in another person or in qualities about them.

On the surface, half of what Shakespeare says looks like flattery. He flatters men, women, the way a sparrow hops, the way the "morn, in russet mantle clad" comes toward us. And yet we sense a stark accuracy in what he says, as if he were speaking from all of our hearts.

Like other seeming overstatements, such flattery may sound dishonest. But in this case, it isn't. The person is speaking from his heart, is swayed by his mood. If we judge what he says by purely objective standards, he is grossly exaggerating. But if we think of him as expressing his emotions, and allow that he is speaking subjectively, he is telling the truth.

In the natural rush of feeling, just as our fears become exaggerated at times and we express them, so does our pleasure and admiration become heightened, or at least they should in the balanced personality.

Our feelings, like our dreams, are often "good" exaggerations. Both may express unconscious happiness. Why should we not express this happiness? Why can't we call someone beautiful if we feel that way?

What seems like flattery to another person may be a genuine statement of our vision at the moment we're speaking. Friendship and love itself would be impossible without flattery. Both require assertions, made in all honesty, which delight the one making them as much as the hearer. The literal person who comes along and corrects them is missing the essence. In the play *The Winter's Tale,* a king says of a country girl:

This is the prettiest low-born lass that ever
Ran on the green-sword. Nothing she does, or seems,
But smacks of something greater than herself . . .

An exaggeration? Not if it seems that way to the speaker. Any lesser description would be a disservice to what the person wants to say. And if we can accept this in poetry, why not in real life?

In a sense, the very essence of love is flattery. The lover sees the beloved as more exalted than he or she actually is. For the person in love, the other person is the most beautiful, the most talented, the most magical, the brightest in every sense.

With love comes a natural impulse to praise the loved one. If we go a little further than literal truth permits, this can be counted as one of the freedoms that love bestows. Flattery is a natural expression for the lover and is a gift to the beloved.

Flattery is so linked with love that a person even expects his friends to flatter him or her on his very choice of a lover. Anyone who has ever acted lukewarm about a close friend's new lover or who failed to say something complimentary has been a disappointment. A true friend will join in the other person's flattery as part of his happiness.

In Shakespeare's play *The Two Gentlemen of Verona,* one of the gentlemen, Valentine, tells his friend, Proteus, that he is in love with a "divine" and "heavenly" woman. Proteus replies that he will not flatter her. To which Valentine demands, then "flatter me for love delights in praises."

Valentine is so pleased with the woman he loves that he assumes that all the world will recognize the greatness of his love and praise him for it.

It is not always true, however, that all the world loves a lover. Some people will resent us for our love, and will envy us. But we certainly expect our close friends to delight in our happiness when we are in love and, ideally, to flatter us.

The greatness of Shakespeare is in part his flattery of all he surveyed. Flattery, in "pure Shakespeare," means to ennoble by a special vision. Such visions and such flattery are everywhere in Shakespeare, as in a sonnet where he writes:

Full many a glorious morning have I seen
Flatter the mountaintops with sovereign eye,
Kissing with golden face the meadows green . . .

- ◆ The person who on principle never flatters others is probably incapable of loving anyone, including himself. He's a boor and he's drab, pretending to be scrupulously honest when in fact he is either lacking imagination or is pathologically stingy or both.

- ◆ If you're afraid to overstate how good someone looks or how good a job they did, you won't do yourself any credit.

People will automatically migrate to others with, perhaps, less talent than you, but who cause them to like themselves. The aim of much of life, the aim of hard work and of accomplishment, is to elicit the respect of others. If you withhold flattery, you rob people of much that makes their lives happy.

The embarrassed person, the tight person, shuns anything that feels to him or her like excess—and this includes flattery. Such people, because they are too embarrassed to go after what they really want in the world, typically belittle anyone who tries to praise them in high-flown terms. They inflict their own embarrassment on others; they would teach us never to flatter them.

I still occasionally meet a boyhood friend of mine, Max, a violinist, who lived in my neighborhood. I grew up with a very wise-guy crowd; we thought we were the smartest generation in the world. Most of us, including myself, were afraid of girls. When in the company of an attractive young woman we tried to play it cool, which meant never complimenting her and doing what we could to imply that we had plenty of others where she came from. This "I've seen better" approach got us nowhere, and we spent more time than we wanted to in purely male company.

Enter Max. His family had barely escaped Hitler and he was just learning English. He was poor at sports and some of us mocked him. But whenever we saw him he was with a spellbinding young woman. Why? I wondered. He was good-looking, but so were others in our group.

Being an amateur psychologist even then, I studied Max. I observed him when he met a dark-haired beauty whom I would have been afraid to talk to. "Wow. What gorgeous eyes you have! I've never seen anything like them," he said to her spontaneously, falling backwards as if struck.

I knew he wasn't kidding because as he spoke I realized that I felt the same way. But neither I nor any of the other kids would ever have dared say such a thing. I was always amazed when the girl responded and when a few days later I saw Max walking with her down Broadway.

I began to see that my misgivings about honest flattery were ill-founded.

Rather than make me look stupid and inexperienced, my expressing such flattery would made me look courageous and polished. Once I overcame my inhibition to verbalizing my flattery of delight, it made a vast difference in my life. I now see how necessary it is to express this form of flattery in all contexts.

Flattery as a Gift

The best psychotherapists are those who can revel in their patients and enjoy their strengths. When those therapists address their patients' problems, the patients are highly motivated to change, both because they trust the therapist and because they have a sense that they themselves are worth fighting for, worth improving.

The poorest therapists are those who never enjoy their patients' strengths, who see their patients as "problemed people." Their patients don't enjoy themselves in the sessions and, before long, they typically lose motivation and end up getting nothing from the treatment.

When you are really moved by a person, force yourself to say flattering things, even to exaggerate deliberately, and to feel foolish once in a while. You won't really be foolish. Other people will respond to you favorably as they never have before.

Shakespeare liberated me to romanticize in this way, and I think that an aim of life should be to do so as much as possible.

To tell people how attractive they are or how much we enjoy them or admire their talents can only enrich our experience of them.

Is this counsel to live an illusion rather than in reality? Shakespeare didn't think so. Don't worry—if we romanticize life, whatever mistakes we make will rarely cost us much.

We can certainly tell the difference between poetic statement and real inaccuracy well enough to allow romantic exaggeration, including flattery, into our lives.

Though not inso many words, most of have been taught not to trust flatterers. If we have in mind only the first two kinds of flattery—especially the first— that sounds like a good policy. But as for the third kind of flattery, what I call "the flattery of delight," never trust a nonflatterer.

You deserve better.

7

MARC ANTONY'S ART OF ARGUMENT

HOW TO PERSUADE OTHERS

Before Marc Antony met and fell in love with the temptress Cleopatra, he'd had a long and successful career as a leader in Rome. When he met Cleopatra in Egypt, he had gone there as part of Rome's governing triumvirate. As many know, his adoration of Cleopatra cost him his status in Rome and, eventually, his life.

Marc Antony had achieved his status in large part through his association with Julius Caesar, a relative and also a trusted friend.

As Caesar rose, Antony did, too. And when Caesar was killed, the conspirators naturally went to Marc Antony to whitewash what they had done. Wrongly imagining that Antony thought them justified in killing Caesar, they permitted him to address the people. The murderers hoped to be converted into national heroes if Marc Antony, Caesar's friend, spoke in their favor.

The conspirators never dreamed that Antony, instead of applauding them, would turn the crowd against them. Brutus, the best known of the band, had spoken first. He had made the point that Caesar was ambitious and wanted to be emperor, which would have ended the Republic. The crowd had believed him, and it seemed that once Antony spoke they would be totally persuaded.

But the conspirators were wrong in assuming that Antony was on their side. And even worse for them, they had no inkling that Antony had within him a speech that would resound through Rome and become a monument in history.

Antony faced a crowd that had been staunchly convinced by Brutus that Caesar wanted to be a dictator and that the conspirators had no choice but to murder him. When Antony began, the crowd was in a mood to kill anyone who spoke against Brutus, and Antony had been allowed to speak only by permission of Brutus, who had introduced him before departing himself. Yet despite these constraints, somehow Antony converted the hostile crowd to his side. So successful was he that even before he had finished addressing the citizens, they went berserk with rage, seeking Brutus and his cohorts in order to kill them on the spot.

Shakespeare Gave Antony His Own Voice

History does not record Marc Antony's actual words, only the fact that he spoke under the most adverse conditions and swayed the multitude over to his side. Shakespeare based his play *Julius Caesar* on a brief account by an ancient historian. Shakespeare was faced with the task of re-creating Marc Antony's incredible speech from nothing.

The characteristics of Marc Antony's speech, as written by Shakespeare, are virtually an anatomy of how to persuade. Great as the real speech must have been to achieve its end, it's almost certain that Shakespeare's version is greater.

Shakespeare's version of Antony's speech, once studied and memorized by millions of schoolchildren, is one of the first great monologues by the Bard that people learn. It stands as a magnificent example of how to make an argument, of how to persuade one person or a crowd of listeners of some point of view.

The real Marc Antony had some solid training in debating and speech-making. Rome was famous for its oratory. For the ancient Romans, renowned for their mastery of the art of persuasion, debating was one of the more important subjects in their "collegium," where two students would be assigned to defend opposite points of view. After debating for a time, they would be stopped and asked to switch sides. If you could win the debate on both sides, you were a master.

The Art of Persuasion Is Really the Art of Presenting Any Idea

Today we hardly teach the art of persuasion.

But we need it more than we ever did. It's true that unless you are in a very specific kind of job, there is little call for public oratory. You may never address a big group with the need to persuade them of anything.

Nevertheless every day you will be persuading people around you of something. Our society is complicated, and many of us lead several lives. In one day, you may need to sell a proposal to a client, convince your child's teacher that he or she belongs in a different class, argue with a store that delivered a wrong item, persuade your mate to take a vacation instead of refinishing the family room.

Our society, in general, allows much more room for debate and discussion and change than there ever was before.

Fifty years ago, in many quarters, only heads of households and bosses and famous figures, of course, had a voice. Today, however, nearly all of us have occasion to try to convince others of what we think and feel. We have to sell ideas or ourselves on a daily basis. We need to put together a convincing argument whenever we ask for a raise or to be given more responsibility. Most parents would rather persuade their children than command them, and there is a never-ending supply of books and articles on how to persuade our partners of what we want in love relationships.

Proper articulation counts in presenting even the most intimate arguments. Being human, people are convinced not only by the logic of an argument but by many other factors that you can control.

Shakespeare, with his boundless understanding, realized what these key factors were.

By analyzing Marc Antony's speech we have been able to identify a set of principles which gave Antony his power of persuasion.

We can use them ourselves, modified to our purposes, in everyday life by borrowing a bit of Shakespeare's power and making it our own.

1.　Plan long to speak briefly.

Your aim should always be to keep your presentation as brief as possible. If you have to fill a certain amount of time, fill that time and no more. Planning a speech that is both cogent and brief will take you longer than if you settle for a long, rambling presentation. But it will be worth it.

The great Roman orator Cicero once apologized while addressing the senate, saying, "I'm sorry that this speech has to be so long. I didn't have time to prepare a short one."

Obviously, it pays to prepare even the briefest presentation. Even if you're planning to discuss an idea of yours at an informal meeting with your boss or a colleague, set down a few points and memorize them.

If you have to deal with a sensitive matter over the phone, rehearse your part at least once. Take advantage of the fact that the other person can't see you by setting down as many notes as you need.

Marc Antony planned even his props in advance, arranging to bring out Caesar's corpse at just the right moment. Even if we weren't told that Shakespeare's Antony had carefully planned his speech, we could have inferred that he did from its precision and its buildup.

2.   State your purpose and leave no doubt about it.

If it's worth arguing for, it's worth stating. And if it's worth stating, don't worry about repeating it. Don't be afraid to state your purpose in the speech often and in different ways.

Don't expect your listeners to sympathize with you to the point of granting a wish that you yourself haven't made clear. If you want to marry someone, tell him or her that that's the purpose of your statement. Failure to adequately assert what you want is usually a sign that you yourself are conflicted about your right to it. If you're conflicted, how can you expect another person or a whole crowd to give it to you?

Marc Antony's purpose was to persuade the people of Rome that Caesar loved them, that he was not ambitious, and that those who slew him were murderers, nothing more or less. He used the word "ambitious" five times and he used the word "ambition" twice in a speech that lasted no more than a few minutes.

3.   Begin on whatever common ground you can find.

Start with the beliefs and desires that you share with the other person. Even if you're talking to a group whose purposes are radically different from yours, find (if necessary, artificially) some common ground. You both believe in truth. You're both humane. You both care about the community. Make clear that you recognize the other person's genuineness in this regard.

Without being condescending, indicate that you understand the other person's needs. "I understand why you think that Jones might be a detriment to the company, and we both have the company's future in mind. But I do think that Jones can change, and let me tell you why I think we should give him another chance."

Once the other person feels that he has been heard, he or she is far more likely to listen to you. It's remarkable how in everyday life people who don't feel heard will contest you even in small matters. If the boss feels that you're trying to roll over her by being a champion of Jones, you and Jones may both be looking for another job. The boss needs to feel that you've heard and digested her point of view, and that you still feel you have something new to add.

Even when you're making a speech and the audience is mute, do the same thing. Throughout his whole speech, Antony kept repeating that he understood the crowd's point of view. "You want a Republic. I want it too," was his message. "And, believe me, Caesar felt as we do."

4.   Keep your demands down to a minimum.

You've begun on common ground. Now keep your differences down to a minimum. Realize that you can gain only one or two points in any presentation. If there are five things wrong with your marriage or with your job, don't bring them all up in one sitting. The other person will feel overwhelmed and hopeless. Choose the one, or at most two, that matter most. And, as you present what you want changed, keep going back to the common ground.

5.   Appeal to greed, but don't identify it as greed, or the person will surely resist you so as not to look greedy. Make your appeal implicit.

For many people, greed is the strongest motivating emotion, though almost no one admits it.

Lay out how your listener will benefit, but don't say this in words or imply that he wants to benefit. Having conveyed to your listener the clear benefits of his doing what you want, if you can, supply the person with high-minded, emotionally loaded reasons to go along with you. This will give him the chance to feel noble while acting in his own self-interest—the ideal combination for the majority. ("Well, if Jones leaves, of course, then two of our major clients will be upset and might leave with him. Do we really want to let our clients down like that?")

The true greatness of Antony's speech was of course his appeal to the emotions of the Roman people. He appealed to their greed by reminding them of how much money and how many captives Caesar had brought them, and presumably could have continued to bring them. The murder of Caesar cost them money.

6.   Appeal to the listener's emotions, but look as if you're appealing to reason.

It's a common mistake, made especially by bright people, to make a purely logical argument. You should use whatever logic you can: Logic has its own emotional charge. People love to feel that they're reasoning things out (even if you are doing it for them). But understand that emotions are what really move the other person. This is true no matter how divorced from emotion a matter may look to you.

The impact of the emotions on what people decide is so strong that our legal system has tried to safeguard against it. A lawyer cannot simply defend his client by bringing forth people who love him or her or who would be sorry if the person went to jail. Lawyers often get around this restriction by bringing on witnesses for pseudo-purposes when they are really there to tug at the heartstrings of the jury.

Though all of us are driven by emotions, no one likes to admit openly that he is. Therefore, when you are making even the most emotional argument, phrase it as if you are talking simple common sense. Avoid raw emotional words. Don't say, "Jones should have another chance. He really *loves* the company, and with his new child he can't afford to be out of work." Instead say, "I think we should consider Jones's commitment to the job. He has worked many weekends and he did agree to forgo his raise in the early years when we weren't showing a profit." This might sound like part of a list of pros and cons, even though you are recalling old times in order to appeal to sentiment.

Having made clear how the people lost out by Caesar's death, Antony then spoke to their basic humanity. He decried the death of this gentle, noble soul that was Caesar (who was, in reality, even greedier than they were).

After describing Caesar's gentleness and concern for everyone, Antony appears so moved that he can not go on for a time. His voice cracks and he weeps profusely for his dear, departed friend. He begs of the people time to collect himself:

> *Bear with me,*
> *My heart is in the coffin there with Caesar,*
> *And I must pause till it come back to me.*

It is fascinating that at this moment, as the people are themselves moved to tears for Caesar, one citizen says:

> *Methinks there is much reason in his sayings.*

Others in the crowd agree that Antony has used good logic and given them good reasons to sympathize with Caesar and reconsider his murder. They prefer to be moved by Antony's logic, though he has moved them almost entirely emotionally.

7. Never tell your listeners how to feel.

People have an instinctive, fierce resentment when anyone tells them what their experience of something ought to be. "You should be delighted with the raise you got last year." "You'll feel terrible if you fire Jones."

"You'll regret it all your life if you break up this marriage." If the other person has any backbone at all, he or she will take this as a dare to do his worst—that is, to defy you. The most you can do is to describe a situation and experience it yourself. The other person can then join you in your experience or not.

Marc Antony was careful not to tell the populace what they ought to feel, but he did invite them not to block up their natural feelings. He wondered aloud: Since they loved Caesar only yesterday, could they not still love him today?

> *You all did love him once, not without cause;*
> *What cause withholds you then to mourn for him?*

8.   Don't whine.

Never communicate self-pity. Don't whine either in words or tone. For one thing, it makes you look like a loser.

Also, to complain that you are being treated unfairly is to accuse the other person of being unsympathetic or brutal. You are by implication calling the other person ugly. No one wants to be that, so the person will almost surely justify his treatment of you and commit himself to it even further.

Even if you do move the person by whining on this occasion, you have disposed him or her to want you out of his life. People are hesitant to give responsibility to known self-pity addicts. If you're a whiner, you'll have to overcompensate by working twice as hard as other people to get where your talents can take you.

9.   Build your case.

Lead your listener by presenting the evidence in a methodical way. State your purpose clearly, but then present your case so that the listener can draw your conclusion for himself. The evidence must seem to speak so that the person doesn't feel that you are forcing him to go along with your position.

Don't say, "We have to keep Jones. It would be brutal to fire him and what would happen to the company?" This is in essence demanding that the other person go along with your speculation. Instead give the evidence. "I think we should keep Jones. The clients like Jones better than anyone else. And look at all the personal time Jones is willing to give the company. A new person might not do that. And don't forget that Jones has a lot of special knowledge."

Ideally, the other person will come to draw the same conclusion that you did. But be sure to allow him the sense of power that comes with drawing it himself.

Antony's speech stands close to perfection as a model of building an argument and getting an audience to draw the conclusion one wanted. So successful was Antony that his audience went wild with rage against Brutus and the others who murdered Caesar, even before Antony had finished his presentation. Antony had literally to plead with the crowd not to run off and kill the assassins but to stay and hear him out.

10. Don't look like an orator.

Coming across as dazzlingly articulate, as a wordsmith, will often hurt you. You may think that you're impressing people, but people who aren't sure of their own intelligence will have a strange reaction. They will feel suddenly on guard and suspicious when faced with what to them is fast speech. If you want them to fully grasp your idea and consider it their own, you must make yourself as low profile as possible. When they see your point, especially if they feel you are not an orator but a simple person like themselves, they may even help you.

Shakespeare's Marc Antony pauses during his stunningly articulate and compelling speech to point out that he's a regular guy. He does not want the people to consider him a great speaker—quite the contrary, he wants them to think of him as merely one of them, a common man. This helps them to seize his point of view as their own and to embrace him as one of them. He assures them:

> I am no orator, as Brutus is;
> But (as you know me all) a plain blunt man
> . . . I have neither [wit], nor words, nor worth,
> Action, nor utterance, nor the power of speech
> To stir men's blood; I only speak right on . . .

11. Imply that there's more than you have told them.

Leave them feeling that you have much more in reserve. Imply that you don't want to trouble them with every detail and every reason you have for your position. "Listen, we don't even have to go into Jones's full record or the problems of replacing him. I don't need to bore you with that." This is a powerful ending when it caps an already persuasive argument. Spare the listener and let him know you're sparing him, that you are taking a little from a lot.

Doing this has the further effect of inoculating the listener against any counterarguments.

*   *   *

Shakespeare has various characters who make powerful, persuasive arguments, not always for a just cause. Many modern historians think that Caesar really was a would-be tyrant. They are on the side of the conspiracy. Our reaction to Marc Antony's speech is, therefore, all the more credit to the speech itself and to the power of persuasion.

Stage Three
SELF-RELIANCE

LIVING BY YOUR OWN STANDARDS

Having defined yourself and having worked on becoming empathic, you are in a position to trust yourself.

The world offers many challenges to our sanity. Most of us must account in one way or another to a variety of people—bosses, teachers, relatives, lovers, and, in a sense, even to our children.

We are faced with an unending array of decisions.

We meet at least some people who are more successful than we are, or more attractive. We may, in some cases, be tempted to run away from such people or to despise them or to fall into the habit of putting ourselves down when we are with them.

In order to keep our highest sanity in a world full of adversity, we must repeatedly engage in great acts of self-trust. First, we must acknowledge that we are doing the best we can. Then we must set our own standards and live by them rather than constantly judging ourselves by how much approval we are getting minute by minute. We must rely on ourselves and on our own self-estimation.

Other people's moods will change, and so will yours, but your self-acceptance must be a constant. This means going ahead with what you consider right and best without obsessing about how others estimate you.

After giving your best thought to a decision, you must learn to live with the risks involved and stand behind it.

It makes sense to study other people who are doing well—all successful people do this, but do so privately. In public, speak well of yourself if you speak of yourself at all.

If Shakespeare were a therapist practicing today, he would doubtless enable his patients to trust themselves, to learn from others but not to be unduly swayed by them. The fully "sane person" interacts freely and often lovingly with others but maintains a strong center. He or she is not thrown off course by the inevitable changes in life or by changes in other people's moods.

Self-reliance is the stage of maintaining your individuality while leaving room for growth. It allows for self-expression based on an understanding of your circumstances and environment.

The self-reliant person has two strong qualities. They are: (1) Self-trust, and (2) the energy to take on life. These two facets go together and virtually belong to the same trait.

After you know who you are and you have learned to pay attention to how you impact others, you have the obligation to gamble on yourself. With a clear sense of others' unconscious needs, you need to feel free to move in the world without being overly concerned about how you are faring with them moment-to-moment.

After all, the aim is not simply to avoid offending people. It is to live your own life and be happy.

If you are unevolved in this third stage you may constantly scrutinize others who are important to you. You may live and die by their moods.

People lacking in self-reliance may make a study of their boss's attitude or of their mate's facial expressions to see how they are doing at every turn. They hope to do better with others by anticipating what other people will like and dislike. They calculate the ideal moment to ask the boss for an extra vacation day or study their mate's mood before telling him that they want to spend some time alone with a friend.

The self-reliant person no longer needs to act in this dependent way. He or she has learned that such tactics don't help in any case.

Your real worth and entitlements are what count, and you must stand behind them. If you feel that you deserve an extra vacation day because you've put in a lot of extra time, ask for the day. Don't time the request as if it were illegitimate.

If you gauge other people's moods before you act, you will over time give yourself the sense that you are unworthy of the things that you want and of the good treatment that you deserve. You will go on seeing yourself as someone who is lurking on the sidelines of life, watching the real people make the decisions. Obviously no one can be right all the time about other people's moods anyway, and it's a shame to waste your force and your imagination trying to do this.

The self-reliant person has learned that it is far more important to let others see that she trusts herself and is willing to gamble on herself. This person speaks well of himself or herself, never falling into self-depreciation even in fun. He or she is known as a person not prone to second-guessing important decisions.

*   *   *

Having the energy to tackle life is the second component of the self-reliant person. This person is willing to take chances, to make mistakes and pay the price for them in order to live. He or she is decisive and has learned that life improves with living. To such a person, the indecisiveness of others seems an appalling inertia.

Rather than staying at home psychologically and emotionally, the self-reliant person is willing to try new things, even if they look very unsure. He is willing to do things badly at the start in order to master them later. Perfectionism seems cowardly and overly idealistic to such a person. Trial and error is a surer teacher.

This high psychological energy level makes the self-reliant person appear sexy and forceful to others—and truly makes the person that way. He or she seems fearless and others see this person as successful even before he or she is.

Part of the person's energy goes into a willingness to learn from others, even those who momentarily make the person feel envious or hold the mirror up to his or her faults.

When the self-reliant person sees someone else doing better, he or she does not fall into a listless pattern of self-hate or of hating the other person. Instead the self-reliant person makes an effort to find out what the other person has and to study how he got it.

Others see the self-reliant person as flexible and as always evolving, even though they recognize his or her strong center. They see that this person trusts himself or herself and they are therefore more likely to trust that person. To the self-reliant person go authority, friendship, and love.

Many of Shakespeare's most riveting characters are highly evolved in this area. His kings and rulers and generals and even lesser folk bring energy and decisiveness to the stage. In other cases, as with Hamlet and Macbeth, we see people acquire self-reliance right in front of us. Both suffer from indecision early in the play, Hamlet until nearly the end, and we feel the excitement as they take over their own lives.

This aura of excitement is ultimately the mark of the self-reliant person. He or she is at the center of the universe.

To the person unevolved in self-reliance, it is as if "Others are free and make the decisions, and I wait and follow."

The self-reliant person sees herself or himself as a central figure and acts accordingly. This outlook becomes a self-fulfilling prophecy.

8

HAMLET'S DILEMMA

MAKE UP YOUR MIND

Hamlet is perhaps the best-known character in all modern literature. Hundreds of thousands of pages have been written on him in every living language. His personal complexity has made him a primary cultural figure. Just as we never tire of seeing Hamlet on stage or talking about him, psychologists never tire of analyzing the forces that make him who he is—in Laurence Olivier's words, "a man who could not make up his mind."

More actors—and actresses, too—have wanted to play the part of Hamlet than any other role. As Hamlet, the actor gets the chance to reel off brilliant monologues. The actor playing Hamlet is the world's most articulate human for the evening or the afternoon and the greatest psychologist ever.

The play is so well-known that it's hard to keep audiences from participating when Hamlet is talking. Olivier observed that the hardest acting role is to play Hamlet in January: "If they're not mouthing the words with you, they're coughing," he explained.

Dozens of phrases from Hamlet have entered the language: "Something rotten in the state of Denmark," "Not a mouse stirring," "Murder most foul," "Foul play," "Primrose path," etc. There's an old joke about a man who criticized Hamlet after a performance, saying that it was one cliché after another.

A person who overacts on stage or in life has come to be known as a "ham." This is the one play to which people go mainly to see the lead actor. In some productions, like Richard Burton's in New York in the 1960s, the other actors tended to do their parts from the back of the stage, and we were left almost with the impression of having seen a one-man show.

More studies have been done of Hamlet, the Prince of Denmark, than of any Dane who actually lived. Hamlet is seen somewhat differently in every era, just as he is acted differently on stage as customs of acting change.

A Likable Hero?

But though Hamlet fascinates us, he was a despondent and basically miserable human being. He was friendless and lost. He was the person we all have been in moments, but whom few would want to be for long. He is someone whom no one would want as a friend.

However we choose to see Hamlet in our "mind's eye" (a phrase from the play itself), whether he is thin or fat, tall or short, he fascinates us. As everyone agrees, this is partly because we see ourselves in him—and not ourselves in our best moments.

Hamlet is the epitome of a man who can not make up his mind and act.

He represents the depressed narcissist. He expresses despair about people, about women, about his country, about the world. But all this despondency, this sour view of life, is Hamlet's reaction to his own failure to be decisive in his own life.

To hear him talk, the world has broken its promises to him. But in reality, we see—and Hamlet himself knows only too well—that he has broken his promises to himself.

The Royal but "Melancholy" Dane

We find Hamlet in acute despair, full of self-pity and self-hate. His father, the king, has been murdered, and within a month of his burial, Hamlet's mother has married the dead king's brother, Claudius. The two now reign in Denmark.

Hamlet is full of irony and innuendo. Dressed in "inky black," unable or unwilling to enjoy his princely privilege, he expresses for all human kind the great disappointments that we all experience. We feel his despair and lean forward in our seats to understand him. No one could complain so eloquently about how the world has gone awry without enjoying his genius of observation and expression, and doing this appears to be Hamlet's one remaining pleasure. Being so good at it, he does us all a great favor by giving words to our sorrows.

Then the ghost of Hamlet's father appears. Hamlet, accompanied by his friend Horatio, sees the ghost, who tells him to take revenge.

Meanwhile, in his wretched state, and hating women, perhaps more than usual because of his mother's treason in marrying Claudius so soon after his father's death, Hamlet takes to abusing Ophelia, a woman he once loved.

He mocks her and hurls her to the floor, acts which the audience has traditionally sympathized with because of Hamlet's own despair.

Hamlet has strongly suspected Claudius of having killed his father, and now the ghost fills him in on the details and begs him to revenge his "most foul murder." No doubt remains in the audience's mind that it was murder or that Hamlet, under the obligations of his station and of his period in history, must avenge it.

At this point, loaded with self-hate, Hamlet indulges in indecision. He simply can't kill King Claudius, or won't. He mainly runs around the court, cursing brilliantly and finding reasons why it might be wrong for him to kill the king.

Being imbued with Shakespeare's psychological genius, Hamlet even realizes that he is substituting words for action. With another anti-female slur, he likens himself to a "whore" and contents himself with batting women around—Ophelia, and then his mother, whom he blames more than the actual murderer.

Hamlet hates himself increasingly as evidence against Claudius keeps coming in. Like other of Shakespeare's figures who fail in their own ethic, he has bad dreams. He even contrives a test of Claudius, which Claudius fails, giving him yet more evidence. But because he is afflicted with indecision, Hamlet keeps telling himself that he must wait for more certainty before acting.

Every postponement of action leaves him feeling more wretched, more impotent, and more depressed. He deflects his self-hatred onto the world, finding it wanting and derelict because he knows that he himself is wanting and derelict.

Hamlet's Decision to Do Nothing

Of course, the failure to act, to take a chance, is in the most important sense itself a decision. Hamlet's failure to do what he must makes him brutal to others. He injures everyone except his true adversary. He drives Ophelia insane, and she commits suicide. He torments his mother to near madness, and would have done worse had not the ghost returned and begged him to go easy on her. He kills the king's advisor, Polonious, by mistake. He distresses all those who care for him, including his supposedly dear friend Horatio.

Being utterly preoccupied with himself, Hamlet doesn't truly care about anyone else. We, the audience, find him fascinating, but we aren't his friends.

In the end, after Hamlet uncovers the king's plot to murder him and foils it, he does take his revenge. There is a grand mop-up of virtually everyone. Hamlet, who has finally acted decisively, may savor that fact for a moment before he dies too.

The play *Hamlet,* is, among other things, the greatest study of indecision and its consequences in literature. Indecision breeds self-hate and self-preoccupation. As Hamlet curses the world, he also senses that the one he really hates is himself.

Do You Have the Hamlet Syndrome?

If you find it hard or impossible to make decisions, ranging from those on the job to deciding on what restaurant to go to, you are suffering a hell on earth. What for other people weighs a few ounces is for you a terribly heavy weight.

You'd like to go back to school but don't know what to study, and so you don't go. You'd like to get married but can't force yourself to meet people. You'd like to get divorced but the time never seems right.

You go back and forth in your mind, as if you were the victim of a torture invented for you by the ancient Greek gods. You squander your energy, wasting precious time thinking about what you might do, while you do nothing.

- Since you judge your future by your past, you feel hopeless.

- The person who constantly changes his mind and who can't act becomes a victim in life. He or she falls into the job that happens to open up, marries the person who has aggressively chosen him or her and spends a lifetime bemoaning the consequences. Every act is the outcome of a hundred vacillations.

- The indecisive person loses force, sexuality, self-esteem. The other person is a motorboat. That person can go where he or she wants, and when. The indecisive person is a sailboat. He goes where the winds push him.

- The person who undoes himself, who has a history of erasing resolutions, loses belief in anything that he states to himself or to others. No matter what he resolves at eight in the evening, he knows that there will be a thousand vacillations and reconsideration before tomorrow. Such a person loses the ability to clarify anything. He loses the courage of his or her opinions and the ability to think clearly.

◆ The person who doesn't make decisions forfeits the golden opportunity to learn from bad decisions.

◆ People with the Hamlet Syndrome are always depressed. Typically, they obsess about age and the passing years. They may feel that others are simply gifted or lucky. Because of their indecision and their need to have others make decisions for them, they are underachievers. They work for other people when they have more than enough talent to work for themselves. They are told when to come and go, often by people who have less judgment but more decisiveness than they do.

Are You Married to Someone with the Hamlet Syndrome?

A man came into my office whom I'll never forget. He was furious at the woman he was living with because, as he put it, "she won't let me work." He was a would-be writer, suffering from terrible indecision over how to proceed. He never knew what he wanted to write next and so he didn't write at all. But instead of admitting that he had a problem, he cursed the woman for making noise in another room.

In therapy it came out that he had done this over a period of twenty-five years with three different women, making their lives miserable because he couldn't go forward.

If you're emotionally involved, married or otherwise, to someone suffering from the Hamlet Syndrome, you are very likely the object of his deflected rage.

If you love the person, then watching his despair and seeing the person fall so short of his or her potential will itself be awful. But even worse, such people are almost always blamers. After letting themselves down by their indecision and inaction, they often blame others for preventing them from reaching their potential.

I sometimes think about those women involved with the would-be writer, mistakenly imagining him as great and themselves as obstacles to his progress. "If it weren't for me . . ."

Don't buy into this kind of attack. Remember how Hamlet treated Ophelia. Playgoers tend to neglect her. But don't *you* neglect yourself. It is never your fault if another person can't make up his or her mind, and as a result feels cheated in life.

Decision Makers Have Tremendous Personal Appeal

The media are full of tips on how to develop sex appeal. Many of them are valid. But we all know people who don't fit the conventional model and yet are incredibly desirable.

They have in common that they are decisive people. Sexiness is in large part a matter of energy.

The sense of youthfulness, of force, the sense of being a winner in life, of getting what one wants—this whole package belongs to the person who makes decisions without always reconsidering them.

This person, male or female, is the gambler on life, the gambler on himself. This person gives us the sense of getting what he or she wants, and this in itself is magnetic.

Being decisive suggests success, and it's an adage that "Nothing succeeds like success."

The great sexologist Alfred Kinsey reported, based on his research, that for every person, no matter what that person looks like or wants sexually, there is someone out there who is a perfect match.

I often thought about this assertion that whatever you are, someone wants exactly that, and I repeatedly saw its truth in my office. A very coarse woman was happily married to a genteel man who loved her coarseness. A sadist found a masochist, and so forth.

Then, one day, I found an exception. A man, both wealthy and handsome, brought his girlfriend with him to my office.

Whatever the woman or I asked him elicited only indecision on his part. At one stage the girlfriend asked him if he enjoyed sex with her because he didn't seem to. He shrugged. He couldn't really say that he did or he didn't. When she threatened to walk out on him, I asked him how he felt. He wasn't sure. He had already told her she wasn't his type, but expected her to remain attracted to him. At the end of the session she thanked me for seeing her, and ended the relationship with him.

I realized then that Kinsey was wrong. There may be someone out there for *nearly* everyone, but not for everyone.

◆ Indecision is the one form of identity that appeals to no one.

◆ Whatever our fantasy is, the other person must assume some position to satisfy it. The indecisive person is nowhere. He or she gives so little back that you can't even have a fantasy about that person.

Why You Should Make a Decision

As a matter of course, it is better to make *some* decision than none. There are so many benefits from making decisions that the few mistakes you make are more than offset by these benefits.

- Making decisions will dispel your sense that the world is against you.

    Even small decisive acts bring hope. As soon as you begin to act you give yourself a sense of possibilities. Your despair, which seemed to be over the universal condition of life, suddenly appears not as universal but as local. And it appears unnecessary. You can make a difference.

    I remember a drug addict I worked with who understandably felt trapped and helpless in his condition. He had kicked the habit but felt hopeless and was indecisive about his future. He had always wanted to be a writer but couldn't take the first step. I prevailed on him to start by learning five new vocabulary words a day, and after only a few days his whole outlook changed.

    Anyone who has broken a habit can recall the huge difference in his or her outlook after even a few successful days. The past loosens it grip on you, and you no longer feel that how you are is how you must always be.

- Life improves with practice. If your decision works out well, the benefits are obvious. If it works out badly, at least you've learned something. The worst feeling of all is that you defaulted on something that could have been. You achieved nothing and you learned nothing. Only by acting can you refine your performance.

- Indecision is the only thing you can't learn from.

- By making decisions, you learn that mistakes aren't so bad. Every successful person makes plenty of them. If you make only one big decision a year, a mistake will seem devastating. But if you make many decisions, you can take most mistakes in stride.

- Making decisions is a prerequisite of love.

Taking the risk of loving begins with choosing someone we love instead of someone we merely feel safe with. But it also means that once we have chosen that person, we must risk allowing chords in us to be touched as they had been only in dreams and in fantasies. The risk of loving and declaring our love is that we render ourselves vulnerable to ridicule and rejection.

The indecisive person waits. Perfectionism and the refusal to take risks become his advisors. Hesitance sets conditions. A better deal will come along, someone who moves him or her more, later. If the other person loses weight, or makes more money, or behaves in some specified way, then we tell ourselves that perhaps we can love that person. But not yet.

The simple lines in a Shakespeare song, quoted many times down through the years, tell us that now is the time:

> *What is love? 'Tis not hereafter;*
> *Present mirth hath present laughter;*
> *What's to come is still unsure.*
> *In delay there lies no plenty . . .*

Three Enemies of Decision Making

Perfectionism. Perfectionism usually takes the form of saying, "Why bother, if it won't be perfect!" Or, "Why bother? Other people do it better."

The greatest enemy of decision making is perfectionism. You have an ideal in your mind. If you were destined to go to school at all, you would have gone to a first-rate university and done so when you were young. Now you put off taking a few business courses at the local community college, which would greatly help you move up to management in your job.

Perfectionists tend to look at other people as role models and ideals, and this breaks them in half when it comes time for their own lives to advance.

Fear of Failure. The fear of failing creates inertia. Perhaps you are afraid of being wrong, of looking foolish, or of looking hysterical.

Perhaps you fear that people will say you were silly to marry your first boyfriend. Or that you hysterically jumped at your first job offer. But you are the only judge of whether your choice was expedient or hasty—or really was your heart's desire.

Don't fall into the classic trap of doing nothing to avoid making a mistake. Many people subconsciously stay on the periphery. If they avoid jumping in and getting their hands dirty, then they can't be criticized. They fail to see that everybody at the top has had the courage to try new things and leave himself or herself open to criticism over and over again. Indecisiveness, a deadly fear of making mistakes, is the surest route to failure.

The Need for Limitless Options. As children, our fantasies for the future may run wild. Everything is open to us. Nothing is decided as yet. You can be a movie actor, a scientist, an explorer. You can marry someone rich, someone exotic, someone beautiful. But as you get older, you have to make choices, and many of these choices eliminate alternatives.

The problem with dating someone you like is that once you're connected with that person, you rule out others. This is, of course, still more true in marriage. Every decision is a doing away with alternatives—for the present, if not forever. There are people who become so distressed by this fact that they become paralyzed by the need to make decisions.

The desire for limitless options is a powerful deterrent to decision making. If you have this problem you feel the panic of being hemmed in by decisions, as if you were forfeiting more than you were gaining. Even the most romantic decision seems to require that you give up your potential with others.

"TO BE OR NOT TO BE"—FINDING THE IMPETUS TO MAKE DECISIONS

1.   Understand that every decision to do nothing is itself a decision.

2.   Realize that few decisions are irreversible.

There are a few exceptions, of course, like taking a major health risk. However, outside of dangerous risks, life is far more forgiving than many of us realize. Careers can be changed. You can relocate. Lovers can be changed if necessary. If you're an indecisive person, you are apt to forget this and to imagine that even small decisions will leave a permanent mark.

3.   No blaming.

The more you pick on other people, as Hamlet did, because you aren't happy with your life, the more it will seem that you are in an utterly helpless place.

A step toward decisive action, Shakespeare tells us, is to be sure not to blame anyone else for our circumstances. It has in our century become almost a custom, enhanced greatly by modern psychology, for people having trouble making decisions to blame their parents. "If I'd had a different mother . . ." "If only my father hadn't been away working such long hours, I would have had the confidence . . ."

It is certainly true that our parents, and the opportunities we did or didn't have, set us on a trajectory. If we were beaten or humiliated for making mistakes, if we were considered second-class in the home, decisions may be harder for us now.

But patterns can be broken. Blaming another adult is even more demoralizing than blaming your early life. It amounts to turning yourself into an infant. The man who blamed the women in his life for keeping him from writing was declaring his impotence and his inability to control his own future.

4.   Remember that no one is so small as to be exempt from challenges and the sense of "What I could be doing with who I am?"

5.   Everyone is just a person. The ladder is eternal. Everyone settles somewhere.

Virtually whatever you do will involve some compromise. Others will do it better and have more, just as others will do it worse. There is always room for improvement. Your idols, doubtless look up to others and feel themselves deficient in many ways, but it doesn't stop them from going ahead.

Every step up the ladder brings its own challenges. The only way to avoid them is to stay at the bottom. Don't worry that a faulty decision will reveal you as imperfect. Everyone knows that you are anyhow. The less pretense you have about yourself, the less you will be blocked.

6.   Do it badly.

For people who suffer from indecisiveness, who can't choose a job or a restaurant or their clothes in the morning, a good motto is "Do it badly." After reasonable deliberation, it's more important to take a position, to act, than to put up the perfect defense against error.

A group of Hollywood screenwriters I knew used this phrase in their creative sessions. For instance, when they found themselves blocked about suggesting possible endings to a movie, they would preface their suggestions by saying, "A bad way to end this film would be . . ." The first three ideas were in fact bad. But the fourth suggestion, given with this preface, was great. The suggestion, "Do it badly," had freed them to take risks and arrive at the ending they wanted.

7. Make small decisions first and the big ones will be easier later.

The Decisive Life Is Rich and Rewarding

The decisive life is rich, and though it admittedly contains more errors than the indecisive one, few errors are as great as indecisiveness itself.

A kind of self-acceptance underlies the ability to be wrong. Part of the game is learning to forgive ourselves. As Shakespeare reminds us, even the best of us are "moulded out of faults."

Remember that doing your best and failing is a minor defeat alongside defaulting. *The greatest failure is not to give your utmost to what you aspire to.* Even if no one ever recognizes that you defaulted, you will know that you have.

There is no fullness, no love, no possession of joy, no serenity without decisiveness. The motto of the decisive person is simple enough: There is no time but now.

9

RICHARD III'S TYRANNY

DON'T LIVE BY OTHER PEOPLE'S MOODS

In Tudor times, when Shakespeare lived, to be on the wrong side of a king or queen was bad business. Those around the throne commonly moved in and out of favor on almost a daily basis. Serious disloyalty could mean death for oneself and dishonor for one's family. Even small slights to the king, like the denial of some personal whim, could cost a person his home and property. The penalty for any wrongdoing was determined not by how serious it was, but by how the ruler felt about it.

If you had something to say to the king or queen, and especially if you had a favor to ask, you had better do it when he was in a good mood.

Not surprisingly, those closest to the ruler compared notes on his or her mood from day to day. When the governing council of King Henry VIII received word that the king's new, adored, teenaged wife, Catherine Howard, had deceived him about her virginity, they thought long and hard before deciding who should tell him—or if anyone should.

They finally decided that if King Henry found out and discovered that they'd withheld the information, they would be in worse trouble, so they picked the gentlest soul they could find, a man known for having no courtly interests.

Thomas Cranmer, the Archbishop of Canterbury, was singled out to break the news to the king. Cranmer, even though he was in high favor at the time, was so freaked out by having to pass this news along that he finally slipped it to King Henry in a note right after chapel. He apparently hoped that the king would still be too absorbed with heaven to turn on him and make his life a hell.

As a result of this careful planning, only four people were beheaded: Catherine Howard, of course, her two former lovers, and her lady-in-waiting.

Cranmer himself wasn't burned at the stake until he slipped up with a later Tudor ruler, Queen Mary.

How many businesses operate something like this, without actually killing people, except through heart attacks and other stress-related means?

"The King Doth Gnaw His Lip" Syndrome

Today, millions of people live or die according to someone else's mood. For most people it is their boss, for others it is a client, their main customer, their teacher, their banker. For some people a lover's or mate's state of mind dictates their own. Their own sense of security rises or falls with what the Bard several times called the "tempest" of another person's "frown."

Such dependency upon another person's state of mind is excruciating, whether it's justified or not. Even the most successful people fall prey to it at times. Most often it occurs when we're in a needy position, as in a romantic relationship, when we crave the other person's love or when the other person has say over our job security or our finances.

Often this dependency is justified, as when a person critical to us is truly whimsical or cruel. More often, it indicates basic shakiness within us about our own worth.

When one of my patients comes in desperate about how someone "feels about me lately," they often follow it with a remarkably subtle examination of the other person's mood.

"My boss looked annoyed at me when I walked in. I think he had just gotten off the phone. I figured this wasn't the time to present my report, so I went back downstairs to my office."

"When they came out of the meeting, my boss seemed preoccupied and didn't say hello. I had this terrible feeling that she was telling them she was thinking of replacing me."

"My wife is always distant with me when she gets home from work. I have a feeling she's getting bored with me."

Patients, obsessed with what they see as irregularities in the expression or behavior of someone vital to them, often try to drag me into the guessing game. Sometimes they try to draw on my credentials as a professional. "What does it mean when a person . . . ?"

Often I quote for them a certain passage from Shakespeare's play *Richard III*. King Richard III was as fierce as any of England's rulers, at least in Shakespeare's version. He is presented as a tyrant whose whimsical mood could mean life or death. Richard's courtiers must surely have studied his every expression before approaching him.

Shakespeare conveys this by having one of them say in terror to another:

> *The King is angry,*
> *See, he gnaws his lip.*

When I quote this to patients who are engaged in similar scrutiny, it often brings a smile, which is what we need at such a time, and afterwards the line serves as a shorthand between us. I want these patients to recognize it when they are scrutinizing another person in this way and to stop, both for their own sakes and for the success of the relationship.

In treating patients with this syndrome, the most important thing for me to remember is never to join the patient in his minute evaluation of his status. Obviously, I must not comply when he asks me to help him put together all his data in order to arrive at my best conjecture regarding how he or she stands in the relationship. Instead I must help the patient see how self-destructive this behavior is.

The Symptoms

The overwatchful state is characterized by a pattern of symptoms.

- You compulsively study the other person's mood, surveying him for facial expressions and the smallest signs of favor or disfavor. Your imagination does the rest. The person's tone or the fact that he didn't compliment you or include you in some way may be all that you need to fall into despair.

- In dealing with the person, you're apt to swallow your pride, as by holding still for bad treatment or by withholding legitimate questions or reasonable demands.

- You may fear that you are transparent and that your neediness itself is apt to put the person off.

- You indulge contradictions of all kinds.

- You find yourself watching for the perfect moment to speak.

- You are overconscious of how you're coming across to the other person. You're anything but natural.

Maybe you actually are in trouble with the person or maybe not. Or maybe this vigilance is just a habit you've developed with anyone in authority. Either way, it's a nightmare. You feel in grave danger.

This may hurt most in a case when you've helped someone to the "crown"—to improve his status or to gain recognition in the world. This might be the person you married, your boss, or even your child—and now you are gauging your status by his gestures. Even if you haven't helped the person tangibly, your love, your devotion has ennobled the person and put him above you in your own mind. It's as if you devoted yourself and now you need that person's smile or compliment for you to feel whole.

What's Wrong with this Behavior?

Obviously, it can never be right to treat another person like a king and yourself like a loyal subject to be dispensed with as he pleases.

- ♦ If you think this way you will be utterly demoralized, and nothing that you do will feel important for itself. Your acts will become nothing more than mirrors, reflecting the other person's wishes or what you think are his wishes.

- ♦ At worst, if you pursue this course you will become paranoid and, ultimately, lose your identity.

A patient of mine, a major war hero, was hired to be a consultant for one of the richest men in the U.S. His job was to troubleshoot in management, looking for slackers and dishonest employees. By degrees, this man became identified with his "master," executing his every wish and getting top dollar for it. He went from hiring and firing help to assisting in his boss's personal life. So closely did he identify with his master's wishes that, as he rose in status, he became empowered to buy clothing for the master, using his own discretion.

He came to see himself as so reliant on his boss for status, money, and a social life that he lost his own identity entirely. He would look at a necktie in a store, and instead of saying, "*I* would like this tie," he would instantly think, "*He* would like this tie." His own personality evaporated, and eventually he had to quit the job to retain his sanity.

- ♦ Too much scrutiny of someone else's wishes will rob you of imagination and independence.

- ♦ You will develop the sense that no matter what you achieve, the

other person can pull the plug and there will be nothing left of
you.

More important to the sufferer, however, the scrutiny will not help you
do better with the other person.

Quite the contrary. You will come across as stiff and the other person
will see through it after a while.

◆ You don't look like a self-motivated person, or a central figure,
   because you aren't.

◆ It begins to look as if you cannot be depended upon as a takeover
   person. If the other person suspects what you are doing, he or she
   will lose respect for you, disdaining you as a hanger-on. And of
   course, a great drain of energy goes into your scrutiny, which
   would be much better spent doing your job and being creative.

THE CURE

If you are prone to imagining that you are in the court of Richard III—
if you suffer from "the King doth gnaw his lip" syndrome—it's important
to take steps before you become paranoid and wreck your own peace of
mind and the relationship.

A caution about the following guidelines. Unlike certain other measures,
you must try to follow these to the letter. Whatever bad habits you have,
you must give up cold turkey. Small indulges will keep you hooked, as with
physical addiction. But if you follow these rules precisely, you will liberate
yourself fast.

1. Stop dwelling on the worst.

Fight against worst-case-scenario fantasies. "If the boss really is sick
of my ideas, how will I pay the mortgage?" "How will I get clothes for the
kids?" Suddenly in your mind, you're out on the street, and everybody feels
sorry for you.

A patient of mine, a thankless type who truly didn't befriend people on
the job, so convinced himself that he was about to be fired that he cleaned
out his desk on a Friday and had to bring everything back the next week.
Instead of concentrating on his drafting job, he indulged in so many fantasies
about his boss's prejudice against him that he fell hopelessly behind in his

work. His boss was actually a forgiving type who simply sat down and talked to him about better ways to meet deadlines.

You can't help the thoughts that come to you in unguarded moments. But you can put a stop to them each time once you become aware of them.

The more you fight them, the freer of them you will be.

2.   Stop all scrutiny.

Play your own game on the premise that maybe it's good enough and you're good enough. This will give you confidence and at the same time convey the message that you are both independent and worthwhile. In turn, you will become more attractive to yourself and to the other person.

3.   Stop thinking about how you look to the other person.

Don't time your interventions with him or her or try to wedge your statements in when the person is in a good mood. Stop censoring what you say or do. Don't watch your phrasing.

The first few steps you take in this direction will liberate you tremendously.

A patient of mine, a student nurse, was working very long hours starting at four in the morning. When she took her brief break one day at 10:00 A.M., she sat down at the nurse's station and browsed a newspaper.

Just then her supervisor came to the station. The nurse's impulse was to drop the newspaper under the desk. But then she realized that she was doing nothing wrong. This was her time. The supervisor smiled, chatted with her briefly, and obviously accepted the nurse's right to relax when she had a moment.

That small encounter was a turning point for the nurse, who felt happier on the job. She felt appreciated and understood, and some paranoid thoughts which she'd had about not being wanted disappeared. If she had hidden the paper, this would have exaggerated her fears, increasing her then mild concern that her supervisor was a tyrant who disliked her.

4.   Don't check with other people about how well you are faring. Or about how well they are faring.

Besides intensifying your own anxiety by these acts, you are also advertising to everyone that you fear you are in jeopardy.

If people didn't have the idea that your status was borderline, you might well be suggesting it by this behavior. Besides, what people tell you will often be wrong, either because they're trying to mislead you or because they're anxious, just as you are.

5. Don't ask for reassurance of any kind, either from the object of your scrutiny or from others around you.

If you're really anxious, then when the boss's secretary tells you that you're doing fine, you won't even believe him or her. You will think, "Of course the administrative assistant was told to fend me off." And now you will have the added fear that your question will get passed along.

6. Try not to replay conversations you had with key people in order to reinterpret them or look for small signals.

Since you are suffering from a kind of delusion anyhow, you are the last person to make judgments about your status. If you replay conversations you will only imagine things and add to your own paranoia.

7. Don't tolerate bad treatment just because you care, especially with a lover.

Don't make a habit of swallowing your pride in order to keep the relationship going. It never works. If you really think your lover is surly or disdainful, don't just cower. Bring it to his attention.

Beware of conceding undue power to someone who does not reciprocate with love or respect. Possibly the other person is withholding appreciation of you and has come to take you for granted. Instead of looking for signs of where you stand with the person, watch the person for signs of how he or she may be defaulting in the relationship with you.

You will probably be happier, look better, and fare better. If it turns out that you really aren't loved or respected, there's no sense pretending. In such a case it is better to have loved and lost than to hang on interminably and hate yourself.

8. Act as you would with a well-meaning friend.

Think about the person you are most free with, someone with whom you express yourself freely. Consider how you act with that person.

Act the exact same way, take the same liberties, when you are with the lover or boss or friend you think you can't live without. Ask yourself how you would phrase things to that trusted and robust friend. Take no precautions with this "king" that you would not take with your friend.

Withdraw your scrutiny and use the energy that went into it for another purpose—to make yourself whole again.

9. Study exactly how you feel when you make these recommended changes.

Stopping your scrutiny cold turkey, for instance, will almost surely make you feel quite anxious.

By studying your feeling you will be able to determine if there is some deeper fear at the root of your anxiety about the "king." Feelings of fear that seem random will almost surely beset you. If you examine these feelings, you will find that they, in fact, direct you toward one underlying fear.

You may find that something you barely suspected is amiss and at the root of the trouble. For example, if you are terrified of displeasing your boss you may discover that in reality you are afraid of letting down your mate, who is putting great pressure on you to earn a big title at work or maintain a position that you yourself don't even want.

Or you may secretly feel that your boss regrets having hired you. Perhaps you exaggerated on your résumé or you aren't as educated as you let on. Fear of being fraudulent and the paranoia that follows can do you a lot more harm than being caught out in a distortion.

Whatever you're afraid of, you've gambled. Keep gambling on yourself. Stop scrutinizing your boss and instead give the job your best effort and let the chips fall where they may.

10

HORATIO'S BAD HABIT

DON'T PUT YOURSELF DOWN

Like the rest of us, Shakespeare varied in his self-estimation from day to day. His sonnets suggest that at times he considered himself a great writer, whose works would last forever:

> *Not marble not the gilded monuments*
> *Of princes shall outlive this pow'rful rhyme.*

At other times he felt utterly incompetent and lacking in imagination:

> *Why is my verse so barren of new pride?*
> *So far from variation or quick change?*

We who aren't poets run through similar radical shifts in our self-appraisals. Even the most balanced of us undergo mercurial changes in how bright or capable or well off we think we are.

Creating Your Own Image

Appreciation and depreciation occur in the realm of personal images as surely as they do in the world of cars and houses.

How you refer to yourself gives others subliminal clues as to what they should think of you. How you control what you say about your own ups and downs will do much to decide how other people will see you.

Many people invest a great deal of time working toward achievements or acquiring items that will represent them in a certain way. For some people, their identity is in their success—in their title of "manager," or in their I.Q., their Ph.D., or in their solid family unit. Still others value themselves by how much money they have or by certain status items that they own—jewelry, good clothing, a certain make of car, a big house. By their choice of symbols they announce to the world the image that they prefer— that they are sexy, old-monied, sporty and young, or "arrived."

To a great many people, image is all. And to nearly all of us, image is important to some degree.

It Isn't Charming to Put Yourself Down

People whose self-esteem rises and falls with their professional or financial ups and downs take extraordinary safeguards to protect their props. We see some staying with companies that treat them miserably because their affiliation looks good to the outside world. Others take expensive precautions against depreciation of their property. Still others hang on to unhappy marriages in order to present an image of family stability to the world.

However, many of these same people think it is disarming or attractively coy to put themselves down lightly in company. Some do it because they think it makes them look young and unassuming. Others do it because they are subconsciously trying to steal thunder from their adversaries.

A woman who actually thinks that she might be a half-pound too heavy for the slinky dress she's wearing might say, "Oh I feel just huge today." She is actually seeking to create the opposite picture in her listener's mind. By describing an extreme that is far from the truth, she is hoping to conjure up an image of herself as physically smaller that she actually is.

It may be that the woman would like her listener to verbalize reassurance, to compliment her. Or it may be enough for her to feel that she has neutralized any negative thoughts that others might have.

There are big problems, however, with the woman's seemingly subtle ploy.

- ◆ First, people inevitably feel burdened, whether they realize it or not, by anyone who puts themselves down. There is an implicit demand on the listener to pick up the person's spirits, to reassure him or her, to chivalrously oppose the self-attack.

- ◆ Secondly, no matter how well the person is disposed toward you to start with, your talking negatively about yourself is giving the person ideas. Few are so steadily on your side that they are immune to a steady barrage of negative insinuations, especially when they come straight from the source.

If you want good press from others, you have to give it to yourself—not by bragging but by maintaining an implicitly positive self-appraisal.

The aim is to look steady, comfortable in your own skin, and satisfied with who you are.

Up to a point, humility is a virtue and others appreciate it. But humility can be overdone, just as bragging can. Be careful not to cross the line from self-possession into the realm of giving yourself a few gratuitous knocks and hoping that someone will dispute you.

Dealing with the "Oh, I'm Not Very Good at . . ." Personality

The other side of the picture, just as important to understand, is how to handle others when they put themselves down in your presence.

Most of us feel uncomfortable when others disparage themselves in front of us. However, it is sometimes tempting to imagine that if your boss or someone you want to connect with puts himself down, you are gaining status as a confidante.

Again, the opposite is true. Actually a subtle psychological law comes into play. *By allowing a person to put himself down in your presence, you are making an enemy of his subconscious.*

You have been a witness to the person's lowest moment.

You are connected with that moment in his or her mind. When he's in better spirits, he will want to rush away from you to other people who will see him in a more glamorous light. People like to be where they look good.

The person who disparages himself repeatedly in your presence will dislike you for another reason. Upon reflection, it may seem to him that you have dragged his negativity out of him or her. If not by something you said, then by some contrast that you represent—a behavior of yours or a fact of your existence. A woman feels poor in your presence because you have a better job or old because you stress youth so much. Maybe you're more athletic or have a younger mate.

Therefore, stop them.

If you possibly can, prevent people from disparaging themselves to you.

Self-Deprecation Is Just a Bad Habit

Certain of my patients have the habit of deprecating themselves, which I can see in the very first session. They preface comments with, "I'm probably wrong, but . . ." or "I know, I'm not very smart, but it seems to me . . ."

As a rule, they don't know that they're doing this, until I point it out. The habit is so ingrained. I always bring it to their attention. Sometimes I ask a person, "See if you can talk for a whole session without putting yourself down." Usually they can't, and when they lapse into such a self-assault, I bring it to their attention.

Sometimes after making the person aware of the habit, I use a technique called "joining."

My patient has just said, "I know I'm stupid, but I think . . ."

"It doesn't matter what you think. You're stupid," I comment. We both laugh, but I have made the point.

As with any unwanted habit, when you try to stop, it's as if another creature inside you were out to defeat you, working at cross-purposes with you. I might explain this to the patient.

Often I add, "Suppose another person, say a friend, were in the room with us and took the role of saying what you yourself say. 'You're stupid. You're probably wrong.' "

Or in one case, after a woman said, "I'm an old lady, it doesn't matter what I think," I observed, "Suppose someone else said that about you."

Obviously these people who put themselves down all agree that they would detest anyone who said those same things about them.

"The person who said those things about you would be a terrible enemy," I observe, and they invariably agree.

I realized this after studying a beautiful passage in *Hamlet*.

Never Speak of Yourself as an Enemy Would

Hamlet's dearest friend Horatio who is actually a scholar and an accomplished youth, has a bad habit of putting himself down. At one point, he calls himself a "truant" by nature, a person who doesn't meet his responsibilities.

This is definitely not so. He is a good and loyal friend to Hamlet and anything but irresponsible.

Hamlet rushes to defend Horatio against his own put-down. Hamlet tells Horatio that if anyone else had said this about him, Hamlet would not allow it. Hamlet would stop anyone from defaming Horatio in his presence.

Since this is so, Hamlet says in effect, do not subject me to such an attack against you.

> *I would not hear your enemy say so,*
> *Nor shall you do my ear that violence*
> *To make it truster of your own report*
> *Against yourself. I know you are no truant.*

Hamlet virtually implies that it is unfair of Horatio to force him to listen to such talk.

By Depreciating Yourself, You Depreciate
Your Lover

Many people have a habit of putting themselves down early in relation-ships. They feel a bit fraudulent and they're afraid of being discovered, so they say the worst about themselves. This is an instance of trying to disarm the other person in advance.

Men might belittle their income, "I should really be making more than I am at this point."

Women might disparage their appearance, as by saying, "I always hated being so tall. It makes me feel awkward."

Or they talk about themselves in the past tense. "I used to be a good dancer, but I haven't tried in years."

These people are planting the idea in the other person's mind that he or she is gawky or out of date.

It's important to realize that when you put yourself down in a love relationship, you are depreciating your partner's value as well as your own. People, if anything, want to be envied for the mate they have chosen—not pitied. They certainly don't want to be told by their lover, in effect, "You should have done better. Nobody else would want me."

When your parents, or other people you're close to, put themselves down, they make you feel impotent. It's as if you should be helping them in some way and you're failing them instead.

A FEW PRINCIPLES

1. Any performance can be devalued.

No matter how good your performance is, it can always be helped along by pride in it and in yourself. On the other hand, you run the risk of nul-lifying even the best performance if you run it and yourself down.

Even a tangible success—for example, a great meal that someone has cooked—can be ruined if the chef puts himself or herself down.

I dined at a friend's house recently. He loved to cook and had prepared a marvelous meal. However, he put a damper on the dinner party by "hum-bly" announcing what a poor cook he really was. He kept saying how much better his wife would have cooked if she were in town. The end result was that we all felt somewhat foolish for delighting in the meal.

Bear in mind that it is never charming to put yourself down. Other people will feel taxed by the need to buoy you up, and at worst you will be giving people ammunition against you that they hadn't realized existed.

2.   Practice handling compliments with style.

Consider the following. One woman, when told she looks great, says simply, "Thanks so much." She is conveying a positive view of herself. The person who complimented her feels glad for what he or she said and sees the woman as even more attractive. We like people who validate our conclusions.

A second woman, when given the same compliment, says with a slight whine in her voice, "Do you think so? I've been trying so hard to diet. I think I could lose another ten pounds." This woman is virtually telling the other person that she is basically unattractive. He gets the message and becomes more prone to see her this way. He feels that he has shown poor judgment in complimenting her and will be careful not to do so again.

In another case, a man, when told he did a great job at work, says, "Thanks. I had a lot of terrific help from the people in my department." He is agreeing that he did a great job and adding that he's proud of his achievement and those of his staff. He knew it was a good job before being told that it was. Whether he actually did it or supervised the doing of it is irrelevant to the person who complimented him, and the man knows it.

We expect more high achievement from this man. By his own self-appraisal he is teaching others how to appraise him.

3.   Stop others from putting themselves down.

Disagree with them as lightly as you can. But make clear that you are not on the side of their adversaries.

For example, the parent who says, "We're old. This sofa should last longer than we will. Why buy a new one?"

Many of us have parents who, often depressed, disparage themselves, calling themselves old, and this is hard for us to take. For some of them doing this is a major personality trait. "I don't even look like the person I was when I was forty. Nobody really wants me at that wedding."

When people we're close to talk this way, we feel pressured to compliment them, to talk them out of it. But telling them they're bright or good looking never lifts them for long.

If someone's running himself down and demoralizing you, you need a direct approach. In some form or other, you've got to ask the person not to talk that way. You can tell the person that his comments only imprint an unnecessarily negative image of himself in his own mind.

And you can add that you don't like hearing him or her talk that way. You can say that his making such comments isn't fair to you.

And how should you handle the colleague or boss who says, "I'm good with numbers but I'm terrible with people"?

In a business situation, people who run themselves down are their own worst enemies. They are spreading hurtful propaganda against themselves. Many would indeed turn in anger on anyone else who talked about them even half as virulently as they disparaged themselves.

Obviously, it would be a major mistake for a business to let customers know, "We're collapsing" after a bad stretch, and then expect business to go on as usual. Yet a great many people in business run down their own personal stock by saying such things about themselves.

Using the Hamlet approach, you will help the other person feel better about himself by not going along with his self-assault, even implicitly.

People will often deeply appreciate your taking this tack. It's a great way to lift someone's spirit and improve your relationship at the same time. Just say, "Hey, cut it out. I don't like to hear you put yourself down."

You can do this even if the person is your boss or someone you report to. Few will object to it, and most will like you better for your spunk and loyalty.

This doesn't guarantee that the person will stop, but if you do this repeatedly most people will get the idea. And even if they don't, you will be doing yourself justice, and will be less apt to feel manipulated.

Remember, don't be your own worst enemy. Never talk about yourself, even in jest, in a way that would delight your enemies and injure your friends.

11

FORTINBRAS'S FORTITUDE

PROFITING THROUGH OTHER PEOPLE'S SUCCESS

A few years ago, Carole, a patient of mine, came in with what she believed to be a very strange problem. It was right after the Christmas holidays, and she had just returned from Ohio where she had spent a week with her family after a long absence. As a child she'd had good relationships with her siblings and had made many friends in the small town where she grew up. This year she had returned laden with presents, and eager to see her new nieces and nephews.

But most of her family and certain friends in her Ohio hometown had been stunningly cold to her.

Carole was baffled by this reaction. She hadn't been back for three years, but had kept in close touch with everyone. She had sent generous gifts on birthdays and holidays.

I asked her who among the people had been cold to her and who had not. As we went through the list we looked for distinguishing traits between those who had welcomed her and those who had seemed bothered by her very presence.

The main difference that we found was that the people who considered themselves successful and happy in their own lives were still friendly, and the others were not.

Carole had come from a loving but unaspiring family. They'd had no money for higher education. Only Carole and one sister had gone to college. They had worked hard and paid their way through college in the evenings.

Carole had come to New York City, and over a ten-year period had built a good-sized business. She was close to the top in a very competitive market, and had made enough money to be considered rich by her siblings. She had never flaunted her success and was eager to help out. Clearly she had the wherewithal to do this, which the others didn't.

Now she was the one supporting her parents in their retirement, with little help from her two brothers and two sisters. One of her two sisters and both of her brothers had settled for almost nothing. They had taken jobs well below their capacities and never sacrificed comfort for a minute in order to improve themselves. They had shunned school and avoided anything that looked novel or taxing.

Only Carole's other sister had remained vital. She now had a family she loved and a teaching job that she enjoyed. That sister stood apart from the others, who all had a tired quality about them.

Carole observed that those siblings and even her father, now dependent on her, had been distant and sarcastic with her. They talked about other people's birthdays and about christenings and about the stuff of their lives, never asking her about herself. Only her mother and the one sister who strove in her own life were truly delighted to see her.

The others actually seemed to resent the animated conversations that Carole had with that sister. They took potshots at Carole whenever they could. One brother made a nasty crack after Carole's mother had complimented her on her appearance. "When you got money, it's easy," the brother had said.

Carole had a sense that they all wanted her to disappear, and she was terribly hurt.

I first thought that Carole's siblings and some of her old friends were simply envious because she was doing so well.

But Shakespeare offers a subtler explanation and one that I have found widely useful:

Carole's success, and, even more, her personal energy, had forced these people to see that they had not needed to be so helpless, so inert, in their own lives. The others, too, might have worked their way through college, as had both sisters. Or they might have taken challenging jobs and tried to excel. But they hadn't, and they were doing their best to imply that life had never given them a chance.

Carole's success *informed* them of what they might have done with their lives—of what they might have become and still could become. By her exuberance and the success she had attained, she was, without meaning to, showing them that people can overcome obstacles and shape their own lives.

By her very presence, she was *informing* them about their own laziness and low incentive. This is why they took her presence as a personal insult.

It told them that they had been responsible for their own lives and could still do a great deal more.

The Arrival of the Informant—Fortinbras

Shakespeare introduces the notion of "informing" and of the psychological "informant" in *Hamlet*.

In the play, Hamlet is tormented over his own failure of resolve. His father has been murdered, and, according to the morals of the time, Hamlet, as the son, must avenge his death. But he keeps putting off the necessary act. He fails to muster the directed energy, and throughout much of the play, Hamlet mopes about in articulate uncertainty.

Much of the time Hamlet does what many people do when they are unsatisfied with their own performance in life. Instead of blaming themselves, they find reasons why they are so far below their own standards. Like Hamlet, they blame the world for being a disappointing and dishonest place. They find tricks of rationalization to convince themselves that there was nothing they could do—that there is nothing anybody can do.

But then, as happens with all emotional shirkers, people appear in Hamlet's life who, *by their very existence, prove that something more can be done*.

In Hamlet's case, the major informant is Fortinbras, a young man Hamlet's age, also heir to a throne and nephew to a king.

Fortinbras, from neighboring Norway, does not waver as Hamlet does. He has already proved himself a valiant general, and has repeatedly rallied and fought for causes, some of which were small matters of injured honor.

As Hamlet languishes, unable to rally himself for his own urgent and very personal cause, Fortinbras appears in stark contrast to him. Fortinbras is passing through Denmark, leading an army, and is about to risk his life for a tiny plot of land which he feels is rightfully Norway's property.

The sight of Fortinbras shocks Hamlet by reminding him of his own ineptitude. As Hamlet puts it, Fortinbras, with his courage and energy, "informs" against him, making it impossible for Hamlet to hide from himself his habit of postponement.

Fortinbras has no idea that he means this to Hamlet, but he has that meaning nevertheless. His existence is a rebuke to Hamlet. Others before Fortinbras have informed against Hamlet this way, showing him how hesitant he has been.

Hamlet remarks to himself:

> *How all occasions do inform against me,*
> *And spur my dull revenge! What is a man,*
> *If his chief good and market of his time*
> *Be but to sleep and feed?*

Hamlet concludes, after contrasting Fortinbras to himself:

> *O, from this time forth,*
> *My thoughts be bloody, or be nothing worth!*

Whenever you have an unresolved problem—for instance, you don't like yourself for being untidy; or, like Hamlet, you put off what you must do; or you've made excuses to yourself in any department—you are apt to meet informers.

An informant is a person who started out in your situation, or was worse off, but who has managed to overcome the problem that right now is conquering you.

The person may not even know about your situation, but, by his or her very presence and accomplishment, forces you to face your shortcoming.

It's as if the informant told your own higher mind that you are letting yourself down.

Like Carole's siblings, you see that someone else who started out poor has worked their way up. Or you see that someone with no more time than you works out three times a week.

How Can You Recognize a Psychological Informant?

You can often recognize that someone is informing against you by your having a vague sense of disquietude in his presence. You may dislike the person and not know why.

After some reflection, you may realize that the person has accomplished something that you yourself wanted to accomplish.

You feel stung by the message that you sold yourself short.

Unconsciously, you have been viewing the psychological informant as an unwelcome messenger telling you that you are guilty of some default. You instinctively dislike or fear him or her because this person has deprived you of your ability to rationalize your mistakes.

The informant probably doesn't want to harm you, and most likely does not even know that he is playing a role in your life.

Carole, who unwittingly informed against her three siblings, certainly had no intention of making them feel bad about their own lives. She yearned for closeness to them, and had passed no judgment on their success or failure in life.

When we inform against people we incur disfavor for seemingly no reason.

Are You an Informant Against Someone Else?

Understanding the nature of informants will also help you to understand why certain people dislike you on sight when you seemingly did nothing to offend them.

Donna, another patient of mine, who was in a miserable marriage to a financially successful man, left after twenty-two years. She took her two kids with her, received very little financial help, but proved that she could get a job at fifty-two and look after her teenage children. Donna's new, husbandless household was happy and prosperous. However, two longtime woman friends of Donna's, also unhappily married, suddenly became irrationally furious at her.

Why? The two friends had been rationalizing their need to stay married, in one case to a man who never talked to her, and in the other to a man who had continual affairs. They had told themselves, and each other, that the dismal life they both led was the only one possible—and that they owed it to their children.

Donna's courage and her success informed against them. It shook their rationalization and invited them to reconsider their own choices.

You may unknowingly inform against people in virtually any aspect of their lives.

The other person is unlikely to understand why he or she is angry at you. The person's denial of his or her own failure may be too deep for him to identify it.

But his or her unconscious knows of the failure and knows that you represent the opposite choice. To quote the Bard, you are "holding the mirror up to nature."

What Have You Done (not Wrong but) Right?

Whenever you find yourself irrationally despised or shunned, ask if you have done anything to hurt the other person. Obviously, this question should always come first.

As often as not, you can definitely answer no. In many cases, you upset the person before he even got to know you.

Next, ask yourself, "What have I accomplished or what do I have which might be a torment to the other person?"

It could be simple. Maybe you improved your vocabulary or you're able to talk about subjects from which the other person feels excluded. Or it could be that you have a freer lifestyle than the people who resent you. Perhaps you are openly and happily gay or you have chosen to put off marriage and live with someone instead. Perhaps you are financially comfortable. People who feel trapped in their own skins resent you.

In other cases, people resent you for some achievement which they think was easy for you. They may have no idea of the years of application and sacrifice that went into your achievement. They may imagine that good breaks just came your way. You seem to inform against their inadequacy, but if you inform against anything, it is simply that you worked a lot harder than they did.

It is critical to identify that you are an informant whenever this is the case.

Unless you realize that this is your effect, you may do a great deal of painful soul-searching for no reason at all. In reality, you will have done nothing harmful to the person—except exist. You simply represent some truth that upsets him or her.

DEALING WITH INFORMANTS

1.   If you find that someone is causing you acute discomfort and you don't know why, the person may be informing against you in some way.

This is especially likely if you can't honestly say that the person is doing harm to you or anyone else.

2.   Fight any urge you have to disparage the informant.

It may take guts to refrain from condemning the person long enough to discover that he or she is bringing you some painful, but true, information about yourself. But you can put that information to good use once you have it.

3.   If you can tolerate whatever discomfort the informant is causing you, you are in position to make important discoveries.

Indeed, every informant is a potential godsend, as with Hamlet and Fortinbras. This person is bringing you information which, once understood, can lead you to make a great improvement in your life. Very likely there is still time for you to do this, just as your informant improved his or her life.

4. Ask, "What freedom or attainment has this person which I would like for myself?"

You may discover nearly anything, from small differences to gigantic ones. For instance, the person is confident enough to say that he or she is good at something which you can do even better. But you've been too timid to mention your expertise.

Or the person has social courage, which you have been resenting him for. Or the person has chosen a lifestyle that you envy.

5. Hold yourself accountable for whatever you don't like about the course you've chosen.

Understand that at this stage your aim is not to blame yourself or beat yourself up. It to understand that you have power over your future life. The value of knowledge is that it can bring hope. You can change your life for the better. Almost whatever you've left out, you can add.

Your aim is to use the informant as a source of valuable knowledge.

The very people that you might have wanted to annihilate because they upset you can serve as your ultimate guides to improving your life. But it is up to you to use them to your advantage.

6. If you find yourself upsetting other people inexplicably, very possibly you are an informant in their lives.

Perhaps there is some freedom or latitude which you have taken and which they haven't. Or you have achieved something they always wanted but were afraid to strive for.

You are their Fortinbras. If these people are critical in your business or important to you in daily dealings, keep a low profile because almost surely they aren't going to like you.

If such a person is close to you, or you hope that he or she will be, sooner or later you will have to talk about the tension between you. If the resentment continues, you are in trouble. But if the other person can overcome his or her resentment, you may even be able to help the person to attain what he has always wanted.

In the worst-case scenario, nothing that you say will bridge the gap. The person simply doesn't overcome his enmity. If this occurs with someone you hold dear, you will doubtless experience shock followed by a period of mourning. You may continue to be friendly with the person on some level, but that person's inability to accept you will limit what you can have together.

7. Even if you have to low-key it around business associates, don't change anything intrinsic to your nature or important to you.

If you realize that you have the role of informant with a business associate or, worse yet, with a superior, you may have to low-key that aspect of yourself in order to survive. But be aware that you are doing this and don't low-key yourself where you don't have to.

It's a too common practice for people to mutilate themselves so as not to upset other people by presenting contrasts. Don't do this to yourself. Be careful never to sacrifice traits that are valuable to you simply because certain other people don't approve of them or are upset by them. You must subject your behavior to your own ethical standards.

Stage Four
PRESERVING YOUR "SELF" IN RELATIONSHIPS

BE ACTIVE, NOT REACTIVE

Unfairnesses in relationships, imbalances, can sneak up on us. Even the most defined, empathic, and sensible person may realize one day that a particular relationship is draining him or her and is heavily weighted in favor of the other person. You have forfeited some of your "self" in your attempt to please the other person.

Such imbalances may have been there at the very start of a relationship. You may have chosen the relationship for the wrong reason: The person, lover or friend, looks good on paper. Or you imagined that other people would respect you or envy you for landing such a partner. Perhaps they do, but this is no help to you if the relationship is wrong.

Very likely you didn't realize at the start that the person you chose was toxic. Or perhaps the person, not necessarily a lover but a relative or an old friend, has been in your life so long that the matter of who chose whom has long been meaningless. Now you find yourself stuck with a chronic complainer or a jealous friend or a narcissist.

If the toxic person in your life is a lover, he or she may make a practice of finding things wrong with you. You may find yourself in a constant struggle to "change" in order to win the person's love or stave off his or her disappointment with you.

Relationship imbalances come in many guises, and unless you address them they are apt to become worse.

Being defined and empathic and sane doesn't make a person immune to losing some of his or her hard-earned sense of self in a relationship. In fact, a highly empathic person may be especially likely to do this.

But being empathic should not make you a pushover. Setting your own standards in relationships is as important as setting your own ethical and moral standards.

*   *   *

As a self-reliant person, you are in a position to interact lovingly but robustly. Preserving your sense of self in relationships certainly means not taking advantage of other people. But it also means not allowing yourself to be bullied, even subtly.

It requires receiving a flow of good responses from others and not merely sending out warmth to others. It means being as free as possible to be yourself with people—and certainly with those with whom you spend time voluntarily.

Over a lifetime, if you are to preserve your sense of self with people, you must actively revise many of your relationships. Just as you draw certain people closer to you because your experience with them is fulfilling and self-enhancing, you will find it necessary to demote certain other people in intimacy.

Think of your friends and acquaintances down to the most insignificant in your life as in a stadium. Those dearest to you are in the front row, witnessing your life and involved in it. Others are farther back, in more remote tiers of the stadium. Still others are so far back that you can barely make out their contours.

You have "tiers of friends," and over a lifetime, you will find it necessary to shift some to different tiers and to exclude certain ones from the stadium of your life altogether.

To preserve your sense of self in relationships, you must be the one who does this. It may hurt at times, as when you must usher someone close to you out of your life. But your own interpersonal balance requires it.

There are two main phases to this accomplishment of keeping your balance in relationships.

The first is starting out with that balance.

It means that you—and you alone—have the right to choose your friends and lovers, and have the obligation to do so, since you are to spend your time and emotions with them.

The second is to retain that balance in relationships. You can be free in your relationships only so long as you recognize your constant right to decide who stays in your life and at what level of intimacy.

When choosing your friends and lovers, it is important to realize that they are a luxury in your life, an addition, and not a necessity. They should be an enhancement of what you already have, of who you already are—and should not detract from you in any way. The ideal is for you to feel richer because of them and not poorer.

These people, whom you yourself choose, are those with whom you should be most natural. You may learn from them and modify yourself. But you should never feel the need to change who you basically are in order to win their approval. You have learned to stay friends with other people's unconscious, and now you have the right to expect them to stay friends with yours.

You have learned to enjoy people as they are. Now you have the right to ask for the same respect for yourself.

Self-reliance taught you that your major concern should be keeping your own center and not winning the good opinions of others. You should choose your friends and lovers based on your own interests, your own needs, your own desires. They should not be chosen to make other people happy or to induce them to think well of you.

Your friends and lovers are not possessions to be flaunted. Nor should you be ashamed of them if they make you happy but they don't live up to other people's expectations. And no one has a right to a lifetime commitment from you unless the person has earned it.

You also have the right to decide which people should stay close to you and how close they should be.

The person who is highly evolved at preserving his or her sense of self in relationships virtually never bends himself or herself out of shape for another person.

He or she understands that no one has the right to use tactics on someone else. For example, no one has the right to withhold love to force a change in you. And no one has the right to persist in being a negative influence, as by inflicting bad news on you all the time, or by complaining continually, or by making little of what you stand for.

It is never an obligation to go on enduring negative people in your personal life.

It is important to be able to identify it when someone in your life, a lover or a friend, is making you feel miserable on a regular basis.

For instance, someone who talks about tragedy all the time may induce panic in you; someone who boasts continually may cause you to question your own worth. A lover who continually implies that he or she would prefer you in an improved version can induce constant anxiety. It is important that you identify this anxiety and not confuse it with the excitement of love.

Finally, if you are highly evolved at keeping your balance in relationships, you are probably a person who has learned to confront people early when something is wrong, and to do it without bitterness.

You have learned that it is easier to talk to a friend about an injury as soon as you identify it than to let resentment build up in you. Confronting a friend or lover who is treating you badly takes courage. But you are not a brooder, and you are not fearful. You have the energy of the self-determined person.

Working on your relationships requires both the willingness to tackle life and a belief in the robustness of other people. It requires that you trust yourself and that you believe in your inherent worth.

Shakespeare, like all dramatists, enjoyed using imbalances in relationships as the subjects of his plays. They are naturals for the conflict that makes for good theatre. In his tragedies, these imbalances lead to disaster. In some of his comedies, they are rectified and the audience learns the folly of letting a relationship get out of hand.

In still other of his comedies, like *The Taming of the Shrew* and *All's Well That Ends Well,* the imbalance is never truly straightened out. Instead it is institutionalized.

In *The Taming of the Shrew,* the woman surrenders her spirit in what is truly a sexist play. After marrying a man, she succumbs to his unwholesome mastery over her, and agrees to let him dominate her life.

In *All's Well,* the heroine practically stands on her head to make a man marry her. When he does, we leave the theatre feeling that despite his protest that he loves her, the woman has ended up with a bad bargain.

Now we are going to look at several characters of Shakespeare's including one of his most abused and one of his most abusive. You will see how relationships can twist out of shape and what you can do to bring them back.

12
FINDING ROMEO

RECOGNIZING LOVE WHEN YOU SEE IT

A young woman, the sister of a close friend of mine, had a deep love affair in college. At first she and her boyfriend talked about marriage, but in time the woman began to sense that her Junior League friends weren't impressed: the fellow wasn't on the right upward track. She wanted a man others would envy her for, and reluctantly dismissed this fellow, who didn't fit the bill.

She was in pain for a time, but consoled herself with the thought that she was young and there were plenty of other men to choose from. Her family was well connected socially, and at holiday celebrations throughout the year she managed to meet plenty of eligibles.

Soon after graduating, she took up with a classically handsome man, athletic, careful about his proportion of body fat, a *Law Review* student. He fit everyone's requirements—parents', friends'—and the two moved in together. The woman had chosen her partner the way some women pick jewelry, not by how much they like it, but by its impressiveness. This guy looked expensive. But from the start she sensed that there was nothing between them—none of that intangible, inexplicable stuff every woman yearns for. Out of ennui they broke up.

Next came a suave, outstandingly gorgeous gigolo. Although my friend's sister was only in her late twenties, this man had targeted her the way he would a rich elderly widow at the country club. Another friend of mine caught him going through the labels of the guests' coats strewn over the bed at one of her parents' parties. He was evaluating the crowd. The young woman imagined that everyone envied her for the match; she was seeing the relationship through other people's eyes, or at least what she thought were other people's eyes. Then without warning the gigolo dumped her. Possibly he had checked out her family's net worth and found her wanting.

After that she dated several different men. Once or twice she put the brakes on her feelings when the man loved her but didn't fit her social template, when his prospects or appearance were not what she thought other people would admire.

At thirty-five, with resignation, she resumed with the *Law Review* lover who now had a successful career. When last I talked with her brother, he said that the wedding date was set, that she was sporting a huge diamond, but that she went on crying jags whenever she thought about the marriage. She knew that she didn't love her fiancé, she didn't even like him, but the match looked good on paper.

I imagine that now that she is married, she doesn't even dream of finding Romeo anymore.

Hers has been the eternal mistake of seeing too much through other people's eyes.

A Face in the Crowd

Shakespeare constantly saw this mistake as the way love could go wrong. He portrays numerous characters, especially women, who feel under pressure to marry in order to please other people. To bystanders the marriage looks like the perfect match, but the woman doesn't truly want to marry the man.

However, Shakespeare's heroines, unlike my friend's sister, have the wit to know what they really want and the courage to resist choosing the wrong person in order to look good to others. They will not give up their own center in a matter as important as love.

In *A Midsummer Night's Dream,* a heroine, Hermia, comments:

> *O hell, to choose love by another's eyes!*

And a youth in *As You Like It* comments desperately:

> *But oh, how bitter a thing it is to look into happiness*
> *through another man's eyes!*

Finding Romeo has more to do with sharpening your own judgment than with logistics. You will doubtless meet Romeo. The odds are greatly with you. Most women do meet their Romeo, more than once in their lifetime. The reason that they are still actively looking for him anyway is that they didn't allow themselves to recognize Romeo when he appeared.

The majority of women have access to meeting many men through friends, through hobbies, at work, or by coincidences of different kinds. The key to finding Romeo is the art of singling him out from the crowd of available men—of knowing who he is and of trusting what you know.

This does not imply that you should "settle" in any way. If you have a particular set of standards, by all means identify them and, if you wish, write them down, as many relationship guides suggest you do.

You Will Meet Romeo. Then What?

Lately, in my psychotherapy practice I have identified an interesting phenomenon. Many women patients of mine have told me that at least once in recent months they have scrutinized a woman acquaintance over forty who has been happily married for many years to a man who seems incredibly suited to her. Among those husbands are many successful, often self-made men. My patients have often marveled at these very natural-looking relationships, saying in so many words, "When I was twenty-five I would never have looked at that guy."

Their reasons ranged from, "I wouldn't have pictured him amounting to anything," to "He wouldn't have been my type when I was young, but now he looks so sexy." Or, "He's still not my type but I don't know who my type is anymore. And I find something very attractive about this guy."

The wives they are admiring seem to have had a homing device, a geiger counter that years earlier helped them go below the surface and select and enjoy the right man. Their secret technique was that they learned early how to combine two seemingly impossible goals:

◆ Not settling and

◆ Trusting their own judgment, rather than basing their decision on what other people thought.

The Art of Love Is Recognition

Contrast the story of my sister's friend with the greatest love story ever told, Shakespeare's *Romeo and Juliet*.

In Verona, Italy, in the fourteenth century, there really lived a couple named Romeo and Juliet. Their respective families, the Montagues and the Capulets, harbored a great enmity toward each other which gave rise to constant mockery and to fights when they met in the public square. These vendettas resulted in occasional deaths. To befriend a member of the opposite clan was taboo, so that when Romeo and his Montague buddies crashed a masquerade given by the Capulets, it was risky business. Were their disguise to be seen through they would be in big trouble.

Juliet, the Capulet, was nearing fourteen at the time and had already been betrothed to Count Paris. She was being pressured to marry this handsome and acceptable youth. But Juliet's homing device had told her that Count Paris was wrong for her. She did not love him, and it is uncertain if he loved her—such was the nature of marriage in those days.

When Romeo talked to Juliet at the ball, though she could not see him because he was in disguise, love was there for her as it was for him.

After that, not all the pressures brought upon her by those close to her could change her mind or delude her. Young as she was, Juliet had a clarity about what she wanted. In her parents' eyes, of course, Romeo, being a Montague, was the worst possible choice. On the other hand, if she would marry Paris, it would be an easy life for Juliet. In those days a woman like Juliet who married whom she was told received honors and a huge dowry, and lived the upper class existence without obstacles. But the concern of others wasn't about to distract Juliet from heart's desire.

Shakespeare does not presume to explain love, but he does not doubt its inexplicable and compelling nature or the notion that when it is felt it must not be denied, whether or not we choose to act on it every time. He constantly questioned whether love is in the eyes or in the mind. He believed that love can transcend the senses. Elsewhere Shakespeare has a lover say:

> *Had I no eyes but ears, my ears would love*
> *That inward beauty and invisible,*
> *Or were I deaf, thy outward parts would move*
> *Each part in me that were but sensible;*
> *Though neither eyes nor ears to hear nor see . . .*
> *Yet would my love to thee be still as much.*

Romeo and Juliet fell in love at once. It was an overwhelming, intangible, inexplicable experience for both of them, which is what love should be.

Shakespeare has written:

> *Whoever loved that loved not at first sight?*

Juliet recognized her feeling for Romeo immediately. The fact that he came from the wrong family did not deter her.

*   *   *

After another skirmish in which Romeo was banished for killing a man, the two contrived to steal away together. But the forces of the two great factions, the Montagues and the Capulets, were too great for them. As the result of bad luck and brutality on both sides, Romeo and Juliet were destroyed.

> *For never was a story of more woe*
> *Than this of Juliet and her Romeo.*

Was Juliet crazy to choose a man so wrong in the eyes of everyone she knew?

You decide.

Don't Turn Yourself into Juliet

In the era of the play, and still in Shakespeare's time a century or two later, failure to comply with society's wishes in marriage often resulted in brutal punishment or in ostracism. Women were routinely consigned to house imprisonment in nunneries for the rest of their lives when they didn't go along with a parent's wishes.

But Juliet followed her heart anyhow.

Nowadays, of course, neither parents nor friends can force you to choose anyone as a lover or a mate. That is, unless you're willing to surrender your life to avoid being disinherited. Still, few parents will truly disown their own children for long. Any parent or friend who disapproves of your choice will probably come around to accepting it if you are happy.

The strictures we face these days are self-imposed. But the criteria that millions of young women and men impose upon themselves can be every bit as fierce as those imposed by the Montagues and Capulets. I am talking about rules that people set in their own minds, the demands they make of a lover because they need others to approve of that lover.

Do you want a husband who loves you and whom you love? Or do you want a husband whom people will envy you for having?

Who is more deluded—Juliet, who risked everything for her Romeo, or a modern Juliet who allows the opinions of others to put someone into her bed for a lifetime?

To the degree that your search for Romeo is blurred by the need for other people's good wishes, you can literally ruin your life.

Be Sure Your Standards Are Your Own

I've had women patients stop themselves from loving men for such reasons as age—the man had to be someone between their own age and five years older—for not having a flat stomach, for not riding a bike and playing golf every weekend, for not being interested enough in a healthy diet, for not making as much money as their friends' husbands made.

The issue is not the standard itself, but whether it is truly your own standard. If you make a good living, is it critical that your Romeo does so as well? Or is it simply that you would feel embarrassed at having your friends know that you're the breadwinner? Are you so immersed in diet that you would reject a man who likes hamburgers? Or are you simply afraid that your friends will consider your boyfriend sloppy or low class?

Even in the most intimate concerns, make sure that your requirements are truly yours.

Perhaps you require that the man wants children. If it's because you yourself really want them, great. But if it's only because you would feel left behind by certain friends if you didn't have them, go for love and let your friends make the adjustment.

The only standards you should stick to are those that are truly yours. Perhaps it is crucial to you that the man desires a monogamous relationship or that he is a good communicator. Fine. Those are things that will impact your life every minute.

The only criteria that you need to accept are those that would affect your happiness even if no one else knew about them.

"Tell Me Where Is Fancy Bred, Or in the Heart or in the Head?"

I'll always remember a patient of mine, a man in his thirties, a lawyer. His first wife looked like the wives of the successful partners in the firm—she had the requirements of being social, upwardly mobile, slender, and stylish. My patient bossed her around a lot: He constantly monitored her eating habits, insisting that she remain as svelte as the wives of the other partners, with whom they socialized half a dozen times a year. The woman complied willingly, happy at living "the good life" in a quiet Connecticut suburb.

After six years of marriage, my patient had begun an affair with a woman much like his wife. She lived in New York City, where he worked. After he became a partner, in no small part thanks to his first wife's social grace and likability, he divorced her and married the other woman. Within four years he had moved this wife to Connecticut and was stamping his system on her, regulating her behavior, and, in particular, her eating habits. This woman had a tendency to put on weight, and he blasted her for lapses and put her on a strict eating regimen, so that his partners and others would admire her and by implication would admire him.

Then, one day on the train to New York City, he struck up an acquaintance with a truly obese woman, and began an affair with her. When he came to see me as a patient he was desperately troubled. He told me that he'd never had better sex than with this hugely overweight woman.

Almost in tears, he told me that his sexual fantasies had always been of fat women, and this woman was an ultimate experience for him. He dreamt about her continually. He confessed that he had always had sexual trouble with his slender wives, and had no sexual desire for this wife, any more than he'd had for the last. Even apart from the two wives, his whole previous sexual history had been with slender women, and it had been poor.

For all of his life, this man had selected women for their appeal to others. He was living his love life for them. In response to a question of mine, he readily answered that he would surely have risen in the firm even if his wife had been overweight. He had been concerned about getting relative strangers to respect him as a lover, a man who could snare desirable women. He had spent a lifetime pursuing women he didn't find attractive because he lacked the courage to pursue what he wanted.

I could not help him. He left after a few sessions, mortified at what he had acknowledged to himself. He hated himself for his taste because it wasn't the mainstream preference. But he could not give up the only sexual happiness he had ever had. So far as I know, he continued his affair, opting for the agony of a life of subterfuge because he lacked the courage to accept his real wants.

Mastering Your Fears of What Others Will Think

In many other cases I have been able to help people identify their real desires and to master their fears of disappointing others, or of being looked at askance for their choice of partners.

Remember that if you're with a person whom you don't love, all the approval in the world will only make you feel more lonely. The envy of others will only make you see your "successful" relationship as more of a mockery.

And if you're with the right person, even the most scathing assaults can hardly dim your happiness.

You alone know how happy you are, how fulfilled. Critics, both real ones and figments of your imagination, are impotent to harm you.

What Every Lover Must Answer

Stick to your true inner standards, the ones that are really yours. If you feel that you are in love, ask yourself two questions above all others.

◆   How does this person make you feel about yourself?

The answer should come to you at once. Either the person makes you feel that you are wonderful, attractive, intelligent, and kind. Or he makes you feel that something central is missing. Certainly, at the start of a long-term relationship, the person should idealize you to some degree. If, instead of feeling that you are this person's Juliet, you find yourself wondering if you are young enough, pretty enough, educated enough, muscular enough, or if you dress well enough, you are off to a bad start.

Such insecurities indicate that you feel unloved or unworthy of the person. Look out. Go slow. Romeo did not tell his friends that Juliet would be perfect if only she wasn't so tall or so short.

◆   Can this person *evolve with me*?

Any of your secondary requirements that are not being met right now may be met in the future *if* the person can change and grow. He may evolve away from hamburgers if they disturb you or he may get with the program and decide that he wants a better career. He may take to your interests in a variety of ways, as you may take to his.

You are going to be with this person a long time. At least that is the plan. You yourself will learn and change and grow. You will make discoveries about other people, about yourself, about the world. Your interests will evolve. For a relationship to survive over time, both people must have the capacity to change and entertain new outlooks.

The new relationship vow ought to be "to love, honor, and evolve with." I have seen more divorces occur because one person changed outlooks— for instance, went back to school or changed professions or interests—while the other refused to accept these changes, to evolve himself, than for any other reason.

How can you tell if a person has the capacity to evolve?

You can see in part by whether the person has grown in recent years, by how open he is to new ideas, to new interests, to admitting it when he is wrong, to meeting new people and hearing them out. But most of all, you can tell by how well he hears you out, by how well he accepts your new ideas and, above all, your feelings.

As long as the other person is willing to keep talking, and disclosing his true feelings without always being defensive, that person can evolve.

Above All, Make Sure That the Magical Elixir of Love Is There

When a couple in trouble comes to my office, by far my best gauge of their prognosis is the presence of this elixir. I will ask each person, "Do you love him?" "Do you love her?" When I get an immediate yes on both sides, I can be pretty sure that things will work out, that I can help the couple, no matter how at odds they are. But sometimes I get less than a yes. For instance, the man says, "Well, it's hard to know what love really is," or the woman says, "I would love him if only . . ." Then I know there's trouble ahead. Without love, even the smallest obstacles are gigantic hurdles. Real love is by its definition a highly personal experience, so who is better fit to judge Juliet's love than Juliet herself?

Don't miss Romeo simply because other people can't see him. Finding Romeo is a lot easier than other people think. Having the courage to recognize him, to see him totally through your own eyes and to trust your own judgment, this is the essential part.

13

IAGO'S TOXICITY

LOOKING FOR THE POISONOUS PEOPLE IN YOUR LIFE

One of the most interesting people in all of Shakespeare's plays is Iago, the second lead in the play *Othello*.

Although Iago is not a title character, he has been analyzed more and has been the center of a greater mystery than almost any of Shakespeare's characters. He is a villain, but unlike Richard the Third or Shakespeare's other wrongdoers, his motivations are not obvious. Iago is essential to the tragedy of *Othello*. He is the one who moves the play—he brings about the evil. But no one in the play or in the audience can ever figure out why he does it.

Over the centuries, scholars have tried to explain why Iago so devotes himself to destroying people's lives. The explanations that critics offer for Iago's evil say as much about those doing the explaining as about Iago himself.

The Original Iago

Iago is on stage when the play opens. He is the first of the main characters to speak. We learn that he is the trusted friend and aide of Othello, who is soon chosen to command the forces deployed in Cyprus. The audience learns that Iago and Othello have long been together. They have easy mutual references and, clearly, a history. Othello depends on Iago, values him, and trusts him to the extent of often calling him "honest Iago."

Iago, however, while outwardly presenting himself as returning Othello's friendship and trust, has a very different agenda. From the start, Iago does what many of Shakespeare's very entertaining villains do—he makes us, the audience, his real confidants. He lets us in on his treacherous plans, even as they form in his mind.

This, in a sense, is Iago's one generous act. He gives the audience the gift of allowing us to watch his evil mind work. He tells us that he is determined to destroy Othello, among others. He never doubts that we will join him in celebrating every time he ruins the life of another good guy.

When we meet Iago, he is already at work as a one-man wrecking crew. Othello has just eloped with his young bride Desdemona. Because Othello is much older than Desdemona and a Moor, her father is against the match. Iago, who prefers to have others do his dirty work, has arranged for a third party to awaken Desdemona's father and turn in the lovers. In spite of this effort, Othello and Desdemona marry, and Iago's role in the attempt to interfere is never found out.

This pattern is repeated throughout the play. Iago works behind the scenes to ruin people, and he covers his tracks carefully. His masterpiece will be to wreck Othello's life by convincing him that Desdemona is betraying him with another man. He plants evidence, tells lies ranging from subtle to blatant, uses innuendo, and misleads Othello through coincidences that he contrives.

Even his most outrageous acts go undetected. Not until the very end of the play, when Desdemona is dead, and Othello, mad with grief, is about to take his own life, does it come out that Iago is the cause of all the evil. Iago's own wife, who has unwittingly been used by Iago as part of his plot, furnishes the final proof that Iago has framed Desdemona.

The play ends with Othello and Desdemona dead, and the audience still not understanding exactly why Iago wanted this.

What Drives Iago?

How are we to explain Iago's treachery?

Iago himself gives various reasons in the play. He says he hates Othello for having promoted the handsome, younger Michael Cassio ahead of him. He says that Othello slept with his wife, though he also implies that he doesn't believe this. At another time, he says that he hates Cassio for having

> *a daily beauty in his life*
> *That makes me ugly.*

And Iago also tells us that after letting various people in on his diabolical plots, he must bring about their death or be found out. These reasons contradict one another, and Iago himself doesn't seem to be convinced of any of them. He seems almost to be making up reasons just to amuse himself and us.

Different scholars have accepted one of these reasons or another, and they have also put forth some of their own. By the late eighteenth century, the Iago question had a life of its own. Then the poet Samuel Coleridge made the startling assertion that Iago had no reason at all. Coleridge described Iago's conjectures and in fact the whole play as "The motive hunting of a motiveless malignancy."

Though the phrase was often quoted, modern psychology disallows motiveless acts. If we personally had to choose a motive, we would select Iago's own statement about his being made to feel ugly in the presence of beauty or of other people's happiness in love. But obviously, the greatness of Shakespeare is partly that he gives us latitude to draw our own conclusions about his characters. And you will draw yours.

As much as Iago shocks the audience with his cruelty and total lack of conscience, he delights us with his charm. He is witty and lighthearted, and he has a magnificent knowledge of human beings. Although he employs all of these good qualities in the service of evil, those around him don't realize this and are taken in by him.

Iago in Everyday Life

Iago is a heightened character, but Shakespeare must have known the type in life. Shakespeare merely exaggerated Iago's essence—he is a negative force, a creature who goes about undermining people.

In the drama he causes two people's deaths. In real life, people who create negative force fields do damage on a smaller scale, as a rule. They lurk in our lives, exerting a slow but sure effect.

Many of us feel uncomfortable around certain people who have made themselves fixtures in our circle. It is sometimes hard for us to pinpoint exactly what the person's negativity consists of.

Why do we feel so depressed after we see a certain relative?

Why do we always feel as if we're going to lose our job after we meet a certain old friend?

Why, after chatting with a particular neighbor, do we imagine that our mate is interested in someone else?

It's hard to blame our sudden depression directly on the relative or old friend or neighbor. But good detective work would show that the particular person was always there right before we fell prey to our anxiety attack or bout of self-hatred.

Iago, in *Othello,* represents the whole spectrum of negative people who appear in everyday life.

Shakespeare, the ultimate psychologist, understood that these people are by their very nature subtle and hard to pin down.

- Iagos often work through other people.

- They use innuendo and do much of their dirty work behind your back.

- They are often people who have been in your life for a long time. They have a way of adhering to you; they may sink into the background of your life but they remain with you.

- Even as they drain you, it's hard to picture life without them. Like Iago, these people often make themselves indispensable to you in some way. Or, they play on the fact that since they are close family or relatives, you will not disown them.

- Many of these subtly negative people share Iago's desire to slash at anyone else who is happy. But they rarely show this openly because, for one reason or another, they want to remain in your life.

- Others don't attack you purposely, but their very presence is toxic, and you suffer while in their company.

The Iagos you know, those subtle negative forces, are much more dangerous than people who are openly hurtful to you.

At work, most people are political enough to figure out which coworkers would use treachery to get their job. You can spot a neighbor who is out to steal your husband or wife. Or a teacher who takes an instant dislike to one of your kids. You are willing to see these people as enemies. You can eliminate them or at least keep close watch over them; in the long run they pose a minimum threat to you.

But the real danger of the secret Iago lies within you yourself. You are loath to get rid of the person because he or she has been close to you for years. Perhaps the person has done some favor for you, or you are attracted to that person. More likely, he or she is profiting by some hold on you— seniority in your life or a blood bond—that you are afraid to challenge.

Looking for the Iago in Your Life

You may not have to look very hard to ferret out your more open enemies. At least, they aren't trying to pass as friends.

*　　*　　*

But the Iago in your life may actually *believe* that he or she is your friend. Your relationship with that person may be the closest thing that he or she has to intimacy. As a matter of fact, you may stay with the person partially because you feel responsible for him. It may actually be that you feel that you are that person's only true friend. You notice that others shy away from this Iago character because he treats them badly. You may imagine that you are the only one he treats well.

With every Iago, however, your unconscious mind knows what your conscious mind is trying to ignore. Instinctively, you may avoid introducing the Iago in your life to your new lover or to your boss. Or you do it anyhow, holding your breath. Later you feel that something went slightly wrong, that your boss got a bit cold with you afterwards or your lover seemed unusually quiet.

You may look forward to having lunch with this Iago type, forgetting that after leaving him or her the last ten times, you felt bad or worried about your future, or you wondered if you looked older. When such a person is one of a group or is invited to a party, the whole event may lose its luster.

These Iagos have demoralizing aftereffects on you, and the aftereffects of people ought to be important criteria of whether you want them in your life. Typically, after leaving a Iago-type friend, you feel worse about yourself and more insecure.

You may try to discount this feeling. You simply struggle to your feet and resume your life, returning to your good mood after a while. You are only too glad to put the experience behind you. Feeling that you could handle whatever damage was done, you keep the person in your life.

But Iago types can actually do you lasting harm.

The Negativity Factor: Iagos Crush You

Negative people can break your spirit; they can demoralize you not just during the time you spend with them but even when you're alone. With such a person in your life, you can feel hopeless about new ventures. You will be less likely to take chances or attempt to improve your life.

Iago types can impart a sense of "What's the use?" about all your ambitions. They can cause you to disbelieve in yourself, to conclude that you are unworthy of opportunity. If you have a potent Iago in your life, you may eventually develop a "so what attitude" yourself. You may end up believing the worst.

You would be astonished to know where your life might have gone without such a person.

It is vital to learn to spot your Iagos before they get very far in your life. You need both sensitivity to these types and the courage to label them properly.

The instant you identify a Iago for what he or she really is, you have neutralized much of the damage that this person can do. Now, when he or she tries to spread the "so what attitude" or criticizes you obliquely, you will realize at once that he is pulling his negative act.

Many people are negative almost by nature. If you tell them you're in love, they say something disdainful. If you announce that you just got a good job, they imply that it won't last or that it isn't as good as you think. And if you express a hope for your life, they will imply that it's a pipe dream and can't possibly come true.

A great many of these people aren't just pessimists who mean no harm. Among them are people who from the bottom of their hearts wish you the worst. They don't dare say, "I hope you fail. It would make me sick to see you happy or successful." If they did, you could discount them. Instead they try to tell you that they are only being "realistic." They imply that they are trying to save you from being shocked and disappointed when things don't work out.

Most of the Iagos that we meet simply make our lives a little worse; they draw a cloud over our better days. But there are Iagos who truly set out to destroy us, psychologically and even physically. Such people in real life can reach cinematic proportions. I knew one who encouraged a long-term friend's drinking when the other man was near death from alcoholism. He had nothing material to gain from the friend's death and no apparent grudge against him. This man was in the tradition of the motiveless, vicious Iago.

Maybe you don't want to attach a public nickname to the person you have identified as Iago in some form. But attach a nickname in your own mind. If the person is very important in your life, perhaps you will want to discuss what he or she is doing and why you would like the person to stop.

In other cases, you may decide that the Iago in your life isn't worth the trouble, that there isn't enough compensation for his influence. In those cases, you will prefer to back away from him or her.

However, whether or not you decide to confront the person with his or her behavior, don't forget what you've concluded about the person. In the case of Iago types, self-immunization is your best defense against the poison.

The "So What" Iago

As with every Iago, look to your own feelings first in order to recognize the negative type that you are dealing with.

Your first clue to the "so what" Iago is a feeling of hopelessness—a "pointless" feeling about what you are doing or plan to do.

For instance, you have just told the person excitedly that your new co-worker is terrific, or that you're in love, or that you were asked to join friends on a vacation, or that you were given a raise. Suddenly you feel foolish about the whole thing. You feel as if you're running off at the mouth, and that you look immature and silly. Now, whatever excited you for hours or days doesn't seem very important.

You may even wonder if it was worth telling the person at all. You feel that you imposed on him and you should be quiet.

The key here is to pinpoint that the drop in your enthusiasm came when you interacted with this particular person. After talking to him or her, there seemed nothing left to be excited about.

"So what if I'm in love? People fall in love every day. It probably won't last."

"Why should I be so thrilled about a new coworker? What difference does it make if I like him? I sound ridiculous going on about it."

Next, ask yourself why the drop in your enthusiasm? What did the Iago character do?

First, he didn't share your excitement.

Secondly, and even worse, he said or implied that you are childish and naive for being enthusiastic. Think about it and you will see that he often makes you feel immature and overexuberant.

Dealing with the "So What" Type

Save your exuberant moments for people who light up the way you do. Those are the people who really care about you. If someone is truly on your side, he or she will want to have highlights in your life. A good friend will help you to celebrate good moments, even though you both realize that on occasion things won't work out.

Why start out something as wonderful as a love affair, picturing defeat? It's only too easy to picture. If you are destined to fail, at least you will have some good moments. At least you won't be a lifetime cynic like your Iago.

◆   Don't fall prey to this Iago's implication that the mature person
    never gets excited.

◆ And worse yet, don't let him or her tell you that you're better off armed with a picture of the worst. Too much time spent envisioning worst-case scenarios can short-circuit your life. A friend should lighten your load, encourage you, and enjoy your triumphs and aspirations, whether they all work out or not.

◆ If you decide to keep this "so what" person in your life, be especially careful about telling him anything you wouldn't want other people to know. Realize that he is professionally unimpressed by anything. Accept his negativity and it won't hurt you as much.

You have the right to point out his "so what" attitude if he persists. And maybe it would be a good idea to see him less, if at all.

Remember that anyone can say, "So what" about anything. The art of life is to make things important, not unimportant. This Iago type can whittle you down over a lifetime unless you take defensive measures.

The Narcissist

This type of Iago also ignores your achievements. You tend to feel worthless around him, too. But he is definitely not a "so what" person. Quite the contrary. To him or her, many things have great importance. The problem, so far as you are concerned, is that these "many things" all involve him— not you.

When you try to tell the narcissist that you got a raise at work, he tells you about a promotion that he is up for. If you tell him about the vacation plans you made, he immediately tells you about his own. You may be tempted to think that he simply didn't hear you, but of course he did. The proof is that he instantly took up your subject and referred it to himself.

If you call the narcissistic Iago with a problem, he either doesn't hear it or compliments you right away, saying that you can handle the problem easily. He uses this compliment to switch to his only real topic—himself. You may enjoy the compliment, but after you've hung up the phone, you realize that you talked about him and not you.

As with all Iago types, you first spot the narcissist by your own feeling. You feel second-rate, as if your life is essentially unimportant and his is vital.

Once you suspect that he is breaking your spirit this way, you can check out your suspicions. How much time have you spent talking about him or her, as opposed to time spent on you?

As a further test, push your own topics. After you've spent a half hour on the phone, talking about his or her relationship or business venture, bring up your own. The narcissist will dismiss it. Bring it up again. Keep pushing your own subject. You will identify the narcissist—or rather he will identify himself—by his absolute refusal to give you anything like your share of time and attention.

Dealing with the Narcissist Type

Once again, identifying what you are up against is more than half the battle won. Once you realize that you can never truly capture his attention or interest, you are free.

Beware the temptation to keep trying to get this person to talk about you instead of himself. Doing this can only demoralize you. At best, he or she will hear you out the way one waits for a train to pass, so that he can go on talking. He will look at you dully while you hold forth and light up when his or her turn comes.

Your only hope is to confront the person, and this is worth doing only if he or she is very dear to you. You must tell the person that he or she seems disinterested in what concerns you, and that you feel discouraged about telling him anything.

The true narcissist will ignore you, since this argument involves you and not him. But if he or she is an imperfect narcissist or an incomplete narcissist, you may get some response. The narcissist will say you are wrong.

Next you must talk about yourself, and when he changes the subject, point out what he has done. He won't really listen to you but perhaps he will pretend to. That's a start. Someday you may get through.

If you decide that the narcissist in your life is just too wearing on you, and you are ready to end the relationship, that's easy. Just keep talking about yourself and don't switch to him. He will soon stop calling and drop out of your life.

The Jealous Iago

The jealous Iago resents your success. Jealous Iagos often belittle what you have in order to injure you. They imply that you haven't done well enough when they are actually seething because you have what they want.

"Oh, I didn't think you were going to buy such a small car." Translation from the jealous Iago—"I am dying with envy that you are able to buy a new car every two years. I've had mine for ten."

Jealous Iagos typically resent your happiness. They try to puncture your good mood. They often disguise their negativity by pretending to offer you advice, implying that you need it. But their advice is meant more to wound you than to help you.

Many compulsive advice givers are jealous people at heart.

"You should save your money instead of taking such costly vacations."

This may seem to express concern, but it is often a jealous person's attempt to rob you of your enjoyment by making you feel guilty.

The jealous Iago can have a problem with nearly anything in your life. He or she can be jealous because you're single, because you're married, because you have a responsible job, because you're at home with the kids and not working, because you are younger, or because you are older and more advanced in your career.

Truly jealous people can be miserable even when they have more than you do or exactly as much. A woman twice as rich as her friend can resent the friend's buying a piece of jewelry which she could easily afford five of.

With this negative person, you feel guilty about everything good that happens to you.

Sometimes the jealous Iago plays injured at your good fortune. They do this by acting hurt, as if you've been neglecting them by spending time or money on yourself. They pull poor-mouth in various ways. "Well, on my salary I couldn't go to that restaurant."

Worse yet, they can systematically put down everything that matters to you, because this is the only way they can deal with their envy. They make you feel like a loser so that they won't feel like one.

Dealing with the Jealous Iago

When with such people, you will detect in yourself an impulse to conceal good things that happen to you.

You'll feel an impulse not to describe your new lover because the jealous Iago will make you feel guilty for having a love affair, or else will put your lover down.

I have seen people so victimized by jealous Iagos, whom they have not identified as such, that they beat them to the punch, disparaging their own accomplishments and friends before the jealous Iago can do so.

- ◆ Resist any urge you might have to disparage yourself to the jealous person.

- ◆ Don't brag. But state freely what you are proud of and what you have accomplished. If the jealous person puts it down, and if you still hope to keep communication open with him or her, tell the jealous Iago that he always disparages you. Ask him or her, "Can't you just enjoy my accomplishment with me?"

◆   Never get caught up being defensive about what you know to be worthwhile. If you rush to the defense of your car or your lover or your friends, you are playing into jealous Iago's hands.

Never limit your own aspirations because another person can't go as far. That would be giving the jealous person more than his or her due. People who don't have nearly the success or money that you do, if they are free of competitive jealousy, will enjoy your success. Real friends will take pride in it as if it were their own. These are the people you need in life—not jealous Iagos.

The Poisoner

Poisoners are the hardest Iagos to identify because their problem seems so much their own and not yours. These people are chronic downers. They are steeped in some particular mood, which over time they inflict on you. Although they themselves may suffer as a result of this mood, they can break your spirit as effectively as if it were their sole ambition to do so.

Their toxicity can be any of various types. They themselves are sad or are angry with the world or feel that their own lives have passed them by. You may feel sorry for them, or they may get on your nerves. Either way, being around them is crushing.

You can get so involved in their state of mind that you don't imagine that anything is being done to you. But they're actually doing you plenty of harm.

The poison that they are using is what psychologists call "induced feelings." What they feel, they are inducing in you, sometimes purposely, sometimes not.

After spending time with them, *you* suddenly feel angry at the world or you feel that your own life has passed you by.

For instance, you spent time with a person who kept talking fearfully about the economy or about your industry. "They'll be cutting down soon, big time," the person said. "Did you read about what happened to———? He's out of a job. I don't think he'll ever get another one."

Without actually predicting that this would happen to you, the person has induced the particular fear in you. He has infected you with *his* fear, and you didn't know this was happening. But now you wake up in the morning afflicted by that fear as if it were your own.

A woman patient of mine came to recognize that after talking with her mother she always spent hours worrying about her physical health and that of her two children. Her mother was an acute worrier, who listened to call-in shows on the radio all day and collected stories about health hazards. "Did you know that a lady ate some shrimp in a good restaurant and three hours later . . ." The stories made her daughter a nervous wreck.

A subtler form of poisoning is usually done with malice. The person doing it is generally miserable or feels that he or she has missed the fast track. So the person tries to put you down and induce in you a similar sense of hopelessness. These poisoners may do this by lavishly praising others, people that you both know or people in the news, celebrities.

When your mother tells you how much she loves your brother's wife and never mentions *your* wife, or when a friend constantly talks about how lovely and thin a certain actress is, you may feel what seems like an irrational annoyance. How can you possibly argue against your brother's wife, whom you actually like? How can you disagree with praise of an actress whose work you enjoy?

The key is to recognize it when the remark is calculated to make you look bad by comparison. It induces in you a feeling that you are second-rate, just as the speaker feels second-rate.

It's as if the person making these comments were simply shoving you out of the way. Even if there were no harm intended, the person could have brought you into the discussion more, and not lavished praise on someone else, to your exclusion.

You leave feeling like a loser.

Modern psychology has studied how one person can, sometimes without even mentioning how he feels, cause another person to feel the same way.

Shakespeare anticipated this, pointing out that certain attitudes are contagious. He has one character, Antonio, in *The Merchant of Venice,* talk about sadness as catching. In another play, *Troilus and Cressida,* he describes how one person's rage can inflame another person to rage. "Rage with rage doth sympathize."

Shakespeare saw both courage and fear as very communicable, almost as if we were herd animals and not individuals at all. For instance, he has Henry the Sixth's wife tell him during a battle:

> *My lord, cheer up your spirits. Our foes are nigh,*
> *And this soft courage makes your followers faint.*

Shakespeare actually uses the word "infect" when he talks about this easy spread of emotions. He credits various leaders in battle with the knowledge that this happens.

Dealing with Poisoners

How should you combat "induced feelings"—the impact of people who, through their own outlook, leave us feeling despondent or hopeless?

As with all psychological problems, the starting place is with insight, with an understanding of what is going on.

Suppose you realize, "I always feel elderly when my husband and I go out with particular friends from his office." You know that you never look forward to those evenings, but after one of them you come away feeling even worse than usual. Investigate how those people induced that feeling.

Perhaps some of them talked about themselves as too old to try for a better job at another company. "Who would hire me at this age?" They acted as if they were invisible and implied that no one even notices people over thirty-five.

Others of them, equally status- and age-conscious, constantly voiced their fear of getting older: "I just turned twenty-eight and I've got this great promotion. I couldn't stand turning thirty and being stuck in a lousy job."

You may have passed thirty decades ago; normally you feel more vital than this person appears. After thinking about it, you realize that the whole group has a morbid fear of aging. They imparted that fear to you and also the idea that there is some magical age, after which you become unhirable and obsolete.

Whether or not these people intend you to feel defeated as they do is irrelevant. Maybe the twenty-eight-year-old was trying to point up the difference between her age and yours and make you envious. Or maybe she was only talking about her own fear of the future. It makes no difference. Your job is to diagnose that these people were inducing feelings in you.

- ◆ As with the other Iagos, as soon as you figure out what the poisoner is doing to you, you have virtually cured yourself.

- ◆ Your very knowing that the other person is a *carrier* of a particular feeling is inoculation in itself.

Once you have determined that someone is a poisoner, say to him or her, "When you go on and on about the terrible illnesses that people can get, I find myself wanting to run away from you. I wish you'd stop."

Or you might tell a friend, "When you constantly rave about how beautiful blondes are, it makes me feel left out."

poisoners have a hard time stopping since what they convey is part of their personality. Feeling cheated by the world, or being cynical about anyone's accomplishments, or feeling that love never works out—these are deeply lodged psychological conditions. You certainly haven't the time to cure the poisoner of his or her deep-seated trouble. The best you can hope for is that you put the person on notice so that when he's with you, he tries to go easy.

Identifying the Iagos in your life is a must for happiness. Unless you do, you will suffer at their hands. You may never know why some of these Iagos act as they do, any more than we know about the motives of Shakespeare's Iago.

Perhaps no one has ever formed relationships without having included at least some Iago types among their friends. It isn't your fault that you allowed them into your life. But it is your duty either to exit them or at least to neutralize them as well as you can.

14

DESDEMONA'S DELUSION

WOMEN WHO TRUST THEIR HUSBANDS TOO MUCH

Desdemona, in the play *Othello,* is one of Shakespeare's great tragic hero-ines. But few people could describe her in much detail.

Shakespeare presents Desdemona as young and pitifully innocent. We learn in the play that she has fallen in love with Othello, an attractive, forceful, worldly man. She knew him from the many occasions when he came to visit her father. She had heard him recount his magnificent and romantic adventures as a soldier of fortune. She fell in love with him. Her love was profound and innocent, and his was, too, when they married.

But Othello was prone to insecurity. He was pained by Desdemona's easy friendship with a younger, handsome man, Michael Cassio, who was under Othello's command. Stirred by lies about Cassio, Othello slowly started convincing himself that Desdemona was betraying him, having a love affair with Cassio.

Othello did not confront Desdemona with these suspicions, however. Instead he spied on her, made innuendos of all kinds, had drastic mood changes, indicated there were many things wrong with her, and left no doubt that she was displeasing him. He was unclear about how. In general he made her life a hell.

Any woman in her right mind would have seen that her relationship was in jeopardy. But Desdemona was painfully slow to perceive the change in Othello. When she did, she hoped it would pass. As it became increasingly clear even to her that there was something grievously wrong, she devoted time to trying to figure out what she had done.

She wondered what she might change about herself to win back Othello's love. It never occurred to her that he might be losing his marbles.

Like Othello, Desdemona failed to talk about the growing trouble be-tween them.

Modern readers and viewers react very differently to the play than did people in Shakespeare's time. In those days, women rarely confronted their husbands with direct questions about their relationships. Highborn husbands openly kept mistresses for many decades and their wives were taught to simply ignore them. Indeed, many of Shakespeare's plots are possible only because of the lack of communication between the sexes.

The Silence of the Lamb

Today, as we read or watch the play *Othello,* a question echoes in our minds, "Desdemona, when you see your husband acting so weirdly, why don't you just ask him what's wrong?"

Or, "Why don't you tell him that you can't believe the way he's behaving?"

We assume that Othello would then tell Desdemona about his suspicions, and that she would straighten everything out by explaining away the seeming evidence against her. She would assure him that she was faithful.

A good loud argument would clear the air, and the two of them would discover that Othello's assistant, Iago, had been telling his boss a pack of malicious lies. Othello would punish the villain. Then he and his wife would go on living happily together, loving each other but having some occasional big confrontations when there were misunderstandings.

If *Othello* were a comedy instead of a tragedy, it would end thus. But in *Othello,* Desdemona played it stupid. Her very silence was part of her downfall. She fell right into the hands of Iago, who is feeding Othello lies about her. Part of the play's great drama is in the alienation between Othello and Desdemona. The audience is on both sides, bridging them, but unable to bring them together.

In a curious sense, *Othello* is a "mistaken identity" play of its own kind. Othello is really the one who is betraying Desdemona by losing faith in her.

And Desdemona betrays herself. She is so busy trying to figure out how to change herself that she loses sight of what is really going on. Her only concern is winning Othello back at any cost. She prides herself on the fact that she would love him no matter what he did to her.

Shortly before being strangled to death, she announces that Othello's:

> *Unkindness may do much,*
> *And his unkindness may defeat my life,*
> *But never taint my love.*

The love part was fine, but her failure to take care of herself was not. Othello calls her a whore. This doesn't motivate her to confront him directly. He hurls her to the floor in front of a visiting delegation of high-ranking ambassadors. They, of course, are shocked, but still, Desdemona doesn't speak up for herself, and, unfortunately, many abused women today behave as she did. She prefers to see the whole thing as a terrible dream.

When Othello finally does tell her what is wrong, they are alone, and he is about to murder her. Then he suffocates her.

But she has a dying breath or two for a last comment to her servant, who comes upon the murder. She denies that Othello killed her, and says instead that she has killed herself, which is indicative of so many women who accept undue blame.

In an ironic sense, Desdemona has killed herself. Desdemona has been willing to bend herself utterly out of shape for a relationship. She has trusted her husband too much, and imagined that if she changed, all would be well. She denied the fact that she was on a collision course.

The Modern Desdemona Complex

Few women today would tolerate such a long-term mood swing in their husbands without comment. Desdemona's was an extreme case, made more so by the fact that she lived in "extreme" time and that Shakespeare was trying to write high drama.

But many of Desdemona's tendencies are common in modern relationships. Many people, more women than men perhaps, are far too willing to bend themselves into unnatural shapes to fit relationships.

Obviously, it is never right to suffer physical abuse for any amount of time with a lover. But people are less likely to spot psychological abuse than physical abuse.

- ◆ It is psychological abuse when anyone tells you that you must change who you fundamentally are in order to conform to some ideal of theirs.

- ◆ A main criterion in any relationship should be how the other person makes you feel about yourself. Ideally, you should feel comfortable in your own skin.

- ◆ By its very definition, love should make you feel better about yourself. It should add something. You should feel smarter, sexier, more capable—and not less of any of these things. You should feel like a movie star, not like a student who has a lot to learn and prove.

- Love should be the end point of whatever efforts you've made in life, not the starting place.

- A lover is a luxury, but not a necessity. You are a whole person without a lover, and the presence of a lover should never make you less.

Don't Confuse Anxiety with Love

It can never be right to twist yourself out of shape for any relationship. We all, however, make concessions and behave "unnaturally" at times in our lives. We sit quietly in school or at business meetings even when we think the speaker is wildly off the mark. We wear formal clothes to work and act in a "dignified" manner that is often unrelated to the looser person we are on weekends.

But to do this in the most intimate area of our lives is self-betrayal.

- Naturalness is the one thing we ought to want most in relationships of our own choosing.

- Try judging your relationship by scoring it, one to ten, based on how much of yourself you feel comfortable revealing to your partner, on how natural you are.

    Almost no relationship is a "ten"—we don't blurt out every random thought even to our mate. But if there's ever a time when we should come close to a "ten," when we should enjoy full freedom of expression, then it should be with a lover.

- Our greatest naturalness should be with the person with whom we plan to spend our lives.

- True romance is not based on unreality. It is not unromantic to reveal your true tastes and preferences, to talk openly about things you despise or fear. Honesty will never mar the fantasy of love. It is vital to a lifetime love affair, because then there are no sudden disappointments.

However, many people find themselves in relationships that keep them constantly anxious and on edge. Their partner has a chronic Othello quality in his or her nature. He or she gives off a sense of being dissatisfied, of wanting more.

If you're with such a person your tendency may be to wriggle into the shape that they say they want. You may confuse the very anxiety that they create in you with the stirrings of passion.

The fact that you can't reach the person or please him or her can cause you to think mistakenly that the person is all the greater. You confuse the happy tension of real love, the excitement of love's unfolding, with this constant sense that you are falling short, that you could be doing better.

Bending Yourself Out of Shape

If your partner is one of those who constantly implies that you're doing things wrong, then you, like Desdemona, may be overly involved with changing yourself. Your partner has distracted you from asking the most important question in any relationship:

"How does this person make me feel?"

Instead you have been obsessing about how well you are faring in his eyes. Your partner has implied that if you change one thing dear to his heart, or a series of things, then everything would be well again.

"Things would be different if only you spent more time with me instead of always putting the kids first."

"If only you were more interested in business and in the world. Why don't you watch *The NewsHour with Jim Lehrer?* Why don't you read *The Wall Street Journal?*"

"Jack's wife plays tennis in a league instead of puttering around at street fairs all weekend. Maybe you should do something competitive like that. You wouldn't be so lax."

Or the person does it by innuendo. Your wife points out, "Dan is always so well-dressed. He takes real care of his appearance. That's why Ellen is so proud of him."

Often these implied comparisons or critiques surface little by little. You feel increasingly lost in the relationship and desperate to make good. One thing after another seems to be going wrong, and instead of seeing the big picture you try to right each one as it pops up. If you look back over a time period, you will see your life as an effort to make good on a series of assignments.

In other cases, however, the need to become someone else arises at the very beginning of a relationship. After the first date you find yourself feeling that you're awkward or undereducated. Or overeducated. You notice yourself apologizing to yourself or to the other person and fixing little things that you had never observed before.

Don't Trust Your Lover Too Much

Don't imagine that if you fix the one or two things he says are wrong with you, then all will be well.

The problem almost always goes much deeper. And the problem is his, not yours.

As the Bard had a character say in *Julius Caesar,* "A friendly eye would never see such faults."

If you find a never-ending sequence of small adjustments that you feel you have to make, there is something else bothering your lover. He or she should be looking at himself, and not at you.

Guidebooks to love often assume that it's advisable to criticize the person you love. These books recommend how to approach making such "improvements." They assume that the wife anguished by her husband's bad table manners has no choice but to correct them until they are straightened out, even it takes a decade and if the husband is desirable in every other way.

They take for granted that the person being criticized repeatedly for poor table manners or sloppiness around the house should forfeit unconditional love and acceptance until the problem is corrected.

Perhaps the husband's shortcoming is real. But the attitude, the merciless implication that he is unworthy of love until he fixes himself, is brutal. You can not criticize a fault of someone's on a regular basis without making that person feel unworthy in a much larger sense.

I've seen relationships destroyed by overemphasis on the other person's failings when the real problem was the accuser's inability to tolerate imperfection.

A woman patient of mine was married to a hardworking, highly successful businessman. When she came to me, she was very disgruntled with her life of luxury and comfort.

Over the next month, it came out that she thought her husband was crass. He worked twelve- and fourteen-hour days and was often too tired to join her at the ballet or opera or the theatre, where they had season tickets. She would regularly accuse him of being "inartistic," and doubtless he was.

This was the *only* shortcoming of his that troubled her. She had loved him when she married him, and she loved him still. But over twenty years she had given him a picture of himself as awkward, heavy-handed, and uncultured.

She was shocked when the husband finally left her for his administrative assistant, a woman without as much education or pretension, but who recognized him as the dynamic, outgoing entrepreneur that he truly was.

This man had tried for years to bend himself into shape for his wife, bridging the outside world of intense, and often harsh, business dealings that he faced with his wife's ideal world of theatre-going. However, her negative picture of him had worn him down at last. He no longer wanted to see himself in the mirror she was holding up.

Unfortunately, I had entered the picture too late to help the woman see that her real dissatisfaction had been with herself.

Don't Side with the Other Person Against Yourself

It is always a major mistake for an accused person in a love relationship to turn against himself or herself. Rather than devoting yourself to changing in order to regain love, you ought to confront your accuser with his or her brutality in withholding it.

It's very hard to change when you're doing it in order to hold on to another person's dwindling respect.

Often when a couple is in my office, one person will logically explain why he is very dissatisfied with his partner. Usually it's the man.

For instance, a man complained that this wife was an overcautious driver. He couldn't stand it when she waited too long to make a turn. Her fearfulness, he said, drove him crazy because it reminded him of how fearful she was in other respects.

The woman took this criticism to heart, too much to heart. She admitted that she was a hesitant driver. She even went on to confess that he was probably right, that she was too hesitant about everything. She promised him that she would change as fast as possible. She said she understood why he was so angry with her.

She was playing Desdemona without knowing it.

Nearly always when people do this, I see a certain look come over their faces. This woman looked wan, beaten, hopeless, even as she pleaded guilty without an excuse, begged for mercy, and declared her love.

I knew that she would get nowhere.

Whether or not she was an overcautious driver was clearly not the issue. As an observer, I could instantly see that the real issue was her husband's brutality in drawing generalizations about her character based on a minor defect he thought he saw. He was essentially mopping up the floor with her by threatening to withhold love. And she was playing into his cruelty by accepting his premises instead of questioning his attitude.

Her efforts to shape up proved to be of no avail. After some therapy, I helped her catch on and see that the only way to renew her status was to demand it.

She confronted her husband with some real alternatives. She would walk out if he continued picking her apart. Suddenly her desirability went sky high.

It came out that her husband had been suffering on his job, and had been taking out his frustrations on her. By standing up for herself, she snapped him out of his self-indulgence, and for the first time became a real ally instead of a follower.

This woman had originally made the mistake of trusting her husband's analysis of her and imagining that if she shaped up, she would improve the relationship. Once she learned to distrust his negative picture of her, she was able to find out what was really at the root of his dissatisfaction. Only then could she regain her balance.

When you feel attacked, ask yourself, "How is this relationship making me feel?"

If the answer is that these days you feel like a sloppy housewife or a loser in business or like someone without imagination or someone sexually unappealing, it is time to look at the bigger picture. Fixing some details, even those complained about, will at best only postpone further criticism. Try to find out what is really bothering the other person.

Is he feeling angry at getting older, which prompts him to poke you to exercise more? Maybe you should exercise more, but for yourself, not for him.

Is he upset that you embarrassed him by not knowing enough about business when you had dinner with his coworkers? Maybe he's upset at his own failure to deliver the goods at work. It won't help him to kick you. And it won't help you to hold still for his kicking.

Try a Test That We Call Role Reversal

You've been with this man for eleven years. Or maybe you just met him last month. The two of you are intimate. You are attracted to him and you love him. Certainly, you could list things that he might improve or that bother you. He eats too fast, he has peculiar taste in clothes. He talks about his divorce more than you'd like to hear about it.

- Can you imagine yourself ceasing to love him for these faults; can you imagine bringing them up five times a day?

- Or giving him a sense that unless he corrects them he is in trouble?

◆   If you can imagine this, then maybe you don't love him. Or
      perhaps you do badger him about details, in which case, stop.

But more likely, these imbalances are nearly always one-sided. He's
doing the criticizing and you're doing the adjusting.

Let's assume, in your role reversal, that you can't picture yourself down-
grading him in a basic way for small faults.

Ask yourself, why not? The answer is that it would be brutally unfair
to him. You feel that the good about him so much outweighs the bad. The
sex life, the camaraderie, the common interests, the laughing together far
outweigh any shortcomings. You might not like something, but you wouldn't
blight the relationship by bringing it up all the time.

If you think this way then why shouldn't he?

Why doesn't he see that the good in you also outweighs the bad? Why
doesn't he go easy? How can he feel as you do and tear you down or make
so much of so little?

Undoubtedly, his criticisms are a pretext. He's lost sight of his love for
you, or he never did love you. In either case, your twisting yourself out of
shape won't help. Nothing can help except confronting him about the way
he's treating you.

You can plead guilty to the misdemeanor that he's been harassing you
about, but he's got to be held accountable for the scope of his accusations
and for his being so relentless.

AVOIDING SUFFOCATION

Shakespeare has been criticized, perhaps rightly, for creating a number
of heroines who take too much male abuse.

Ophelia, in *Hamlet,* suffers grievously because Hamlet is preoccupied
and angry with himself. She is the victim of Hamlet's hatred of women,
inflamed by his mother's marrying his father's murderer. Ophelia is ignored
by Hamlet, cursed by him, and finally driven to madness and suicide. She
ends up floating in a brook, covered with flowers. She could hardly have
done worse with a sturdier approach.

In the play *The Comedy of Errors,* a woman sums up the position of
many of Shakespeare's women—a position that is too often assumed today
though not as extremely as women did back then.

> *Since that my beauty can not please his eye,*
> *I'll weep what's left away, and weeping die.*

Here are some guidelines to help you avert the Desdemona trap, even on a small scale:

1. Reveal who you truly are very early in the relationship.

If your new lover likes athletic women, don't lie and say you enjoy sports even if you really hate them. It will have to come out later or you will lead a life of misery, trying to be a jock when you aren't.

Don't pretend even in small ways to fit into someone else's picture. Differences in relationships are healthy, and if your new lover can't tolerate differences, then you shouldn't tolerate him. Over the years many differences will arise, unforeseeable ones. If he is not a compromiser, you need to know that now.

2. Never accept your partner's withholding love until you make some change.

If you generally feel loved and beautiful, you can give ground. Maybe some criticism of you is valid. But if you have to do something, or change something about yourself in order to win his love, don't make a move. Protest the condition he is setting. If you do make any change, it should be for yourself.

3. Never enter a guessing game about what you might be doing wrong.

If your partner looks generally miserable in your company, or isn't happy to see you, don't fall prey to scouring yourself for faults. There are people who make a practice of looking grim—of "playing John Glum"—to get attention and to get you to ask over and over what's wrong. If he hasn't got the guts to tell you what's wrong, you shouldn't play the game with him of "Where did I fail?"

4. Never trust that if you convert in one way, he will love you again.

The "one-way fallacy" is very common. But if you change in his one way, there will always be something else. If he's giving you a hard time, discuss his behavior and not your own.

5. Set an ultimatum if there is any physical abuse, and stick to it.

Warn the person that one repetition is the end, and if that repetition occurs, go to any means to protect yourself from him. Remember, violence escalates.

6.   Beware of the trap of telling yourself that he's helpless, pathetic, had a bad past, or is in a bad way—however you look at it.

Women have been trained to be caretakers, and this often works to their disadvantage. Past suffering doesn't warrant present abuse. Don't make excuses for a person while you twist yourself out of shape to please him.

7.   Keep your friends.

In the normal flow, there may be some changes in friendships. But it's a very bad sign if your partner invariably despises people who have been close to you for a long time. He may be doing it subconsciously to strip you of allies. Don't allow this to happen.

Even if he's not doing it for that reason, if he is an ally, he should be glad that you have others close to you. Giving up friends is a very common way of turning yourself inside out for another person.

8.   If you're in an unhappy relationship, keep a diary and see how many days a month you are really enjoying yourself and feeling worthwhile.

This is important because if you're a person who twists yourself out of shape, you are very apt to delude yourself by saying, "I have to give ground this one time." There's a tendency to forget how much ground you have been giving. A diary will help you see how much you've been twisting yourself out of shape and how much ground you have been giving over a period of time. It will give you perspective.

Stage Five
KEEPING THE DEMONS OUT OF YOUR LIFE

AVOIDING OBSESSIONS AND COMPULSIONS

Shakespeare often wrote strongly against what he called becoming "passion's slave." As one with superb insight, he realized that in order to be fully whole we must have access to a wide diversity of feelings and desires. For us to allow any single desire or impulse to dominate our personality would be to short-circuit everything else.

A clear example of such a life-thwarting passion would be obsessional jealousy. But there are other examples of overriding passions that are more subtle and just as pernicious. We permit demons to take hold of us as soon as we overstress any part of our personality.

For example, the person who allows his or her need to control others by manipulation gives up a whole range of other emotions, including the vulnerability necessary for real love.

Similarly, the person who becomes dominated by a fear of aging or by a sense of despair over the passing of years becomes the very thing he or she fears. He or she become emotionally shrunken and psychologically old. Self-pity can rapidly become a dominating force which saps vitality and drives other people away.

Even seemingly favorable emotions can turn into trouble by taking too much precedence in your personality. Joy at success and the striving for it can make us forget who we are. True personal success can never come to the person who is overly preoccupied with it. In the end no attainment will be enough, as this person will constantly compare himself or herself to someone on a higher rung of the ladder.

Shakespeare espouses the balance of emotions so that all of them can have their due. Allowing yourself to lose your internal balance for the sake of any single emotion or feeling is cheating yourself out of the fullness and richness of life.

*　　*　　*

As we go up the scale of natural evolution, from the lowest forms of life to the higher ones, we find that the feature that marks the higher-order creatures is their ability to learn.

The ant, for instance, is capable of very complex behaviors, but all these behaviors are inborn. An ant separated at birth from all others of its species will behave exactly like one that has always been with its colony. Ants are capable of learning a little bit, but not much. They can't change their nature.

Our dogs and cats rely on a more balanced combination of instinct and learning. Apes rely still more heavily on learning from experience. And human beings, presumably the highest developmentally of all living creatures, rely almost exclusively on learning and on changing themselves throughout life.

This capacity to change internally, to develop habits and alter outlook and attitude, gives us humans a remarkable flexibility—what the great anthropologist Ruth Benedict called "plasticity." We can live differently in different climates, adapt to different circumstances individually and collectively. Our plasticity, our ability to accommodate by changing ourselves, is our greatest survival trait.

But this very fact, that our individual natures are continually subject to alteration, is also a hazard. We can become alcoholics or drug addicts, we can contort ourselves into compulsive gamblers or into love junkies. We can learn to hate ourselves for features we can't control, like aging. We can distort our entire psychological being in relationships to a degree that no other creature can.

With nothing given to us, we create all. And this means that we need to be on guard all our lives against turning into people we don't want to become.

Becoming highly evolved at Stage Five means being able to retain your equilibrium, your internal balance. This means avoiding psychological devices because they can take you over and possess you. It means not allowing outside events to change your attitudes or your approach to life. And it means never allowing any single emotion or attitude to dominate you.

Internal equilibrium is a harmony between your impulses and your wishes. It requires that you be self-determined, that you have unshakable self-acceptance, that you acknowledge your feelings but recognize the limitations in what you can control. Internal equilibrium is enhanced by solid relationships.

If you have already worked hard on improving yourself and on your own integrity with yourself, then with internal equilibrium you will keep trusting yourself even when things go wrong.

An implication is that you should beware of all deliberate tactics. The instant you begin using any tactic to control a relationship or other people, you automatically start relying on that tactic. The tactic becomes a demon and takes you over. As you do so, you lose sight of who you really are. If you play hard to get in a relationship, for example, you are belittling the worthwhile person you could be. You have failed to preserve your "self" in the relationship by the very act of trying to control it.

When you use any emotional device to control another person you are as much as saying, "I am not good enough on my own." You become increasingly dependent upon the tactic as you convince yourself of this.

In any case, tactics rarely work on others in the long run. People most often see through them, or at the very least you make enemies of their unconscious. If the tactic does seem to work for a time, that is, in fact, the worst-case scenario. It condemns you to keep using the tactic. You make yourself an addict of your own device, dependent upon it and afraid to give it up. You live in fear that if you stop using it, your relationship and your life will fall apart.

Outside events can also distort you if you are subject to obsessive concerns. If you have such concerns, uncontrollable facts of life, like your getting older, can break your spirit.

Even success can knock you off your center. (Sudden great success is listed as one of the top ten causes of suicide.) Those who don't have the knack of looking at the world in perspective become disoriented. They lose their bearings and can't go on.

In general, wherever a single emotion or attitude dominates, the rest of your being suffers. Whether the emotion is jealousy or a feeling of hopelessness about age or the need to be fascinating all the time, you are denying yourself the fullness of life if you give it too much.

People's inner harmony was very important to Shakespeare. He refers to it again and again in his plays and poems. Hamlet praises the person who is not "passion's slave," and in his sonnets the Bard praises that inner mastery which the ancient Greeks revered. Shakespeare's own ability to welcome all emotions bespeaks his belief that no single one should dominate.

In *Antony and Cleopatra*, Shakespeare portrays a woman who relies on psychological devices. In *King Lear*, the distortion is of a different nature. And a minor character in *The Taming of the Shrew* illustrates how easily greed and too much ambition can make us forget who we really are.

15

LEAR'S BLINDNESS

HOW NOT TO BE OLD BEFORE YOUR TIME

Shakespeare's *King Lear* is an eternal representation of old age at its worst. King Lear makes many of the classic mistakes we all fear and pays the maximum price for them.

In folklore, Lear was a king of ancient Britain. He was famous for having given away his kingdom while he was still alive, to two of his three daughters. In Shakespeare's play, he has a rigid requirement that the young praise him, that they tell him he is wonderful and reinforce his feeling that he is still a potentate.

Lear disinherits the one daughter, Cordelia, who truly loves him, when she refuses to make up profuse praise just to please him. He gives everything to the other two daughters, who are totally self-seeking, who lie and cater to him, telling him what he wants to hear.

After Lear has given them his kingdom, the two daughters turn against him and deny him even his retinue of servants. Stripped of all he owned, Lear is left impoverished and becomes essentially a homeless person.

Throughout the play, Lear has an enormous amount of self-pity. He sees himself as "More sinn'd against than sinning." Because of his desperate need to be told he is great, Lear is unable to distinguish who his true friends are. The victim of his own misjudgment, he wanders through the countryside, on the brink of insanity.

The King Lear Syndrome
Lear made most, if not all, of the errors in judgment older people tend to make. He gave too much away and then complained bitterly about his lot. Feeling impotent, unloved, and panic-stricken, he meddled in the lives

of others and tried to control people who wanted to live their own lives. He was opinionated and thought there was only one way to do everything.

King Lear is a great play not only because of its incredible drama, characterization, and poetry, but because Lear himself stands as a monumental example of what can happen to a person who ages badly. Lear, who by his own mistakes drives himself increasingly insane, fascinates us. In real life we would not want to know him. But nearly all of us do know someone like him, and for many of us it is our own father or mother.

Virtually every week some patient of mine, in his thirties or older, talks about a parent who is driving him half mad. The patient's father or mother has retreated from life, not by giving away a kingdom but by declaring themselves elderly before their time and by quitting activities that gave them great joy in life. Instead of continuing to seek pleasure, the parent has resentfully resigned from life, saying in a variety of ways, "I'm old. What I do isn't important. I leave the world to you young people, and you aren't doing it right."

The parent, who may be as young as fifty, tries to substitute manipulativeness of the children for living directly. Even when the parent continues his or her job or relationships with others, he adopts a negative mind-set that he tries to pass off as the inevitable result of his chronological age.

"I'm seventy. What do you expect me to feel?"

Complaints, unfair demands, and self-pity as a way of controlling the children substitute for the engaged life that the parent could still enjoy.

The difficulties resulting from real physical losses should of course never be underestimated. Failing eyesight, loss of mobility, for example, are obvious blights in any life. But, as a character in *Othello* says to another,

> *Take up this mangled matter at the best;*
> *Men do their broken weapons rather use*
> *Than their bare hands.*

Even when losses are real, there is nearly always some possibility for happiness—or at least for reducing some of the impact. Especially at such a time, your attitude becomes more important than your condition. The art of life then, more than ever, is to find satisfactions in what you still have. And doing this is never accomplished by self-pity.

Many more of my patients say they dread the day when their parents turn into "old people." When I question them it turns out that they're not talking about a loss of physical powers or about the onset of illnesses of the elderly. What's on their mind is that their parents will become a psychological burden, depressed, depressing, and isolated.

Some of these people have parents in their eighties who are still contemporary in their outlook and a lot of fun to be with. They are proud of their parents, and hope that they won't change. In effect, they are hoping that their parents won't lapse into the elderly habits of other people their age.

My patients wince as they tell me about their parents' friends who say things that make them a psychological drag.

We can all identify some of these phrases: "All my friends are dying off now. I never thought I'd make it to this age." "Don't buy me expensive clothes; it doesn't matter what an old woman wears."

Being Elderly Is a Matter of Habit, Not of Chronology

However, a more remarkable problem, which is an early form of this disorder, occurs in much younger people. We have all had the experience of being with people our own age or younger who leave us feeling mysteriously hopeless. Why these people depress us may escape everyone who knows them, but others do feel their negative impact, a burdensome quality that takes the edge off happiness in the world. These people make us all feel a bit guilty for being alive. They give off a subtle aura of despair.

When you do your diagnosis of them, you may be the only one who sees why they make you feel so bad. They have subtly removed themselves from hope, optimism, and joy of life. They have the psychological problem of having made themselves elderly.

Psychological signs of passing from vital adulthood into old age can appear years earlier than physical signs. In fact, they can appear during someone's twenties.

The True Fountain of Youth Is in the Mind

In Shakespeare's work we find some excellent advice about how to stay young psychologically as the years go by.

Physically, of course, we look much younger than people of comparable age in Shakespeare's time, and even than people of fifty years ago. Our great advances in understanding diet and exercise, and our improved living conditions have helped a great deal. In Shakespeare's day, medical science couldn't replace a tooth. Michelangelo, who died the year Shakespeare was born, had to live with a deformed nose broken by a punch, an injury that modern plastic surgery could easily have repaired.

But nowadays, with many people cannier about appearing youthful, more subtle factors are starting to determine who passes as vital, young, and desirable in jobs and in relationships.

We live in a society where, unfortunately, it has become a matter of respect and sometimes of livelihood to convey a sense of youthfulness. Spending money by joining a gym, by keeping up a fashionable wardrobe, by attending to makeup, to skin care and hair care—all of this is useless if you subconsciously act old.

Every bit as important as physical health and fitness, which symbolize youth no matter how old we are, is psychological youth. This kind of youth— the youthfulness of the mind—is not just a shallow requirement of the world. It truly does make for a happier life. Psychological youthfulness implies hopefulness, continued exuberance, interest in the world and its developments; it implies a readiness to nourish intimacies and to form new attachments. This is the youthfulness that underlies learning and the belief that one can learn new things.

Cultivating this kind of youthfulness will go far in counteracting fears you might have about aging. Psychological youthfulness defies the years. People will migrate toward you and enjoy you, find you sexy and interesting. They will be attracted to this youthfulness without knowing what it is. Unconsciously they will want what you've got.

If you possess this form of youthfulness you will also make others feel young.

Being Old Is a Matter of Choice

We all make instant judgments when we meet someone. Does he or she give us the sense that we're old or young?

The feeling that we ourselves are old can be induced in us by another person. Or this feeling can spring completely from elderly traits that we ourselves have developed.

Naturally, some recognition that we are older than we were is in order. People who live in abject denial of their age, as by spending their time exclusively with those much younger, suffer more than most.

But beyond accepting the inevitable physical changes that occur with the years, there is no need whatsoever to think about your age.

We have all had people in our lives who stunned us when we found out how old they really were. We had taken them for being very much younger. If we look back on those people we realize that it was not their physical appearance so much as an attitude that made them seem young.

*   *   *

Shakespeare's advice on how to go on feeling young is based on his study of human nature, and this has not changed since his day. Some of it is direct advice and the rest of it is implicit in what he says about certain tendencies he observed in many people as they get older.

There are habits of aging that we fall into—habits that make us feel old—and when we see what they are, we can resist them. If you can rid yourself of these habits, you can be sure that people will see you as younger than your years. If you see any of these traits developing in yourself, cut them out at once.

If you see that one of your parents, or an older person for whom you are responsible, is developing these traits, there are some things you can do. Reassure the person that life still has much possibility and richness.

If you wish, tell the person that it demoralizes you to hear him or her talk this way. Point out that hearing the person speak about himself with "ageist" self-hatred upsets you and your siblings or family. However, resist any tendency you might have to get nasty.

If you have a good relationship and your parent is psychologically aware, you can do a lot more. You can point out to him or her that he is making himself old, and describe how.

You might say that, "When you talk that way, it makes me feel terrible, and I think it makes you feel worse, too. I hate to hear you make yourself old this way."

People don't need to be licensed psychologists to help one another overcome many problems, including this one.

NO ONE SHOULD BE KING LEAR—SHAKESPEARE'S ADVICE ON HOW TO STAY YOUNG

Here are ten specific do's and don'ts from the Bard which can be invaluable if you want to retain a youthful spirit. Use them. And even more important, bring up these items one at a time with your parents or with anyone else who is burdening you with his elderly attitude:

1. Remain a student.
Behind every effort to learn something challenging and new is the notion of tomorrow. The very idea, "I will know more, the world has more to offer

me," is revitalizing. When Hamlet calls his dear friend Horatio "fellow student," I think he means that they were both students of life. Scholars have a hard time gauging Hamlet's age—actors of all ages have played the role, some in their sixties and older. Whatever Hamlet's age, there is a youthful vigor in the two words, "fellow student."

Whether it's a craft or a new language or whatever, giving yourself over to the pursuit or the interest renews the spirit and keeps it going.

The most youthful of Shakespeare's characters are always learning, making discoveries and getting things done. On the other hand, when in *The Tempest,* Prospero, who is probably not truly an aged man, announces that he is going to give up the study of magic which made him so vital, we have the terrible sense that he has suddenly gone from being young to being old.

2. Don't memorialize the past.

Resist announcing to people how vital or capable you used to be or how marvelous people thought you were years ago.

Moments of feeling old, especially in the presence of younger people, may bring out this tendency. You may be tempted to tell stories about your young glory days. However, the stories you tell are almost sure to be irrelevant and to sound out of place.

People may pay you lip service and act impressed, but you are differentiating yourself from the group by these "old person stories," and they will only make you feel older later on.

A Shakespeare character describes this fault.

> *I speak not like a dotard nor a fool,*
> *As under privilege of age to brag*
> *What I have done being young, or what would do*
> *Were I not old.*

The best way to avoid making yourself appear old or feel old is to avoid the kind of bragging referred to, whatever you imagine its motive to be.

3. Stay interruptible.

This may sound like unnecessary advice, but people as they get older often feel that they have definitive answers. They talk in blocks as if they have little speeches prepared. Combine this with a tendency that may set in for them to be impatient with differences of opinion, and you have a very stultifying experience.

In the natural flow of conversation, people break in on one another. Call it a youthful habit, call it a vital part of life, call it bad manners if you will. But the person who simply can't be interrupted, who makes daily orations, looks old and preposterous, and if you do this, you will feel that way.

Shakespeare describes this kind of person as having

> *Purpose to be dress'd in an opinion*
> *Of wisdom, gravity, profound conceit,*
> *As who should say, "I am Sir Oracle,*
> *And when I ope my lips let no dog bark!"*

The worst offender in Shakespeare is Polonius, not very elderly judging by the ages of his two children. People find it hard to last out his lectures, even the Queen of Denmark, who finally breaks in on him, asking for "more matter with less art."

Of course, you have a right to voice your ideas and finish your thoughts. But giving stiff recitations will mark you as old. Stay flexible. Permit interruptions from time to time. Practice going with the flow, and then returning to whatever you wanted to say, if it still seems important.

4. Enjoy and encourage younger people rather than competing with them.

No matter how old you are, you don't need to have the last word. Someone much younger may know more even about a subject that you have studied longer. Your identity is not at stake. If you try to top people, pull rank on them because you are older, they may fall silent and perhaps if they need you, or out of politeness, they will let you go on. They are expressing, as Shakespeare once put it, "due observance to thy godlike seat." But in the process you will appear old and unlike the people you are with. You will feel their deference to your age, which is certainly not what you want.

One Shakespeare character, in *All's Well That Ends Well,* aware of the tendency in older people to compete with younger folk, vowed not to succumb when he got older. He told a friend that he would rather die than presume upon his age in such a way that he stifled younger people:

> *"Let me not live," quoth he,*
> *"After my flame lacks oil, to be the snuff*
> *Of younger spirits, . . ."*

Admittedly, this was a bit dramatic, but after all, Shakespeare was a dramatist. The point is, however, that if we are not to feel aged ourselves we must acknowledge and make room for growth in others. As we welcome them, we feel welcome ourselves and we do not feel that we are in a world that is passing us by.

5.   Don't force unsolicited advice on people.

Doing this is a habit that many people adopt and indulge as they get older. They do it to justify their existence, but the role of unsolicited advice giver only makes them feel more elderly.

6.   Don't substitute philosophy for life—especially for love.

Maybe you found out about love and rejection the hard way. You've made the elderly resolution that you'll never fall in love again or you've been living for years with a mate that you don't love. Whatever your motive, your offering rational wisdom to younger people and expecting them to substitute it for passion won't help them or you. If you have what seems to you a vital insight about love, offer it once at most, and then drop it.

Even without the names, you can guess which of these two characters is the older and which the younger. One of them tells the other to reconcile himself to his loss of his loved one. He advises him to take

> *Adversity's sweet milk, philosophy,*
> *To comfort thee, though thou art banished.*

To this suggestion, the other, who happens to be Romeo, replies

> *Hang up philosophy!*
> *Unless philosophy can make a Juliet . . .*

Allow lust, vitality. Allow mistakes to be made. In all likelihood, they won't be fatal anyhow, as they weren't with you. In fact, there may be a next time in love for you, too. As a character in *As You Like It* said,

> *Men have died from time to time, and worms*
> *have eaten them, but not for love.*

Don't be the person with all the answers where passion is concerned, especially in matters of love.

7.   Develop and maintain at least some artistic or aesthetic pursuit.

It might be literally a love of art, as painting or music, or a love of beauty in nature. Shakespeare, who seemed to love everything in existence, big and small, appeared miraculously conversant with flowers; he wrote extensively about their variousness and beauty.

Seek to possess beauty in some form—and as you do, your own sense of discovery and elation will keep you young. I think this is one of the ideas Shakespeare had in mind when he wrote in *Love's Labor Lost* that

> *Beauty doth varnish age, as if new born,*
> *And gives the crutch the cradle's infancy.*

8.   An obvious one: Don't complain about getting older.

First of all, to talk about yourself getting older borders on implying that you are the only one with the problem. It's a narcissistic as well as depressing thing to do. It will make you feel even older and highlight the subject of whatever your age happens to be.

If you subject people to this, such as your children, who are the usual audience for these self-pitying speeches, they may listen. If they are close to you, they may feel that they have to listen. However, many people will start avoiding you. Those who don't will want to say, as Shakespeare did, but probably in less eloquent language, in the words of a nobleman in *Richard III*:

> *Madam, have comfort. All of us have cause*
> *To wail the dimming of our shining star;*
> *But none can cure their harms by wailing them.*
> *Madam, my mother, I do cry you mercy.*

By "cry you mercy," Shakespeare might have meant, "I wish you the best," but I think he more likely meant, "Please have mercy on me." This is how most listeners will feel.

9.   Don't automatically put yourself last when with younger people.

This should hold true even when with your children, especially if they are grown up. Don't give everything away—for instance, by insisting on paying for everything if the younger person can afford to pay and wants to. Be prepared to acknowledge that certain younger people are selfish if they truly are.

Not letting "the younger generation" contribute will set you apart from them and make you feel old. You deprive them of seeing you as an equal and of developing a sense of their own maturity. You may even convince yourself that you would not be wanted by the person unless you paid for everything.

The greatest exemplar of this mistake in literature is King Lear, who divided his kingdom between two daughters, empowering them and disempowering himself. Lear's doing this amounted to a death sentence in his case, since his daughters turned out to be brutally ungrateful.

Buying people always accents the difference between young and old. It intensifies the giver's feeling of, "I am stepping into old age and uselessness. I don't need pleasures anymore. They're more fitting for a young person to enjoy."

I've seen people thirty and under take this position. A common instance is a woman giving everything to a slightly younger sister as if her own time for happiness were over.

A wise and witty Shakespearean character, the Fool in King Lear's court, mocks Lear when it is too late, after he has given his daughters everything.

> *Fool:*   *. . . I can tell why a snail has a house.*
> *Lear:*   *Why?*
> *Fool:*   *Why, to put's head in, not to give it away to his daughters,*
>   *and leave his horns without a case.*

Lear stripped himself of what he later felt he needed. But even if you can well afford what you give to a younger person, think twice. If your motive for giving includes trying to offset a sense of being older and less deserving of the relationship, then your giving will make you feel older than ever. Trust relationships. Allow balances in them.

10.   Don't talk about dying.

Again, I've seen young people as well as older ones do this, though of course older people do it more.

Obviously, such talk is a miserable experience for everyone concerned. It seems calculated to make the listener feel guilty for being younger or more hopeful, and it is a naked way of drawing attention to oneself.

Who wants to hear Prospero's self-pitying tug at people's heartstrings at the very end of *The Tempest*? After giving up his magic, he warns us that he is going to:

> *. . . retire me to my Milan, where*
> *Every third thought shall be my grave.*

By the way, one of Shakespeare's chronologically oldest characters, Falstaff, who retains a marvelous boyish spirit till the end, never wallows in self-pity. Falstaff, a character whom Shakespeare essentially invented, basing him on scraps of information about a man named Sir John Oldcastle, embodies the spirit of adventure and of what is possible as we get older. Irresponsible; yes, he had that fault. But Falstaff rose each day with curiosity and verve and joy.

When someone asks him when he will quit fighting and drinking and carousing with his friends,

> *and begin to patch up thine old body for heaven*

Falstaff has no desire to go on with such talk.

> *Peace. Do not speak like a death's head, do not bid me remember mine end.*

Shakespeare was not against acknowledgment of death. Characters die right and left in his plays, and they talk about death easily. But people don't wallow in their deaths, except, arguably, Hamlet himself. Most are too young in spirit, too vital for that. And Falstaff, who might be seventy, remains as vital as the youngest of them.

How old we are chronologically is of course not up to us. Shakespeare once wrote jokingly that Time must be bald. But how old we feel is definitely something we have much control over, and the Bard gives us a rich understanding of where this control lies and how we can employ it to our benefit.

16
CLEOPATRA'S MANIPULATIVENESS

THE DANGERS OF TOO MUCH MYSTIQUE

Shakespeare's play *Antony and Cleopatra* memorializes Cleopatra's last love affair, with the high Roman statesman and general Marc Antony. Owing in large part to the Bard, Antony and Cleopatra came to be known as one of the great pairs of lovers in history. Shakespeare obviously had a gift for creating great romantic teams, like Romeo and Juliet, and Beatrice and Benedict.

For Shakespeare, Cleopatra's romance with Antony must have been the most appealing chapter of Cleopatra's life because so much was at stake and because it ended in her suicide at thirty-nine.

However, Cleopatra had a history of passionate, high-profile love affairs. Shakespeare drew on this history to present Cleopatra, the Queen of Egypt, as a woman who is fabulously beautiful, wealthy, and powerful, and is ultra-sophisticated in using her opulence to captivate potential lovers.

The Bard describes her as sensual and wise, able to employ her physical wiles to capture any man and keep him in love with her. He implies that she was schooled in keeping a man sexually aroused and obsessed.

Shakespeare describes Cleopatra's self-packaging as almost magical, as if, at will, she could create and sustain an aura of beauty and glamour.

In a famous passage, he has a character say of her that

> *Age cannot wither her, nor custom stale*
> *Her infinite variety.*

Cleopatra was almost a sorceress.

Shakespeare himself seemed entranced with her, as have many writers over the centuries since. He saw her as supremely beautiful and physically perfect.

The Secret Cleopatra

Recently, however, much has been written about what the real Cleopatra might have looked like. Fragments of contemporary comments and some portraiture now suggest that Cleopatra was actually an ordinary, if not less than ordinary-looking woman. Her features were somewhat coarse and her body may have been on the flabby side. She was no Elizabeth Taylor, that's for sure.

However, recent scholarship also tells us something about the amazingly advanced makeup techniques that Cleopatra would have possessed, and about the mind-boggling enhancements of clothing—weaves of gold, jewel-encrusted headdresses, exotic feathers—available to her. And we know now about the flattering settings that Cleopatra created for herself, all the while controlling the light in the area and the scents that surrounded her.

This dramatic physical mystique that Cleopatra created was matched by an even more complicated psychological mystique, according to Shakespeare, the greatest of all students of human nature.

Shakespeare understood that Cleopatra's love affairs were not pure self-indulgence, but were in her opinion part of her job as Queen of Egypt. She used her wiles to protect her throne.

Cleopatra's father had willed the throne to her, but as a teenager, she was ousted by her brother's guardians. She was about to try to win it back when Julius Caesar arrived in Egypt in pursuit of a rival Roman. Cleopatra saw her chance to enlist the greatest general in the world in her cause and did so by seducing him. She bore Caesar a son and stayed with him until he was murdered in Rome.

When Marc Antony, one of Caesar's successors, summoned her to appear before him, representing Egypt as its queen, Cleopatra promptly seduced him.

Through ups and downs she retained Antony's desperate love for the rest of their lives. She induced him to abandon his wife, Octavia, the sister of the most powerful man in Rome, and to abandon Rome itself to be at her side. For Cleopatra, Antony lost his reputation in Rome, became a laughingstock, and entered a war against Rome and Octavian, who was soon to be Augustus Caesar.

When Antony appeared to be losing the great sea battle at Actium, Cleopatra deserted him, taking her sixty ships with her. Rather than return to Rome, Antony followed Cleopatra. After hearing false reports of her suicide, Antony fell upon his sword. At the last moment he was carried into Cleopatra's presence, where he died in her arms.

Cleopatra then sent word to Octavian, essentially offering herself to him. However, she had finally met a man who was impervious to her mystique, and she had nowhere to turn. In Shakespeare's version, she committed suicide by having a poisonous snake bite her breast. Thus ended Cleopatra but not her myth or her mystique.

Cleopatra's Psychological Mystique

Cleopatra's psychological mystique, as depicted by Shakespeare, is especially unforgettable. The primary underpinning of her illusion is keeping her lover off balance.

At first she is wildly seductive toward Antony. But then she is by turns loving and cold. She carefully arranges that her moods appear whimsical and that she seems to be uncontrollable. By keeping the relationship stormy, she induces anxiety and uncertainty in him that he mistakes for love.

As the play goes on, Cleopatra does not share Antony's experiences but makes herself greater than they are. She demands full attention, no matter what else is going on in Antony's life. She implies that she will withhold her love if he fails to dote on her. She acts emotionally remote and hard to get, even when she is available. She conveys that she is displeased with him.

By her devices, Cleopatra torments Antony, keeping him in a state of high agitation that merges with his passion.

On one occasion, when Antony leaves her to attend to urgent business in Rome, she sends one of her attendants to find him. First, she tells the messenger not to let on that she was sent by Cleopatra. That might show too much interest on her part and relieve Antony's worries that he is losing her. She then tells her attendant:

> *See where he is, who's with him, what he does.*
> *If you find him sad,*
> *Say I am dancing; if in mirth, report*
> *That I am sudden sick.*

An essence of psychological mystique.

Antony realizes in moments that she is playing with his mind. He is able to tell a friend,

She is cunning past man's thought.

But this doesn't halt his obsession.

Few moderns can pull off Cleopatra's type of grand-scale mystique. But many try.

Today, however, physical mystique is so easily achieved that it virtually merges with pride in appearance. Anyone with access to a mall can find the latest trick of cosmetics and perfumes. Most people don't even count plastic surgery or liposuction as mystique-enhancing. Today, mystique is relegated to the realm of psychology. Those who would use it, like Cleopatra, rely on psychological means and not on tricks of appearance and setting.

Mystique-People

People who rely heavily on psychological mystique are basically insecure. However, on the outside mystique-people usually appear confident and polished.

♦ These people are often better looking than average, which gave them the idea that they could get others to fall in love with them or serve them. Over time they added touches that worked.

♦ They tend to name-drop and to gather around them people who make them look good.

♦ They don't have deep friendships with others; they don't reveal themselves enough for that. Many of their friends are simply there as image-enhancers while others are being primed for some service they can give.

♦ Mystique-people tend not to be very precise about anything, especially anything ethical.

The aim of mystique, after all, is to create an effect, to control the other person, the lover or potential lover, by blinding that person to everything except his need and desire.

This semiprofessional use of mystique has nothing to do with the romantic atmosphere that healthy people, capable of love, often try to create. This is not a matter of arranging a candlelight dinner or playing a game as lovers or decorating the house magically for your lover's birthday. This is instead a lifestyle, one

calculated to perpetrate fraud on other people. Men and women
are equally prone to become mystique-people.

◆   Mystique-people have a curious combination of empathy and
    cruelty. They are acutely sensitive to when you are unhappy, to
    when you are ready to give up on them. Their antennae are very
    finely tuned.

    They make the moves necessary to keep you in limbo. If you
    are ready to sign off a relationship, they will suddenly be kind
    and remember details about you. They will use sentiment on you
    to make you feel guilty. But don't be fooled. That empathy is
    never at the service of real caring.

THE FOUR DEVICES OF MYSTIQUE

Remoteness-Mystique

People who use remoteness for mystique play it as being more elegant
and more knowing than you are. They act vaguely displeased with the world
or show no reaction when you would expect them to be enthusiastic or
excited. They seem to be saying, "I know how it's done, and you don't."
"I've been to better places and known better people." "I'm slumming right
now, so I guess you will do."

Extremely good-looking people often pull this. They know from experience that their looks will carry them far, and they feel that they only risk
marring their image by inadvertently saying something wrong or reacting
too passionately.

But others pull this as well, including the very unappealing. By being
unresponsive they guard against rejection.

The whole point of remoteness-mystique is to artificially create a situation in which the other person makes all the effort and takes all the
relationship-risk.

The other person, faced with this remote god or goddess, has the experience of talking too much, of feeling awkward, and of scrambling.

Masters of remoteness-mystique are acutely aware of *who* calls *whom*
and how often. If you meet such a person on the street by accident, your
hello will always be more enthusiastic.

I did an experiment with one (of the unattractive variety), a fellow I'd
known since high school. No one liked him because he gave so little. We
would often bump into each other at a backgammon club we both belonged

to. I would always say hello first. After a while I realized that he was actually calculating his hellos to be softer in tone than my robust, "Hi, Terry."

The next time we met I deliberately lowered my voice, and his reply came back even lower. Over the next few meetings, I reduced my hellos to a whisper, and then to a nod. I verified that he always kept his reply below my intensity. By the end of my experiment he barely moved his head in response to my nod. Now we are down to nothing.

Remoteness is often the last resort of very unevolved people. Rather than risk revealing themselves as empty, they opt to stay quiet, look bored, and let others overestimate them.

The rest of us have a tendency to read depth into remote people. It's so hard to understand a vacuum.

Scarcity-value

There are people who ration out their presence the way De Beers rations diamonds—they keep up their value through scarcity.

They feel that they will be treasured most if they are hard to get.

For instance, the person withholds sex or the time he spends with you or is secretive about how he plans to spend his vacation. The result is that when the person is suddenly free with sex or generous with time, you are supposed to feel as lucky as if you won the lottery.

These people are slow to return phone calls and are often mysteriously busy. Married people engaged in extramarital affairs are especially prone to employ scarcity-value. They imply that their life without you is rich and important and forbidden to you. If you're having an affair with such a person, you're apt to feel inferior—until you find out that the person also pulls scarcity-value on his or her spouse.

Those who base their appeal largely on scarcity-value, like remoteness-mystique people, put themselves forth as more refined and better than you are. They often imply that they have a whole set of friends whom you are not allowed to meet for some reason not made clear.

They may enshrine certain critical days of the year to spend with a "special" set of people other than you. "I always spend Christmas with my old friend Karen. She's a wonderful person. She'd feel hurt if I brought someone else along."

Instilling jealousy

There are an infinite number of ways to do this, and it is always the attempt at mystique used by people extremely unsure of themselves. They try to enlarge their desirability by making it appear that they are the object of a bidding war. By implication, you are lucky to be with them. These people may flirt, have affairs, or simply imply that someone else is desperate for them.

Often they put you in competition with former lovers or mates, instilling what has been call "posthumous jealousy."

We all know this type.

Unpredictability-mystique

This is the mystique of people who put themselves forth as young, care-free, and too light to pin down. They carry themselves as if free of the burdens that "dull" people like you take for granted in your own life—being punctual, sober, responsible, a promise keeper.

This type is often very attractive and charming, and you may discover his or her irresponsibility only after you are hooked. There is much desirable about these people or they couldn't keep you so off balance.

They play upon the eternal myth that the genius, the prodigy is unpre-dictable, that you never know what a truly high-level person will do.

These people often capitalize on the artist's reputation. What they lack is the talent of the real artist and his or her dedication. Most truly great artists are highly disciplined and responsible people.

WHAT'S WRONG WITH RELYING ON PSYCHOLOGICAL MYSTIQUE?

Unconsciously, the person using mystique is making a deal—"I will sub-stitute illusion for reality because my own reality is not enough to arouse the other person and sustain a relationship."

The use of mystique is always an admission of being unable to attract and sustain love.

It is an artificial device, and by using it you are always building a relationship on quicksand. The more psychological mystique, the deeper the quicksand.

◆ Psychological mystique always backfires.

Will you create desire in the other person? Very often yes.

Will you bind the other person to you for a certain period of time? Yes.

But along with the desire that you arouse, and the obsession, you are always inducing in the other person a seething, subconscious rage.

- The other person, even as he or she comes toward you and does your bidding, is learning to hate you.

    What you are doing is abusive, and even as the other person swears undying love, he feels unconsciously that he is the victim of ugly treatment. This is so even if he or she is unable to admit it.

    Your lover may defend you in his own mind for a time.

    Often his friends are the first to realize what you are doing. They may warn your lover to back away from you. Your lover may turn on them in your defense. He or she, still caught up in a desperate desire to reach you, to prove himself or herself, may be your staunchest defender.

    But don't be fooled: Every sacrifice your lover is making, every compromise, is accumulating in his unconscious.

    And, at some point, he will probably get even. It may take a decade for your lover to work up the courage to walk out or to have an affair behind your back, but he will have remarkably little sympathy for you when he or she does so.

- Another hazard of using mystique is that you may be bested by a rival who is open, honest, and comfortably straightforward.

    Mystique thrives on lack of real communication, and there is a basic core of distrust and distance which leaves the door open for someone else to step in.

    Someone else may come along, perhaps less appealing than you but who compliments your lover and satisfies him or her. With such encouragement and support, your lover may come to his senses. Why should he or she treasure someone who makes him grovel when he has someone who makes him happy? Why live in pieces when he can be whole?

    While he or she was under your spell, the person believed himself inadequate. Now someone else has shown him that this was a lie and that you were the one who perpetrated it.

    He will feel immense rage and equally immense relief to get away from you.

- What happens if you get what you want and drop the mystique? If you have been using psychological mystique to trap a particular person, you may let down your guard when you think you have won him or her. You may stop demanding that he jump through hoops to win you. You declare your love. You become available.

Sounds good. But instead of delighting the other person and putting the love affair on solid ground, your sudden availability liberates him, and now he feels free to get even. For every sexual rejection that you inflicted, for every trick of remoteness or scarcity-value that you pulled, causing him to suffer, he will pull ten. He has lived in pain, and now it is your turn.

◆   The last scenario is really the worst because it goes on forever.

You may feel that in order to keep your lover or mate in line, you have to keep your mystique going for a lifetime. Since psychological mystique is always basically a lie, this is an incredible strain. You will feel isolated and lonely, and will feel pressured to keep inventing new versions of your game.

There are mystique-people who play one of the games mentioned their whole lives. They allude to the women who wanted them when they were young, they remain remote with the one person who could understand them. They torment themselves and their lover forever, afraid always that if they showed their love, their truth, the relationship would collapse or their partner would take the revenge they deserve.

If You Are Attracted to Mystique-People

Having this particular addiction will put you in some of the most humiliating and painful love relationships possible.

By definition, the mystique-user's aim is to make you feel continually inadequate. There is no relationship more imbalanced than that between a mystique-person and the person desperately trying to reach him.

Mystique-people are always "users." They are likely to replace you if someone who better serves them comes along. But whether you admit it to yourself or not, it may be worst if they stick with you for a lifetime, indifferent to your feelings and demanding utter devotion.

BREAKING THE SPELL

1.   Ask yourself why you think generous people are stupid.

What would be wrong with really good treatment? Do you feel awkward or embarrassed when someone, especially a would-be lover, is attentive or appreciative? Maybe you don't feel worthy. If so, you may be too quick to label the person who worships you as a fool. Instead you are spending a great deal of energy trying to turn a mystique-person into a human being, a near impossible task.

2.   Practice being with people who treat you well.

Stay open to a new relationship, and if you meet someone eligible and attractive, resist your impulse to write the person off as a loser just because he likes you. Learn to live with good treatment and study your own embarrassment at receiving it.

People who have been treated badly by one or both parents are especially vulnerable to mystique-people. They are unconsciously repeating their childhood efforts to get through to a difficult parent. It's as if they were comfortable with neglect because it is the only atmosphere they know.

3.   Set limits in your own mind.

Would any amount of neglect or game playing be too much for you to take? Suppose the person didn't change his ways for a month, a year, five years. Suppose he virtually never volunteered warmth or extended himself. Could you live a lifetime in the cold? Would it be worth it?

Write down the amount of time you are willing to endure this abuse. Make a promise to yourself that you will stop after a designated period.

Keep a diary so that you can see how long you have been suffering. Each day, write down whether the relationship meets your minimum standard. Note how many times he or she tries to make you jealous or mentions another person as sexually appealing or how many times he forgets an appointment.

At least this way you are facing yourself with a deadline that becomes hard to break. After the designated time, you will have a kind of documentation that the mind on its own would erase, especially the mind of a person enduring abuse from a lover.

4.   Make no excuses for the other person.

Get off the kick of explaining his abuse of you by saying that he was abused, that he had a hard childhood, that he hasn't been loved enough, that he doesn't understand.

Make your position clear to him or her. After that, admit to yourself that if he doesn't understand your position, it's because he doesn't care to.

5.   Define what you are getting out of the relationship.

Does he or she look good and impress other people? Is the sex truly good or is it that you feel so privileged that he considers you worth his attention?

Once you define what you are getting out of the relationship, you will have defined what you will lose if he or she goes. Maybe it isn't as much as you thought, and even if you won't do as well in some respects, you will do better over all.

6.   Are you a competitive person yourself, and if so, is this dominating you?

You maybe won't let him or her go because you've invested so much energy and time. You've made so many compromises that if you broke up, it seems that your lover would come out way ahead. And all your misery would be wasted.

This is the gambler's folly. Every day must be considered on its own merits. If you act now, a year from now you will have your life back again, and you will have cut your losses.

7.   List his real virtues, and realize that no matter what they are, you are overestimating them greatly because he is artificially inflating them.

8.   Are you playing the same mystique game as your lover— for instance, appearing unavailable or making him jealous?

If so, by accepting these tactics in yourself, you are making yourself much more vulnerable to them when he pulls them on you.

Clean up your own act. Learn that these tactics are taboo, that they are kid stuff. Then when he pulls them, you can feel clean enough to hold both them and him in contempt. You will make it very much easier to walk away.

9.   Put yourself in the other person's position, and you will see his behavior in the proper light.

If you yourself would never use psychological mystique tactics, it may be hard for you even to understand that another person—especially someone you love—would stoop to their use.

Ask yourself, "How would I feel if I deliberately waited two days to return a phone call to him or to any friend?" Or, "Do I mention potential lovers or people interested in me?" The answer probably is that you do not, and that if you did you would feel like a devious, manipulative person. Face it. That's what he or she is.

10.   Realize that a mystique-person can cash you in at any time, and that's the end of you.

It's a lot better to have this happen now than to endure bad treatment for years and then to be dumped.

11.   Live your own life.

Never honor the mystique-person's tactics by rearranging your own life around his. Don't cancel appointments with friends just because he keeps you guessing. Don't wait by the phone.

When you're with him, don't hide your enthusiasm or withhold what you think because you are afraid of looking naive or of losing his respect. You haven't got it anyhow. You might as well keep your own.

12.   Realize that if you do break up, the first month or so will be the hardest.

And it's far easier if you make the break than if he does. In fact, when you sign off, he may well try to get you back by mending his ways. But that won't last. Very likely he will dump you so that he can have the final word.

13.   Be glad that you yourself aren't a mystique-person. Your prognosis for real love is a hundred times his.

A great many people who have wonderful relationships have found them only after they have been badly mistreated by a mystique-person. Their generosity, which the mystique-person exploited, is their great strength now. They are happy, and their former lover is still plying his sorry trade without love or anything lasting.

17

SLY'S NARCISSISM

DON'T LET POWER GET TO YOU

Outside a country alehouse, Christopher Sly, a drunken, disheveled beggar, tells the hostess that he can't pay her for the drinks he had. They argue briefly and she goes for assistance. Sly wanders off and then tumbles down in the cold twilight and instantly falls asleep.

As Sly lies sleeping outside the alehouse, a lord and his huge entourage returning from the hunt come upon his inert form. They are all struck by how "foul and loathsome" Sly looks, and, thinking of him as freakishly amusing, they decide to play a practical joke on him. The lord instructs his retainers to carry Sly to the manor, being careful not to wake him up. They are to place Sly in the lord's bed and when Sly awakens they will tell him that he himself is actually the lord and that they all serve him.

They decide that when Sly protests, they will tell him that during a prolonged illness he has been ranting incoherently that he was a useless drunk, but that mercifully he has returned to his senses.

> *What think you, if he were convey'd to bed,*
> *Wrapp'd in sweet clothes, rings put upon his fingers,*
> *A most delicious banquet by his bed,*
> *And brave attendants near him when he wakes,*
> *Would not the beggar then forget himself?*

More than a mere joke, this is to be a test of how gullible the average man is. Can a beggar be made to believe that he is a lord?

After a while, Sly comes to his senses in a room resplendent with paintings and to the scent of perfumes of sweet wood burning in the fireplace. He becomes aware of an attendant wiping his head with rose water and then of the subservient throng looking at him hopefully. When he speaks they cry with delight over his "recovery."

At first Sly protests truthfully that he is a derelict and not their master, but they argue that he has merely been dreaming this and babbling it feverishly for years.

They are astonished when Sly hardly argues back. After protesting weakly he is ready to accept their version of him and seems to completely forget his prior identity. He carries on as if in no doubt of his supremacy or his lordly status.

Immediately Sly begins snapping commands at the lord and his retinue. They are dumbstruck at how fast he assumes his new role as their superior. None of them had expected their prank to work nearly as well as it did.

After giving them a few orders, Sly commands a troupe of performers in attendance to put on a play for his amusement.

Thus begins Shakespeare's comedy *The Taming of the Shrew*. This play, performed for Sly, which we are allowed to watch, had to be a comedy because Sly needed lightness after his ordeal.

Interestingly, after the play is performed, supposedly for Sly, Shakespeare sends the theatre audience home without ever returning to Sly himself.

We never see the beggar undeceived, set straight about who he really is. We can only imagine that some time later Sly is ridiculed boisterously and dumped back out into the world, perhaps the better for a few coins. After that opening scene, Sly is simply gone forever.

Shakespeare's failure to tell us what happened to Christopher Sly is not like the Bard. Those who argue for Shakespeare's perfection, true "bardolators," explain the omission as not Shakespeare's but the printer's. Perhaps there was a staged ending which never made its way into the printed text.

In any event, the failure to dispose of Sly is so glaring that many productions omit the entire opening. Richard Burton's and Elizabeth Taylor's *Shrew* left Sly out altogether.

In one Stratford, England, production, Sly was made to be so obnoxious that we were glad that he disappeared after the prologue.

Sly is performed as a comic figure in a comedy, but in fact his problem is profoundly serious. The "Sly Syndrome" of drawing an identity wholly from externals is a tragic psychological condition which is unfortunately too prevalent in our society.

Many people define themselves not by their personal traits but by their possessions or their status in other people's eyes. Rather than think of themselves as humane or sensitive or concerned, they judge themselves by their

Mercedes or by where they vacation or by the extras that they can afford which their neighbors can't.

In the play, the lord's retinue had anticipated that there would be some sport in convincing Sly that he had always been nobility. That Sly would instantly undertake a whole new conception of himself, as if he had no prior history, was more than they could imagine. Sly's adapting so easily required a near-psychotic emptiness, a failure of commitment to anything past, but Sly met those criteria.

The Narcissist's Delusion

Sly's illness, of completely defining one's own identity by one's external circumstances, has become much more prevalent since Shakespeare's time.

In Shakespeare's England, people had little chance of significantly improving their circumstances. A man like Sly stood out as a particular fool because he imagined that he could rise greatly above his station. Today, however, people can in fact elevate themselves by hard work and sometimes go from rags to riches.

The obvious good side of our modern democracy is the opportunity that millions of people now have to improve their living conditions. The bad side is that many are too ready to judge their inner worth by their place on the social ladder.

Many people now draw their identities from whatever external success they have. These people have lost their bearings entirely.

Obviously, some of us still hold to inner standards, to an ethic, to a purpose, to loved ones, to a goal. However, with increased human potential has come competition on every level. And there has also come this unfortunate by-product, the increased tendency to judge oneself by externals—by money, by clothing, by possessions—the "Sly Syndrome."

Millions of people overestimate the contribution that wealth and other externals make to happiness.

Sly's is therefore the modern narcissistic condition. The cause of narcissism is a gaping lack of personal identity, a failure to have invested in purpose, in commitment, in love.

The narcissist lives his life for other people in the sense that he tries to get them to admire him. To the narcissist, other people are merely suppliers of praise and esteem. They have no other value, and the narcissist dispenses with them when they stop supplying his needs.

The swollen self-importance that we see in Sly, the willingness to believe anything in one's own favor, is boundless in the narcissist. Shakespeare's audience, though they didn't have the term "narcissist," certainly recognized Sly as being like people whom they knew. To them, Sly might have been a symbol of what happens when one is blindly vain.

The Modern Christopher Sly

Interestingly, the modern audience may be less apt to recognize Sly's condition as an illness because it is now so prevalent.

Today people like Sly often pass as successes. Inherit money, marry well, be hoisted to fame, develop even a hint of status, and in proportion to your narcissism you run the risk of forfeiting humanity and judging yourself too much by externals.

If you have the Christopher Sly personality pattern, you are dangerous not only to yourself but to others.

With this problem, you will imagine yourself superior to those who have less than you do. You will expect certain people to see themselves as your inferiors, much as the divine-right kings imagined themselves to have different blood than their subjects did.

If you have the problem, it is only too easy for you to forget your personal past. You will treat people according to what you consider their status. You will be curt or abusive to the waiter or doorman when they make a mistake. And you will accept anything from those you consider your social superiors.

If you are rude or abrupt with people you consider below you and deferential to those you consider your superiors, you yourself will feel second class all your life.

People who are without centers, who suffer from the Sly Syndrome, are also without true self-love, and without honest self-appraisal. Their seizing of opportunity reveals them. Their sense of entitlement is boundless because they never knew who they really were. When allowed to become the favored group in a society, they instantly assume an innate specialness and try to run other people down.

Curing the Sly Syndrome

◆ Judge yourself by how you treat the least important person in your life.

◆ The best way to lift yourself spiritually, to give yourself the sense that you are as valid a person as anyone alive, is to drop all distinctions between people, and treat them all with dignity, even if you disagree with them or decide never to see them again.

   And as with many spiritually motivated behaviors, you will often reap everyday tangible rewards, too. If you treat the boss's secretary respectfully when you make a call, you only increase your chance that the boss will treat you well.

Besides, you save yourself from having to make countless extra decisions. Why should you have to distinguish between who is worthy of good treatment and who isn't? The easiest way is to drop such distinctions.

♦ Mental health requires you to strive for something steady and far away. It requires not just ideals but long-term effort to realize those ideals.

If you want real equilibrium in relationships, you will not betray your own past, for any kind of profit. Bargaining away your connection with your center in order to move up the ladder is a kind of psychic suicide.

Just as a person in love cannot find satisfaction in replacing the loved one, as with someone richer or better looking, no one with any confirmed vision of life can surrender it without a deep sense of loss.

Some of us have been jolted by the defection of a friend or a lover who traded us in for an "upgrade," as if our relationship were not a work in progress. In many cases, this was the Sly Syndrome at work.

♦ For your life to have serious meaning, it must be a work in progress. The very sense of incompleteness that at times haunts most of us attests to the fact that our lives have meaning, and that we are trying to become better or more complete people.

♦ Unless you insert value into your life by striving and by caring, your externals will not keep you happy for long.

Staying Centered

Sly's effortless transition attests to the meaninglessness of his life. Almost surely, even if he had been permitted to continue as Lord of the Manor, he would soon have experienced that void again. He would have become bored with what he had and started wishing for more.

Sly is a fool. From the minute the prank is played, the audience senses that he will soon get his comeuppance. When he is thrown out into the street, he will be doubly dismal because he will imagine that he actually had greatness and lost it.

*   *   *

In modern life, not all Christopher Slys get punished. It is up to you to spot them from afar and recognize them for what they are. And it is up to you to keep your own center, and never allow yourself to lose sight of who you are, no matter how badly things go or how well.

One superstar actor in my office so suffered from this "Sly delusion," he had lost his center so far, that he did not even scruple at giving his venereal disease to women who chose to sleep with him. It was *his* syphilis, after all.

Another actor, even more celebrated, had never forfeited a scintilla of his humanity. He remained a soul, and a sensitive one at that, always conscious of people he had known through the ranks, and mindful of his own early poverty. He suffered when other people were injured or humiliated. He wouldn't have believed for one instant that he was Lord of the Manor, or superior to his servants had they bowed and scraped in front of him for a lifetime.

- In order to contrast with Sly, continue evolving complex purposes in life, and commitments to yourself and to others.

- Honor and perseverance give deep meaning even to a life full of outward deprivation.

Especially in the best of lives, so much is incomplete, so much remains to be discovered and achieved, one has so many commitments to love and work that no one else's life can possibly replace your own.

Stage Six
NURTURING YOUR SOUL

SPIRITUALITY AS THE ULTIMATE
SENSE OF BEING

Unless we nurture our souls, we will behave "mechanistically"—like robots. We may seem successful to others, and yet in the profoundest sense other people never relax with us. We can't love them and they can't love us.

Unless we give place to our souls, no matter how high up the scale of evolution we think we are, we remain a machine and live in a world of machines. Our death does not really matter to anyone, which means that our lives have not truly mattered either, to them or to us.

Shakespeare knew this profoundly, that a king without a soul is poorer and more alone than a beggar with a soul. He was himself a highly practical man, yet he was a romantic and an idealist in the supreme sense.

No matter how many times we read his plays or see them acted out before us, we have a sense that his characters, like real people, have an interior life which we can never wholly know. This dimension is spiritual. Shakespeare's mastery at conveying it is perhaps the main reason why his characters are the greatest in literature.

The spirituality, the essence of the person, can only be suggested and never quite captured in words, even by the Bard.

This is the nature of spirituality. It exists beyond the words. It is transcendent, indescribable, and yet we know it is there and would stake our lives on its presence. Only by experiencing what is spiritual can we become spiritual ourselves.

If you have ascended the first five rungs of psychological evolution as defined by the stages in this book, you are centered and forceful—a master of yourself and wise in relationships. You must have worked hard to develop your sensibility to your own feelings and to those of others.

The sixth stage is that of personal greatness, the one that colors your accomplishments along the way and that gives you a sense of the vastness of life. Mastering it places you in communion with all other people on earth, with those who lived and died millennia ago and those as yet unborn. It bestows upon you a sense of how lucky you are, no matter how ill-starred your conditions. It gives you possibility and hope and an appreciation of beauty at every stage of life.

We are talking about spirituality—the sense of something greater than yourself, the reassuring feeling that you are not alone. Your spirituality is an unseen force within you, which waits for you to accept it and welcome it. As soon as you do, others will feel it, too, and appreciate you more than ever.

Your spirituality nurtures you when things go wrong. Even as it gives you communion with all living things, it makes you remarkably independent and gives you courage. It is with you when, as in the Bard's language, you happen to be "in disgrace with fortune and men's eyes."

Shakespeare, with all his gifts, would not have been Shakespeare without his spirituality. His deep engagement with all human beings glows in his language and in his images. His spirituality is a life-force of its own, enabling him, along with his pure genius, to make magical voyages into the minds of incredibly diverse people. The metaphysical force of his poetry is spiritual.

Spirituality is not designed to be practical, and yet people are drawn to it as to no other trait. They trust the spiritual person, ennoble that person. The greatest leaders in history have been our spiritual leaders. We love people, alive and dead, in proportion to their spirituality. They remain larger than existence, ineffable. They embody all that we cannot express and yet would give thanks for. How could we not aspire to possess such a trait?

Some of us acquired spirituality effortlessly from people who inspired us—our parents, teachers, religious figures, friends who served as guides to us. But some of us, brought up in an atmosphere of acquisitiveness, of brawling, of everyone for himself or herself, were cheated of this most precious stage of evolution. For our own sakes we must strive for it now.

Some keys to acquiring spirituality, to rising to this stage of psychological evolution, are given in the chapters that follow. Prospero, the great magician in *The Tempest,* has one great secret, and one great lesson to teach. Portia, the heroine of *The Merchant of Venice,* has another. And we think we have discovered a secret of Shakespeare himself, one that he used to sustain and enlarge his own spirituality.

These are approaches we can all take to bring the real wealth of spirituality into our lives.

18

PROSPERO'S SECRET

FINDING SOMEONE TO LOVE

Arrange to have at least someone in your life whom you can fight for and give to.

Why create what might seem like an unnecessary burden?

Because you need an echo, even in your own mind.

Does this mean that you shouldn't live alone or that you must get married and have children? Absolutely not.

The point is that you must make yourself in some way responsible for at least one other life. The life you choose may be that of a lover, a child, an elderly person, a neighbor, an animal.

Shakespeare understood that this is not simply a trite moral maxim but that it conveys two deep psychological truths.

- ◆ Your achievements can resonate in your own mind only if you have at least someone who depends on you—on your efforts, on your productivity, on your insight, on your love.

- ◆ No matter what you have or how much you achieve, in the end it will mean less to you unless it also matters to others.

It's not that you need applause or praise from those you give to—they may not even understand what you've done for them or why. Their presence will carry you.

True Refuge from the Tempest

The only omnipotent character in all Shakespeare's plays was the mighty sorcerer Prospero in *The Tempest*. Prospero could cast spells; he could see and control invisible spirits. He could command the earth and trees. Virtually nothing is beyond his power.

Twelve years before the time of the play, Prospero had been the beloved Duke of Milan. But being absorbed in his studies of magic, he had left too much influence to his younger brother Antonio, whom he misjudged. Antonio, who had joined with powerful allies, usurped Prospero's throne.

At Antonio's direction, Prospero and his infant daughter Miranda were set adrift in a small boat without tackle or sail or mast. However, Prospero retained his most important possessions, his conjuring robes and his books of magic.

Duke Prospero and his crying daughter Miranda reached a distant island inhabited by spirits. There the sorcerer released spirits that had been imprisoned in giant trees and enslaved them, making himself master of the island.

As the play begins, Prospero divines that a ship is passing carrying the traitorous Antonio and other nobility. Using the magical powers of the invisible spirit Ariel, Prospero raises a mighty tempest that causes the ship to capsize. With Ariel's help, he saves the passengers and guides them to his island.

There, he conquers his adversaries not with savagery but with peace and reconciliation. Under his spell, his daughter and the young Prince Ferdinand, one of the passengers on the wrecked ship, fall in love.

Prospero, through his magic, has almost unlimited power over the elements. But he realizes a deep truth. Limitless power means nothing without love, without someone else, in this case his daughter, to wield it for.

Not until she is fifteen does Prospero tell his daughter, Miranda, about his banishment. When he recounts their travail in the tiny rudderless boat, she observes:

> *Alack, what trouble*
> *Was I then to you!*

But Prospero corrects her.

> *O, a cherubin*
> *Thou was that did preserve me. Thou didst smile*
> *Infused with a fortitude from heaven . . .*
> *. . . which raised in me*
> *An undergoing stomach, to bear up*
> *Against what should ensue.*

Prospero's omnipotence would mean virtually nothing if he were solitary. Unless he were acting for someone other than himself, for someone he loved, his magic would be empty. It would bring him no real joy.

The Gift of Responsibility

Only when we do our best in life, strive against obstacles, with another person in mind, ideally with many others in mind, can we feel the importance of our accomplishments.

What seems like the burden of responsibility is really a benefit. Even if the other person doesn't know what we've done with him or her in mind, as a small child surely doesn't, we know. We reap joy in the doing. And the knowledge that we have made life better for another person has no equal in all of existence.

When I encounter a truly depressed person, someone who says that his or her life is meaningless, my first question to myself is whether any part of the person's life is spent with others in mind.

If it isn't, my next thoughts concern how to get that patient to take on the responsibility for at least one other life, perhaps even a pet. Only then is real pride of accomplishment possible. Effort becomes meaningful when others experience its benefits.

Such a beneficiary might be a needy child, a friend, or even future generations, people who will never know or appreciate what we've done. It doesn't matter who they are or whether they know because *we know that we have done something to improve their lot.*

The pleasure of having saved the life of a dog or cat now under our protection is fulfilling, though we don't expect gratitude. We can interpret the animal's good health and friendship as gratitude. We are well rewarded for our efforts if they have benefitted others because we ourselves are fulfilled by them.

As the Bard wrote elsewhere,

He is well paid who is well satisfied.

Never Confuse Responsibility with Limitation

Responsibility for those we truly cherish is life itself—it is beyond life, it is reason for living.

A woman in my office, herself addicted to sleeping pills, wealthy but bored, and without anyone she cared about including her husband, expressed pity for her sister.

"Poor thing. She's all alone with two children to support."

Her sister, who was indeed poor but purposeful, was nourished every day by the hungry mouths of her two daughters. Their happiness, their physical health, their tribulations with which she could help them, gave her courage and daily joy.

Millions of us are kept going, virtually kept alive, by those who need us—by our children or by a parent no longer self-sufficient, or by an animal.

No one is so lowly that they can't make themselves critical in the lives of others.

Find someone, whoever it is, to whom you have responsibility, and you will achieve:

- A sense of triumph

- A feeling of being necessary, that carries you through the roughest periods of life

- A heightened appreciation of the value of life. You will appreciate the value of the other person's life even in those low periods we all pass through when you lose sight of the value of your own

- A consistent feeling that the world will be impoverished by your death, which is tantamount to feeling that your life is important.

You can't be a total cynic if you're willing to sacrifice for at least one other person. Even if the one you are helping is too young or too sick or too old to appreciate what you're doing, you can appreciate it. Your making a few extra bucks may be a triumph only to the pigeons that you can now afford to feed during the winter.

What matters is that you appreciate your own efforts, and you will realize that there are other people like you out in the world, other people who care.

Don't consider yourself crafty if you've escaped being needed by anyone. No matter how proud of your seeming independence you are, you will be prone to depression. Unless others rely on you, you will just watch yourself get older, even if it's older and richer.

This is Prospero's lesson.

19

PORTIA'S POWER

MERCY TRANSCENDS ALL

In a tiny museum in Stratford, England, full of miscellany about Shakespeare, is an eighteenth-century oil painting that stays in my mind. The scene portrayed is a well-told tale that is part of the Shakespeare legend. Lore has it that when William was about nineteen years old, he was brought up on charges of poaching a deer.

In the painting we see young William in a velvet gown, with his father at his side, both standing in front of a magistrate. The artist managed to imbue the magistrate with a very serious look, as if he were about to pronounce sentence on the youth who had committed what was at the time a very grave crime. William and his father are waiting before him expectantly and fearfully.

Yet such was the talent of the artist that a scrutiny of the painting shows something beyond the obvious. In those somber eyes of the elderly magistrate I could also see, or thought I saw, a twinkle, as if the magistrate had already decided that this time he was going to let young William go. The artist is letting us know that the magistrate was going to forgive William his first offense. He was making a great show of being on the brink of punishing the youth in order to teach him the seriousness of his crime. At heart the magistrate meant to be merciful.

According to one version of this apocryphal tale, it was to avoid being punished for poaching that young William left Stratford in a hurry. But our artist took a different view. Judging by his fine painting, William, in blue velvet as I remember him, was forgiven, which meant that he left Stratford more voluntarily than the story implies.

It is satisfying to accept the rendition in this painting because of its beauty and because it conjures up a merciful world.

Perhaps being treated with mercy was a factor in Shakespeare's becoming the greatest exponent of mercy ever.

The Quality of Mercy

In the truckload of articles on mental health and so-called mental illness, the word "mercy" appears seldom if ever. Psychologists don't use the word, and yet the cultivation of mercy—toward others and toward ourselves—is at the core of our sense of well-being and entitlement.

"Mercy," according to the *Oxford English Dictionary*, is "the forbearance and compassion shown by one person to another who is in his power and has no claim to kindness."

This needs some thinking about, and Shakespeare helps us.

Mercy, unlike justice, is a purely individual creation, like a painting—a form of grace, if you prefer. It is a voluntary act of sacrifice and kindness toward one who has technically no right to ask for good treatment under the rules of justice.

Mercy alters justice, the way a mannerist exaggeration alters the sheer "accuracy" of an artistic work for the sake of beauty—for the enrichment of all. Mercy breaks with the literal, goes beyond the literal, to produce a result magnificently human at its best, a level of kindness that we can all reach.

The recipient of mercy is in the strictest sense not innocent, but guilty, not right but wrong.

From the point of view of justice, of sheer, blunt justice, mercy is a violation. But its aim is as high as that of justice and there is soul in mercy though not necessarily in justice.

Shakespeare would have us see acts of mercy as artistic expressions, those acts that are, in the strictest sense, adornments and dispensable, but which spring purely from the soul.

Justice may be compelled by law. But no law compels mercy, nothing forces us to be merciful. Mercy must come from the heart or it does not come at all.

Portia, the Eloquent Heroine of *The Merchant of Venice*

Shakespeare has many characters who eloquently plead for mercy. It's almost as if he were trying to teach mercy to the rough crowds that came to his plays.

His greatest speech on mercy is that of Portia, the heroine of *The Merchant of Venice*.

Portia isn't a likable person at the start. Behind closed doors, she and her lady-in-waiting mock the men who have come to court her, outdoing each other in their sarcasm. Portia's father has bequeathed a fortune to her and the man who marries her, but has insisted that her suitors play a guessing game with three caskets. The man who chooses the right casket will win her. The three caskets are of gold, silver, and lead, and the prize, namely Portia, will go to the suitor who selects the lead casket. In her father's view, the one who would choose the lead would be a man not "deceived with ornament."

Portia defeats her father's will by helping her favorite, Bassanio, win the game that her father had contrived. She hires musicians to sing a song which leads him to the right casket. In feeding Bassanio the answer, she makes him the equivalent of a crooked contestant in a modern quiz show.

But Portia more than redeems herself in what proves her greatest moment. Her husband's friend, Antonio, must, under a promise he made, forfeit a pound of flesh because he cannot repay a loan. Portia disguises herself as a man and makes a plea for mercy for Antonio, which has become one of the best-known speeches in all of Shakespeare.

First, she explains that mercy as a quality cannot be forced. It must be voluntary. No one can constrain it ("It can not be strain'd") but must be given freely. She points out that mercy is a great benefit to both people, the one who gives it and the one who receives it, and that the more influence you possess, the greater the gift you render by using that influence to show mercy.

Finally, Portia tells us, there is no one so mighty or important that he or she is not made mightier by showing mercy:

> *The quality of mercy is not strain'd,*
> *It droppeth as the gentle rain from heaven*
> *Upon the place beneath. It is twice blest:*
> *It blesseth him that gives and him that takes.*
> *'Tis mightiest in the mightiest. It becomes*
> *The throned monarch better than his crown . . .*
> *. . . But mercy is above this sceptred sway,*
> *It is enthroned in the hearts of kings,*
> *It is an attribute to God himself . . .*

The Transforming Power of Mercy

Portia, unlikable in many respects, is transformed by this great plea for mercy. She is remembered down through history as one of the most sympathetic and gigantic of Shakespeare's heroines.

Ironically, she has become a symbol of justice, perhaps because in the play she was disguised as a judge and because we root for the character she is defending. But actually she does not ask for justice. Her plea is for a higher value, that of mercy.

Portia's plea delineates the boundary between justice and mercy. Mercy begins where justice ends. For mercy to be pure, the recipient must be undeserving. As for Portia's assertion that mercy transforms the human being from something less to something more in a magical way—she herself illustrates its truth. The effect on the person who shows mercy is a kind of alchemy.

THE PRACTICAL POWER OF MERCY

Though mercy must come from the heart, being merciful isn't merely spiritual; it is also highly practical. Showing mercy has widespread effects in the world.

Here are some arguments for mercy that you may not have considered:

1. When you show mercy toward people, you make friends forever.

Obviously, this nearly always includes the person you've forgiven or helped. But it also includes virtually everyone who witnesses what you've done or hears about it.

You are relieving these people of the need to be perfect in your presence. You are telling people that they have room to err, or to look foolish. For most people, this is vitally important.

I've seen many people without that moment of mercy win a case or an argument, and then overfight their position. By being unnecessarily fierce and crushing the other person, they lost everything, even if they were right.

During the O. J. Simpson trial the lawyer/writer Gerry Spence was appearing on a talk show when a woman called in with a question. "Why doesn't the jury ask the defense . . ." She went on to list a set of questions which she thought the jury should be asking the defense counsels.

Three lawyers on the program competed to reply. They had the answer. The question seemed laughable to them. The answer was an obvious rule of procedure. They all knew what to tell the caller: it was a straightforward matter of law. The jury isn't permitted to ask direct questions of either the prosecutor or the defense, said one of these prominent lawyers, and the other two nodded agreement. They had the expertise, she didn't. They had acquitted themselves like professionals and put her in her place.

The moderator was about to hang up, when Gerry Spence asked to comment. "It's true that the law doesn't permit the jury to ask direct questions like yours, which are good ones. But the jury is certainly asking those questions in their own minds. I'd bet anything they are. It's too bad they're not allowed to verbalize them out loud."

I thought about that woman afterwards. Which of the lawyers would she or the millions of listeners have chosen if they had been in a contest? The answer is obvious. The one who acknowledged her existence and accorded her due dignity. While not disagreeing with his fellow attorneys, Spence had done much more. Unlike the others, he had given the woman a place to stand. She was technically off the mark based on present rulings in this country, but her error was easily understandable and forgivable because she was not a lawyer. She had made an important point.

On the other hand, people without mercy will make enemies, or at best be offputting for reasons that seem inscrutable to others but can actually be pinned down as a coldness at the center of their character. Other people, including superiors at work, will subconsciously fear the person without mercy, seeing him or her as an unpredictable quantity, a wild card.

2.   Mercy is, curiously, an easy road to a great sense of exhilaration and power.

A live-and-let-live attitude will make you go on feeling young and free, no matter how old you are.

Among people who blame others, the worst are those who go into a snit, silent and displeased for hours or days. Usually these unforgiving people want the other person, their mate or a child, to apologize. By their message, "Win me back by groveling," they seek importance that they feel they lack.

But the truly great sense of power goes to those who instantly forgive. They sense their profound effect on others.

True royalty grants reprieves; only pretenders to royalty feel the need to punish every lapse.

Showing mercy is a way of drawing near the nature of the gods, and there is no one so poor that he does not have the chance to express mercy. In the desperate rush for ascendancy over our neighbors and for the acquisition of goods, this much easier route to the sense of self that we want is too often overlooked.

Refrain from any act of power at another's expense—from killing a raccoon or a rat, if you have an alternative—and see how you feel. Forgive a blunder by a loved one or a colleague. Treat the person mercifully, and you will have given yourself a miraculous gift. Any fear that doing this will lead to chaos or that you will reveal weakness and be disrespected is misguided. Nearly always such fears are irrational.

Being merciful is an ultimate way to enjoy a real sense of power.

3. Being merciful toward others will give you a sense that you are entitled to mercy in your own life.

If other people's mistakes are forgivable, yours are too. The merciless person, the scourge, lives under the terrible stress of waiting for others to attack him if he slips.

If someone treats you brutally or unfairly for a mistake you've made, if you are merciful yourself you can handle it. The knowledge that you wouldn't treat someone else that way will see you through.

If you can say to yourself, "I would never turn on someone else like that or bring up that mistake over and over again for months," then you will be at least somewhat immune to such brutal treatment. If you yourself are merciless toward those in your power, then you will suffer terribly from the brutality of others. You won't be able to feel, "I truly deserve better. This fellow yelling at me is crazy."

This holds clearly when dealing with sexism and racism. Don't respond to sexism or racism with more of the same. Oppose injustice by all means, but if *you* become sexist or racist even for a moment in retaliation, you become weaker. You forfeit some of your own feeling that sexism and racism are wrong. You substitute a petty battle for power for what began as a pure desire for a better world.

That we feel we deserve the kind of treatment that we give others is a profound psychological truth.

If we are to have mercy—to feel worthy of mercy—we must render it. Portia tells us this:

> *We do pray for mercy,*
> *And that same prayer doth teach us all to render*
> *The deeds of mercy.*

Unless we can develop mercy toward others, we will never experience self-love. The elation of empowerment that comes with forgiving others is in itself matchless, and it brings with it the recognition that we too deserve forgiveness and that those who don't grant it are deficient and dangerous.

4. **Being merciful toward others will give you tremendous emotional ease and personal freedom.**

I have found that in helping my patients develop mercy toward others, I am helping them live longer, avoid hypertension and other maladies. Especially when I work with people after heart attacks, I want them to give up pouncing on others for mistakes. Life is a "mingled yarn" as the Bard put it; to accept the great diversity among us, to live mercifully, is to live longer, I think.

5. **Mercy toward oneself is also important.**

The person who is pitiless toward himself feels desperately insecure over one trivial default after another, unable to forgive himself or herself.

He affords himself no leeway if a detail isn't right, and makes a thousand unseen, last-minute adjustments as if other people were utterly unforgiving. When the doorbell rings, the host scans the room, arranges a chair or straightens out a box of tissues, in terror that even friends and loved ones will adjudge him brutally for the smallest lapse.

The person without mercy may turn against not just himself but loved ones when things go wrong.

In a flash of hatred a businessman patient of mine called his wife a moron in front of colleagues because she didn't know a particular fact: She couldn't name the capital of the Sudan. Beneath my patient's fury was his terror that his wife had disqualified him in the eyes of his peers. It wasn't the first time he had lost control, but this time his own outburst ended up costing him his relationship with the very people he had hoped to impress.

Not surprisingly, he blamed his wife for failing him, which resulted in her insisting that they go for help. In my office she asked me what she might better have said. Of course it's not a therapist's prerogative to invent dialogue, but I recalled a line from Shakespeare's play *King John*.

> *Why do you bend such solemn brows on me?*
> *Think you I bear the shears of destiny?*

In this man's case of course his own character was his destiny. His inability to forgive himself in life, a mercilessness he displaced on his wife, had long been the torment of his existence.

TO SHAKESPEARE, MERCY WAS ONE OF THE MOST IMPORTANT NOTIONS IN HUMAN DEALINGS

Shakespeare used the word "mercy" ninety-four times, and in thirty-three of his thirty-six plays. A character's whole nature was often determined by whether he was guided by mercy or not. Being without mercy could pull a character down from greatness to being less than ordinary.

We can tell from his writing that Shakespeare himself had almost boundless sympathy for all living creatures, human and animal.

He often repeated the theme that the greatness of mercy is that it must come from the heart. No one can force another person to be merciful.

The instant you try to force someone to be merciful, your very imposition of duress renders the act no longer an expression of mercy. You have made it an act of fear. Neither can you bribe a person to be merciful because this time you are motivating the act by your blandishments. Mercy must retain its own motive force to remain mercy.

HOW DID SHAKESPEARE EVOLVE HIS OWN BOUNDLESS SYMPATHY FOR ALL LIVING CREATURES?

Of course, no one can answer that question fully, but I like to think that he himself received mercy at a critical moment and never forgot it.

Let's think once more about that painting of teenage William in his velvet gown, standing before the magistrate with his father at his side. He has committed a real crime, taken a deer from someone else's property, and has been caught. Such crimes were punished heavily in Elizabethan times: Limbs were lopped off and people were often hanged for theft.

Young William must have pondered his fate with great apprehension at this moment when even he could not acquit himself with words. Mercy was his only hope—the magistrate's mercy, if he had any. How the boy must have thought about mercy then and likened himself to all in his place!

And when the magistrate forgave him that time, and set him free, William would not have forgotten the power of mercy, which he was to proclaim all his life.

I often think about how that act of mercy benefitted all the people in the painting. William's father doubtless took the gift to his son as a gift to himself and saw the world as a kinder place.

As for the magistrate, he benefitted in all the ways we discussed. He delighted in his own kindness, and was surely pleased by the relief and thanks of young William. He could hardly have known the impact he was to have on the world for centuries to come. If he had punished the lad severely, we might well have gone without the plays.

But the magistrate could know, as evidenced by his own act, that there was mercy in the world, and not merely misery. Having acted mercifully, he could surmise that there were others like him. And having rendered mercy, he could expect mercy from others.

William himself was the most evident beneficiary. His most obvious rewards were his freedom and his forgiveness. If he was at that age prone to cynicism, the mercy he received would help dispel it. Having received mercy, he would be more prone to render it and value it. Mercy is passed along, much as vindictiveness is, and such an act as the magistrate's must have enhanced Shakespeare's ample spirit.

Some day he would write the powerful line that "mercy seasons justice," and have a character plead, as we all must:

> *Wrest once the law to your authority*
> *To do a great right, do a little wrong.*

20

MALVOLIO'S MELANCHOLY

REACHING THE HIGHEST STAGE

As a college student I felt sure, as millions of people have over the centuries, that Shakespeare was writing especially for me. With an arrogance that embarrasses me now, I presumed to pass judgment. I informed my teacher at City College that Shakespeare's tragedies were better than his comedies.

My professor had the good grace not to note that I was in no position to judge. He also kindly omitted to say that it didn't especially matter to him how I felt.

I'll always remember the painfully slender, immaculate Professor Burt, a superb teacher, hearing me out. I can still see him wiping his glasses and telling me softly that many people take to the tragedies first, and only as they grow older do they come to appreciate the greatness of the comedies.

Watching myself and innumerable friends and patients, I've come to see three distinct ways of thinking.

First, as small children we rejoice. We look for humor and dispensation. We see serious-minded adults as pointlessly grim. Comedy, slapstick—anything not severe is preferable to whatever limits us or might make us frown.

Then, at some young age, depending upon how our lives go, comes the realization that none of this will last, that not just we ourselves but our loved ones, that the whole world will age, that some day we will die. Perhaps we've already seen death, and even if not, we suddenly have a past to compare with the present, and a future to worry about.

That same Professor Burt, when a student asked him how old Hamlet was, answered cryptically, "He was just at that age when one first considers death as a real possibility." In reality, actors of every age, men and women, from fifteen to seventy, have played Hamlet.

The Melancholy Epoch

This melancholy epoch of life, which follows childhood's innocence, may begin early, and many of us never recover from it. It is a form of reaction to our personal discovery of the universal, which our elders seemed to know about, the truth that, as the Bard put it, "What's to come is still unsure."

In this epoch of melancholy, we consider wisdom and sadness almost the same, the one being a matter of mind and the other of feeling. We look sorrowfully, even disdainfully at other people who still delight in life, as if it were eternal. If these joyous people happen to be elderly, we think of them as dotty.

This melancholy epoch of life, which for many lasts all their lives, masks as "responsible," as "adult," as "mature," as if the only proper verdict of true vision were sadness.

The melancholy stage has several obvious rewards, fringe benefits, what psychologists call "secondary gains." One is that you can't be disappointed if you already see the world as "weary, stale, flat and unprofitable . . . an unweeded garden," as Hamlet put it.

This is the resolution that some of my patients have arrived at, and a few point to human misery with an actual air of wisdom. Moreover, melancholy itself affords very direct pleasure. You can sulk and feel sorry for yourself.

The Highest Stage

There is another stage beyond the melancholy one, however, a higher stage. Reaching this higher level requires that we not fixate on melancholy even though we understand the ills of the world and the frailty of what we love most, including ourselves.

We have seen the world at its worst and also at its best. We have seen injustice, ravishment, ingratitude, disease. At times we cannot help but mourn, as Shakespeare did in a sonnet:

> *Then can I drown an eye, unus'd to flow,*
> *For precious friends hid in death's dateless night,*
> *And weep afresh love's long since cancell'd woe . . .*

But though we see this, we are not yet ready to hurl away what remains to us—the possibility of love, celebration, study, responsibility, laughter. Nor would our loved ones, dead and alive, want us to leap into a melancholy abyss, as Hamlet leaped into Ophelia's grave.

This is the level I always hope my patients will ascend to, one that only superficially resembles the childhood state of blissful ignorance. It is indeed utterly different. It is not based upon ignorance of pain, but it does not cherish melancholy—or dote on it.

Twelfth Night—An Ode to Joy

I'm often struck by the contrast between the plots of two of Shakespeare's plays, as great and eternal as two continents—*Hamlet* and *Twelfth Night*. In *Hamlet* the plot hinges on the murder of Hamlet's father by Hamlet's uncle. Goaded to his revenge, Hamlet is for a time unable to rally himself but finally does. Included among those who die in the play are Polonius, Rosencrantz, Guildenstern, Ophelia, Hamlet's mother, his uncle, Laertes, and finally Hamlet himself. Hamlet has often been described as "the melancholy Dane." Perhaps the play is, as some think, the single greatest piece of writing ever done.

Contrast this with *Twelfth Night*. Three drinking buddies, Sir Toby, Andrew Aguecheek, and Feste the jester, delight themselves by drinking and singing late into the night. They are singing a particular song much too loudly for those already asleep:

> *What is love? 'Tis not hereafter;*
> *Present mirth hath present laughter;*
> *What's to come is still unsure.*
> *In delay there lies no plenty,*
> *Then come kiss me sweet and twenty;*
> *Youth's a stuff will not endure.*

A trivial ditty. But to me as sad as any words that Shakespeare ever wrote. As with some Mozart melodies we delight in their lilt, feeling their sadness without identifying that sadness for some time.

Anyhow, in the play, on this particular night, this trivial night, the truth of that song touches the three very unimportant people singing it.

As they are singing, full of wine and sentiment, Malvolio, the overly serious steward to the lady of the house, comes out in his nightgown and tells them to stop. Malvolio is by nature almost comically melancholy. He represents "maturity" at its worst. His whole demeanor seems to say, "Life is grim and you should be aware of that at every moment." His very name, Malvolio, comes from the Latin word for "wishing ill."

When confronted by Malvolio, who has clearly often been in the position of telling them to behave themselves or they will be sorry, the little group only taunts him and sings louder.

I think that without articulating the fact, or knowing it, the characters are responding to the words and not merely the wine. They are seeing keenly the brevity of life and celebrating what is left to them, and they will not allow Malvolio to stifle them.

Sir Toby, refusing to be held down, shouts at Malvolio:

Dost thou think because thou art virtuous there shall be no more cakes and ale?

Feste the jester supports that argument, railing

Yes, by Saint Anne, and ginger shall be hot i' th' mouth too.

The three are upholding their right to sing and dance—to drink, if to nothing else, then to the brevity of life, and to the courage of human beings to delight in one another despite being aware of that brevity.

We are heroic creatures at best, celebrating and sacrificing for one another while knowing what is in store for us. Why should the band not play, as it did while the *Titanic* was sinking?

Is melancholy a preferable state, a more learned doctrine?

Shakespeare was saying no, I think.

The sum and substance of the plot of *Twelfth Night* is the right to experience joy despite our fragility. We have the irrepressible right to sing, to laugh, like the three very fragile figures who kept on singing.

Their revolt that evening is the core of the play. With the assistance of Maria, a serving woman who contrives a jest at Malvolio's expense, they triumph over the notion that melancholy is superior to wisdom. Theirs is such a good jest, so delightful, that in the end Sir Toby marries Maria for it. A wrong reason to marry if we take Sir Toby's explanation literally, but lightness of heart, in a person who already understands life's tragedies, is the greatest virtue.

How trivial on the surface! How small a theme! If one proposed it as the spine of an upcoming play, it might not pass muster.

What is love? 'Tis not hereafter;
Present mirth hath present laughter.

"Why not?" *Twelfth Night* seems to be saying.

A story is told about Edmund Kean, one of the greatest Shakespearean actors ever and the best of his generation. In 1833 when Kean lay dying, a friend went to his bedside and observed in sympathy how hard it was to die. Kean replied succinctly, "Dying is easy. Comedy is hard."

This highest stage surpasses the first two. We know what tragedy is all about. We have seen the skull beneath the skin. Tragedy has befallen us, but we are not ready on that account to descend to the melancholy view or mistake it as the only form of wisdom. Mindful of the worst, we must rise above it.

I imagine that Shakespeare wanted us to retain our ability to laugh, to delight in beauty and in one another, to take what is given to us. This to me is the highest stage of psychic development.

21

FINAL CURTAIN

SEEING THE WORLD THROUGH OTHER PEOPLE'S EYES

How did Shakespeare observe so much?

Shakespeare understood an extraordinary amount about people. And not just about those he knew. He understood the drives and desires of many whose lifestyles were personally unfamiliar to him. Through some aspect of his genius, which has perplexed millions over the centuries, he was able to infer what diverse people felt and to know what fascinated them. He could talk through the mouth of a farmer—or that of a queen who had never gotten her hands dirty.

It was as if Shakespeare had miraculously found a tape recorder, and interviewed these people for many hours. Beyond that, it feels as if he gave them a truth serum that compelled them to reveal their inmost thoughts.

Beyond observing people, the Bard seemed to know an incredible amount about nature and about the details of everyday experience.

We can account for some of his vast knowledge of nature by noting that he began life in rural surroundings. With his unfailing curiosity and his seemingly perfect memory, he observed the colors of foliage in every season, the behavior of spiders and of the snail.

But other of his observations are harder to account for—the fact that grass grows faster at night, that the flesh of someone who spent his life outdoors in the sun takes longer to decay in the grave.

Shakespeare enthusiasts cite folk knowledge. But even folk knowledge has to come from somewhere. Clearly Shakespeare must have been around people who had a store of information. He must have heard many life stories, or else, as some people think, he must have lived many lives.

Shakespeare's Secret—"Method Living"

In a way, Shakespeare did live innumerable lives, not through actual reincarnation but through an *ability to psychologically reincarnate himself in other people's skins.*

Through his powers of empathy he lived the lives of a great many of the people to whom he had spoken.

I believe that Shakespeare was the greatest master of a technique which I refer to as "method living." It is an extension of the method used by actors and widely known as "method acting."

Method acting is the actor's technique of drawing upon his or her personal experience to find a reaction. The actor's life may have been very different from that of the character he or she is portraying. But there were moments in the actor's past when he or she felt as the character does now. The actor felt the same joy or anguish, or was perplexed in the same way, though the circumstances were entirely different.

To use the method, you would find an experience of yours which was similar to that of the character. Then you would summon it up in its full force. On stage, you would relive it; and through it, you would truly understand and project the character.

Method acting is not mimicry. It is much deeper. It is the way to access the common bond between you and the character you are playing. Find that moment in your own life when your soul's journey was at the same juncture. Experience that moment now, and you will have found your character.

"Method living" takes this technique and applies it in everyday life.

Its purpose is again to find a common bond, to understand another person emotionally. You enter the psyche of another person by finding an experience of your own which is the same as his or her experience right now.

Method living is a conscious and deliberate technique of doing what in many situations we do naturally. We understand a child's pain or feeling of abandonment by recalling our own similar pain under very different circumstances.

When you use this technique, even people very different from you become emotionally accessible to you. You understand their motivations, and in this way give them a profound sense that you understand who they really are.

You are sending a message to their unconscious: "My life is like yours. I have had the same journey, been at the same crossroads. Your feelings are not unnatural and I know that because I have had the same ones."

The aim of method living is to live as many lives as possible. It is invaluable for connecting with people. Its ideal use is to understand another person's feeling, especially when you don't automatically sympathize with it or share it.

Even granting Shakespeare's matchless conversance with the greatest imaginable variety of people, I think he could have produced such richness only by dint of a genius for method living. Others were starting places for his characters; there was, of course, a real Julius Caesar, a real Marc Antony, and so forth. But in the end, all his characters must necessarily have been only shadows of his own spirit. He was all of them, and what we see is his own richness and his own ruthless honesty when looking into himself.

ABOUT THE THERAPIST

WHO WAS WILLIAM SHAKESPEARE?

Because Shakespeare knew so much about us, it is very frustrating that we know so little about him and his life. We have only the barest facts about him.

William Shakespeare was born in 1564, in Stratford, England. His father, John Shakespeare, was illiterate, indicating his name on documents with the symbol of his trade, a pair of glover's compasses. William was one of eight children. In 1568 when William was four, John became Bailiff of Stratford, the town's highest official position, equivalent to that of mayor. We know that John Shakespeare suffered a financial decline while William was still a boy. Young William almost surely went to a free school, the King's new School of Stratford upon Avon.

In 1582, when he was eighteen years old, he married Ann Hathaway, about eight years older than himself and pregnant. Six months later, Shakespeare's daughter Susanna was born, and two years after that his twins, Hamnet and Judith. We are fortunate that the official records have told us this much.

Following the birth of his twins, in the life of young William comes a period sometimes referred to as "the lost years," because we know absolutely nothing for sure about his life. Speculations about this period of his life abound, but no one is sure what he did.

We do know, however, that Shakespeare arrived in London before 1592, when he was twenty-eight. The first mention of him in London is in that year, and he is referred to as an already successful playwright. Shakespeare wrote his plays for a theatre group of which he was a member. He also acted and, like all actors at the time, he helped out in every way from tending the horses to building the theater. Like the rest, he shared in the company's profits.

We don't know exactly how Shakespeare went about writing his plays. All we can say for sure is that he wrote with miraculous speed, two and sometimes three plays a year when he was at full tilt. His earliest plays included histories, dramatizations of periods in the lives of English kings, and a violent tragedy, *Titus Andronicus,* which is very seldom done, and not at all comparable in quality with the rest of his work.

In 1592, a plague hit London. A quarantine was declared, and all the theatres were closed. This brings us to another "lost" period in Shakespeare's life. For two years, he disappeared from sight. Many speculate that he spent the time on the estate of the Earl of Southampton, to whom he dedicated some long poems. After the plague, Shakespeare's co-op company reopened. Multitudes would watch for the flag over the famous Globe Theatre to be hoisted, informing them that, weather permitting, a play would be put on that afternoon. In accordance with the custom of the day, Shakespeare's little band of players consisted entirely of men; men played the women's parts.

Shakespeare had a touch for what the public wanted, he could bring in the money and he knew exactly how to invest it—in real estate. He bought up property in both London and Stratford and by 1600, with the most memorable part of his writing career ahead, he was very rich.

By this time Shakespeare's genius had come to the attention of royalty. Queen Elizabeth the First herself saw at least one of his plays. It is said that she asked Shakespeare to write a play about her favorite character, Falstaff. The result was *The Merry Wives of Windsor.* All along, Shakespeare was also writing his sonnets, which are among the most gorgeous works in any language, though their relationship to his life, and to the person to whom he addressed them, is unclear.

In 1603, after the death of Queen Elizabeth, King James the First came from Scotland to rule. A capricious and vicious man, James slowly stifled the intellectual growth that Elizabeth had fostered. After another decade Shakespeare stopped writing plays and returned to Stratford. Exactly when? This is one of the last unanswered questions about his life. It is estimated that he left London at around 1613, when he was forty-nine. In any event, according to public record, he died in Stratford at fifty-two, on his birthday, April 23, 1616. How he died is our last question about him. We don't know that either, only when—another matter of public record.

Were it not for two friends and members of Shakespeare's company, who loved him and grieved for him after his death, we might not even know his name, so slender was his cable to immortality. The two, John Heminge and Henry Condell, collected his plays and published them in the now-famous *First Folio*, which appeared seven years after he died.

To appreciate his impact, consider that the three major influences on the English language as we speak it today are the Saxon language, the Latin language imported by the Normans, and the influence of William Shake-speare, a single individual.

GLOSSARY OF SHAKESPEARE CHARACTERS

Antonio (in *Twelfth Night*) is an old sea captain who has saved a youth's life and then lends him money. He has a minor role in the play, but makes one of the most beautiful speeches in Shakespeare.

Antonio is "The Merchant of Venice" in the play of that name. When fortune turns against him, he borrows from the moneylender Shylock in order to sponsor his friend Bassanio, who is trying to win the heiress Portia. Antonio can not repay the money and Shylock demands the pound of flesh which Antonio has offered as collateral. Portia's great speech for mercy is in his behalf.

Brutus (from *Julius Caesar*) was a prominent upper-class political figure in ancient Rome. Formerly a dear friend of Caesar's, he becomes a leader of the conspiracy to assassinate Caesar. He is the last of those who stab Caesar, and after Caesar's death leads the opposition forces against Marc Antony.

Cassius (from *Julius Caesar*) is a high-born Roman who believes, perhaps rightly, that Caesar means to abolish the Republic of Rome and become a dictator. Cassius persuades many of Rome's elite, especially Brutus, to partake in the plot to murder Caesar.

Cleopatra (from *Antony and Cleopatra*) is the queen of Egypt, who so enthralls Marc Antony that he neglects his obligations to Rome to be with her. The two share great love and luxury but commit suicide after their military forces are defeated by Rome.

Desdemona (in *Othello*) is Othello's young, beautiful wife. When the evil Iago lies to Othello about her, she is unjustly accused of adultery. Through the play Desdemona remains annoyingly passive and sweet-tempered, trusting Othello even after he physically assaults her. At the end of the play, Othello strangles her and she meets her death uncomplainingly.

Falstaff is a bigger-than-life character created by Shakespeare. He is distinguished by appearing in three plays and being mentioned in a fourth. Falstaff, a jolly, fat, good-for-nothing, is brilliantly witty and charmingly irresponsible. Queen Elizabeth the First so loved this character that she persuaded Shakespeare to give him a vehicle of his own. The resultant play was *The Merry Wives of Windsor*. (He had appeared in *Henry IV, Parts One and Two*, and is talked about in *Henry V*.)

Fortinbras (from *Hamlet*) is the prince of Norway and a parallel prince to Hamlet. His decisiveness and immediate courage mock Hamlet with his own indecisiveness. Fortinbras arrives at the end of the play, and it is Hamlet's dying wish that Fortinbras will rule Denmark, which presumably he does.

Hamlet (in the play *Hamlet*) is the prince of Denmark. He is visited by the ghost of his father, who tells Hamlet that he has been murdered by his own brother, Claudius, who has already married Hamlet's mother and assumed the throne. Hamlet, though required to avenge this murder, becomes unable to act and despises himself and the world as he agonizes over his incapacity.

Iago (from *Othello*) is Othello's right-hand man who wins Othello's trust. For reasons of his own, he sets out to destroy Othello by convincing Othello that his wife is having an affair with a younger man. Throughout the play, Iago contrives to drive Othello insane with jealousy. The mystery of Iago's true motives for his villainy is one of the great discussion points of all literature.

Juliet (from *Romeo and Juliet*) is a young teenager caught between her love of Romeo and loyalty to her family, which is in a blood feud with Romeo's family. Romeo and Juliet secretly marry, and then through a series of tragic happenings and misunderstandings, the lovers die.

Julius Caesar (from *Julius Caesar*) is one of the greatest military leaders in history. He led the legions of ancient Rome over much of the known world. After his conquests, he returned to Rome where as a ruler, perhaps on the brink of becoming a dictator, he was assassinated.

King Lear (from *King Lear*) is an old man, a fictional ruler of ancient Britain, who gives his kingdom away to two despicable daughters, disinheriting the third, the only one who truly loves him. Lear's daughters practice villainy against him but Cordelia, the loyal one, stays on his side throughout. Lear lives long enough to discover his folly, only to have Cordelia die in his arms before he himself dies.

Macbeth (from *Macbeth*) is a Scottish nobleman and warrior who after heroic feats on the field conspires with his wife to kill the king and take over the throne of Scotland. After doing so, Macbeth finds it necessary to murder others to protect his newly acquired crown. He struggles with deep guilt, sees his wife go insane, and is killed in the end by forces loyal to the murdered king.

Malvolio (from *Twelfth Night*) is the servant who manages a huge household for a noble lady. Malvolio has no fun in life except that of correcting others and trying to make sure that they have no fun either. After he scolds Sir Toby and Andrew Aguecheek for making too much noise carousing at night, they plot a revenge scheme that humiliates him profoundly.

Marc Antony is a lusty, loyal friend of Julius Caesar (in *Julius Caesar*). He becomes one of the corulers of Rome after Caesar's death. The great speech he makes over Caesar's corpse catapults him to glory. By the time of his next appearance (in *Antony and Cleopatra*), he is Cleopatra's lover and the hero. His revolt against Rome fails and he kills himself after hearing false reports of Cleopatra's suicide.

Ophelia (in *Hamlet*) is the unfortunate young woman who loves Hamlet. In his rage at women and at himself over what he perceives as his mother's betrayal of his father, Hamlet turns on Ophelia and brutalizes her to such an extent that she goes mad and drowns herself.

Othello (from *Othello*) is a heroic Moorish general who leads the Venetian armed forces. He has married the young Venetian Desdemona. Goaded by Iago to intense and misplaced jealousy of Desdemona, he kills her and then kills himself in his grief.

Polonius (from *Hamlet*) is a minister to the court of Denmark and father of Ophelia, whom Hamlet once loved. He uses his wiles to further his own purposes and acts as a spy for the crown. Hamlet kills him by mistake, thinking that he is the king.

Portia (from *The Merchant of Venice*) is a wealthy and worldly-wise young woman whose deceased father's will has specified that for a man to marry her he must win a guessing contest. Bassanio, the man she loves, wins the contest using hints from her and money he has borrowed. At the end of the play, his sponsor, Antonio, faces a terrible punishment if he does not return the money that Bassanio has borrowed through him. Portia, though full of contempt for people, manages the greatest plea for mercy ever made. Unfortunately, it is not by this speech but by trickery that she saves Antonio's life.

Prospero (from *The Tempest*) is the rightful duke of Milan who was brutally banished with his daughter, Miranda, and set afloat on a tiny boat. The pair land at a small island, where by use of occult powers, Prospero tames the elements and island spirits. In the play, he finally forces a meeting with those who have sent him away, and in the course of events, Miranda finds her true love. Prospero is a great magician and one of Shakespeare's last creations. Some scholars feel that Prospero represents Shakespeare himself.

Richard III was a late-medieval king of England whose true nature remains controversial to this day. Shakespeare portrayed him as a cruel and vicious hunchback who murders many, including his own nephews, in order to take the throne. In both the play *(Richard III)* and in reality, Richard dies in battle, defending his throne.

Romeo (from *Romeo and Juliet*) is a youth from the Montague family in Verona; he falls in love with Juliet, whose Capulet family is virtually at war with the Montagues. Their love affair ends with the deaths of both Romeo and Juliet.

Sly (from *The Taming of the Shrew*) is a remarkably minor character with a remarkably big lesson to teach us through his own lack of vision. He is a derelict who is scooped off the roadside by a lord and his entourage. As a prank, the lord convinces Sly that he owns the lord's manor and has been suffering from amnesia.

Valentine (one of the leads in *The Two Gentlemen of Verona*) falls passionately in love with Silvia, daughter of the duke of Milan. Having been against love on principle, when in the throes of it, Valentine demands that all the world flatter him and his beloved.

INDEX

GEORGE WEINBERG is a psychotherapist in New York City. He has a Ph.D. in Clinical Psychology from Columbia University. He also holds a master's degree in English literature from New York University. He has written twelve books, and has been translated into twenty-three languages. His books include *The Taboo Scarf, Nearer to the Heart's Desire,* and *Invisible Masters,* which are tales of psychotherapy drawn from his practice. He also has written *The Heart of Psychotherapy,* a classic primer on technique, and has published a collection of quotations entitled *Shakespeare on Love.* He has contributed often to popular magazines, such as *Cosmopolitan* and *Glamour.*

DIANNE ROWE coauthored *The Projection Principle* with George Weinberg. She has been an executive in radio and in publishing. She was Director of Publicity for several major book publishers, and was Vice President, Director of Publicity, at Prentice Hall Press, a division of Simon and Schuster. She is now a consultant to several New York businesses.